Sexual Reformation?

Contents

SECTION 2 | BIBLICAL REFLECTIONS

SECTION 3 | ETHICAL REFLECTIONS

List of Abbreviations

AIC's	African Independent Churches
ART	Assisted Reproductive Technologies
BBC	British Broadcasting Corporation
BCE	Before Common Era
Can.	Canon Law
CE	Common Era
DRC	Dutch Reformed Church (of South Africa)
FBI	Federal Bureau of Investigation
FDA	Food and Drug Administration
FTM	Female to Male
GBV	Gender-Based Violence
GHREC	General/Human Ethics Committee
GHS	General Household Survey
HIV/AIDS	Human Immunodeficiency Virus/Acquired Immunodeficiency Syndrome
IAAF	International Association of Athletics Federation
INS	Immigration and Naturalization Service
LGBTQIA+	Lesbian, Gay, Bisexual, Transgender, Queer, Intersex/Intergender, Asexual and Others
MTF	Male to Female
NT	New Testament

OT	Old Testament
PF	Patriotic Front
RCZ	Reformed Church in Zambia
SRHR	Sexual and Reproductive Health Rights
UN	United Nations
US	United States
USA	United States of America
WHO	World Health Organization
WHO-ICMART	World Health Organization-International Committee for Monitoring Assisted Reproductive Technologies

List of Contributors

Ntozakhe Simon Cezula, Senior Lecturer in Old Testament, Department of Old and New Testament at the Faculty of Theology, Stellenbosch University.

Juliana Claassens, Professor of Old Testament, Department of Old and New Testament at the Faculty of Theology, Stellenbosch University, and Head of the Gender Unit of the Beyers Naudé Centre for Public Theology.

Nontando Hadebe, Research Fellow at the Department of Historical and Constructive Theology, Faculty of Theology and Religion, University of the Free State, and Part-time Lecturer at St. Augustine College.

Manitza Kotzé, Associate Professor in Dogmatology, Unit for Reformed Theology and the Development of the South African Society at the Faculty of Theology, North-West University.

Nadia Marais, Senior Lecturer in Systematic Theology, Department of Systematic Theology and Ecclesiology at the Faculty of Theology, Stellenbosch University.

Jacob Meiring, Research Fellow at the Department of Systematic Theology and Ecclesiology, Faculty of Theology, Stellenbosch University.

Jeremy Punt, Professor of New Testament, Department of Old and New Testament at the Faculty of Theology, Stellenbosch University.

SIZWESAMAJOBE (SIZWE) SITHOLE, Doctoral Candidate in the School of Religion, Philosophy and Classics, University of KwaZulu-Natal, and publications manager at Cluster Publications, Pietermaritzburg.

NATALIA STRYDOM, Master's Graduate (Pastoral Counseling), Department of Practical Theology and Missiology at the Faculty of Theology, Stellenbosch University, and full-time ordained Minister in the Dutch Reformed Church.

ASHWIN AFRIKANUS THYSSEN, Junior Lecturer in the Department of Systematic Theology and Ecclesiology at the Faculty of Theology, Stellenbosch University.

CHARLENE VAN DER WALT, Associate Professor and Head of the Gender and Religion program at the School of Religion, Philosophy, and Classics, University of KwaZulu-Natal, South Africa, and Deputy Director of the Ujamaa Centre for Biblical and Theological Community Development and Research.

MIAS VAN JAARSVELD, Doctoral Candidate in the Faculty of Theology and Religion, University of the Free State and the Vrije Universiteit (VU), Amsterdam.

NINA MÜLLER VAN VELDEN, Postdoctoral Research Fellow, Research Focus Area in Ancient Texts at the Faculty of Theology, North-West University.

TANYA VAN WYK, Senior Lecturer in Systematic Theology, Christian Ethics and Spirituality at the Faculty of Theology and Religion, University of Pretoria, and Research Fellow with the Programme for Religious Communities and Sustainable Development at Humboldt University (Berlin).

1

Sexual Reformation?

Theological and Ethical Reflections on
Human Sexuality: An Introduction

Manitza Kotzé, Nadia Marais,
and Nina Müller van Velden

Sex in church is a popular topic of discussion the world over. Moreover, Christian faith traditions and Christian texts of faith—including the Bible—have been everything but silent on sex. Yet the emergence of new sexual moralities is not always welcomed within Christianity, whether in regard to lifestyles, communities, identities, or expressions—which then also includes sexual, gender, and reproductive rights. From the perspective of theology, when we reflect on what it means to be human, we cannot do so without also reflecting on human sexuality; we are unavoidably embodied, and as Susannah Cornwall indicates, for many people this would mean that we are "inescapably sexual" as well.[1] James Nelson emphasizes both the relational aspect of human sexuality, as well as its mysterious nature. For Nelson, human sexuality conveys "the mystery of our creation"; we need to reach out for the embrace of others, both physically and spiritually. This "expresses God's intention that we find our authentic humanness not in isolation but in relationship." As embodied sexual beings, we experience the need for relationship; "the emotional, cognitive, physical, and

1. Cornwall, *Theology and Sexuality*, vii.

1

spiritual need for intimate communion with other, with the natural word, with God."[2] In a similar vein, Stanley Grenz notes that sexuality is related "not only to the incompleteness each person senses as an embodied, sexual creature but also to the potential for wholeness is relationship to others that parallels this fundamental incompleteness." As such, from his perspective, human sexuality can be said to be "the dynamic that forms the basis of the uniquely human drive toward bonding."[3]

Catholic theologian Gerald Loughlin also links the notion of embodiment and sexuality with discussions of the church as the body of Christ. Reflection on the church and sexuality, he indicates, "is a proper concern of the Church with itself as a sexed body." While he acknowledges that this appears an odd way to speak about the church, and one that would strike many people as unusual or even unheard of, he makes the argument that it is actually very traditional and even orthodox: "The Church has . . . understood itself to be the bride of Christ, called to bodily union with him, so that the sexual joining of bodies is also part of the Church's imagination of itself, in her union with, and difference from, the divine."[4]

Inasmuch as "sex" and "sexuality" are not words often spoken from pulpits and in academic theological circles, a vast number of utterances have been made in the name of so-called "Christian values" and "biblical views" on sex and sexuality. These are often given from moral-ethical perspectives, and seemingly very prescriptive: who should have sex with whom, when sex should take place, which purposes sex should serve—and especially, when sex is wrong. Organized religion, Nelson indicates, "has been, and in some ways still is, the major institution of ideological legitimation for sexual oppression in Western culture." As such, he urges churches to deal more directly and imaginatively with a whole scope of sexual issues.[5] Moreover, often there is little or no recognition of the complexities surrounding human sexuality, resulting in what appears to be a blueprint for sexuality, applicable to all persons.

In recent times, movements such as #metoo and #enoughisenough have brought previously concealed sexual violence, harassment, and everyday sexism in different industries into public moral debate—and, to some extent, at least, compelled Christian faith communities to consider their own positionality regarding sexual and gender injustices.

---

2. Nelson, *Body Theology*, 22.

3. Grenz, *Social God and the Relational Self*, 278.

4. Loughlin, "Sex After Natural Law," 88.

5. Nelson, *Body Theology*, 16.

This edited volume contains a collection of theological and ethical reflections on human sexuality by South African scholars, with the aim of exploring what a sexual reformation within Christian dialogue might entail: a reformation which moves beyond narrow moral-ethical utterances toward life-giving discourses which speak to the history of the Christian tradition, the realities of contemporary faith traditions amidst complexity, and a future in which Christian theology might still play a part in how people engage, understand, and speak about sexuality and sex.

As such, this volume builds upon work begun in the edited book publication *Reconceiving Reproductive Health: Theological and Christian Ethical Reflections*[6] and explores in greater depth some of the important themes introduced and/or addressed in this book.

This volume is divided into three sections, drawing on different theological disciplines and offering an array of perspectives by fourteen authors who find themselves in a diverse range of theological contexts. Reflections within the fields of systematic theology, biblical studies, and ethics contribute overall to the theme of sexual reformation.

In the first section of this volume, four contributions reflect on sexual reformation from the field of systematic theology.

In "*Sacramentum Matrimonii*?: Sexuality, Human Flourishing, and the Grammar of Grace," Nadia Marais argues that Martin Luther changed his mind about marriage. She explores Luther's view of marriage—in particular his engagement with the Catholic view of marriage as sacrament in his time—and how he changed his mind about marriage as a sacrament between 1519 and 1522. In a 1519 sermon, Luther still held to the view that marriage was a sacrament. In a 1522 treatise, Luther refuted the theological justification of marriage as sacrament. She asks, how did this happen—and why? Which hermeneutical keys or strands informed Luther's change of mind during these three years? In her opinion, these are important and interesting questions for our time, since a number of (theological) debates are inquiring after the nature and function of marriage. This contribution provides, in conclusion, some suggestions for engaging such debates—with the most important being that theologians such as Luther could reconsider the nature and function of marriage, even in a short span of time; and perhaps so, too, can we today.

Nontando Hadebe discusses "The Crisis of the Sexual Abuse Scandal as Catalyst for Reform in the Catholic Church." The sexual abuse of minors by some priests is undoubtedly one of the worst crises in the history of the Catholic Church. The crisis was (and continues to be) exacerbated by the

6. Kotzé et al., *Reconceiving Reproductive Health*.

cover up, concealment, protection of perpetrators, and silencing of victims. There is no consensus on the causes of the crisis, only conflicting views, two of which are discussed in this chapter: (a) one-dimensional views that focus on one issue, for example, clericalism or sexuality; and (b) multi-dimensional perspectives that integrate multiple intersecting variables such as power, sexuality, clericalism, and institutional culture. These different perspectives reinforce pre-existing polarizing divisions within the church. One point that seems to have some consensus is the need for change in the face of the sexual abuse scandal, however way that change is defined. This chapter will propose the methodology of *Laudato Si* as a possible way in which the sexual abuse crisis can be a catalyst for reformation and change in the church. Four aspects of the methodology of *Laudato Si* will be appropriated: (a) the framing of the problem of sexual abuse of minors as a global issue of injustice and violence that demands accountability and responsibility from every person; (b) an integrated interdisciplinary approach that addresses the causes of sexual abuse; (c) a theological response that addresses underlying issues including sexuality, power, clericalism, and patriarchy; and (d) a spirituality that will sustain a counter cultural context of safety for children and all persons. By appropriating the methodology of *Laudato Si*, this contribution places emphasis on raising the issues without necessarily providing answers.

In the chapter titled "On Bodies and Theologies: The Aftermath of the Sexual Revolution," Jacob Meiring notes that the sexual revolution of the 1960s and 1970s had a deep impact on how the church and theology view the bodies of believers. There were two major reactions in the late 1970s and early 1980s which culminated in two diverse theologies of the body. One was a *theology of the body* of the Roman Catholic Church, which developed out of the Wednesday catechesis of the Polish cardinal Karol Józef Wojtyla, who later became Pope John Paul II and which culminated in his book, *Man and Woman He Created Them*. The other reaction was that of reformed theologian James B. Nelson, for many decades a sole voice in the desert, with his first book, *Embodiment: An Approach to Sexuality and Christian Theology* (1978) followed by *Body Theology* (1992). Meiring explores the difference between these two streams of interpretation and the impact of the work of Wilhelm Reich on the sexual revolution. Reich is sometimes called the godfather of the sexual revolution and he is often vilified by Roman Catholic theologians for his ideas on sexual freedom which, according to Pope Emeritus Benedict XVI, caused a suffering in Catholic moral theology, rendered the Church defenseless against changes in society, and led to "homosexual cliques" in seminaries. Meiring questions the location of body theology or theology of the body in Christian ethics or moral theology and argues that inquiries around body and theology find a more suitable home in contemporary theological anthropology.

This section concludes with Manitza Kotzé's chapter, titled "Reproductive Technology, Sexuality, and Reproduction: Theological and Ethical Reflection." There have been numerous advances in reproductive technology, offering couples and individuals the opportunity to become parents who would otherwise be unable to, whether it is because they are unable to conceive naturally or choose not to for various reasons. With the growing number of people utilizing these forms of technology, however, the number of ethical questions grow as well. In the first section of this chapter, she provides an overview of the ethical qualms that opponents have, especially from a Christian perspective. As part of this volume, the separation of human sexuality and procreation is focused on in particular, both as conceiving children through technology instead of sex, and by making use of donor material. In the second part, she responds to the reservations that critics hold regarding reproductive technology by utilizing theological insights from the notions of embodiment, relationality, creation, and birth, in particular a relational theology of the Trinity. In doing so, certain concerns should indeed be held in mind when reflecting on reproductive technology from a Christian theological and ethical perspective, while others could be contested.

Biblical texts and their interpretations are often drawn into theological and ethical discussions relating to the notion of sexual reformation. In the second section of this volume, five biblical reflections are provided.

In "Voicing Reproductive Loss: Rachel's Cry in Conversation with *The Light Between Oceans*," Juliana Claassens notes that the topic of reproductive loss for the longest time has been met with overwhelming silence. Both in contemporary faith communities, but also in the biblical text, the profound grief regarding miscarriage is rarely mentioned—this despite the fact that it is estimated that one in four pregnancies will end in miscarriage. Moreover, the very few references to miscarriage in the Hebrew Bible (Exod 21:22–23; Num 5:11–31) are always presented from a male point of view. One exception where we encounter a glimpse of the woman's voice is in the figure of Rachel, who in Genesis 30:1 exclaims as follows about her struggles to conceive: "Give me children or I'll die!" Rachel's grief regarding reproductive loss has come to represent on a metaphorical level the grief of a nation mourning the loss of its children (Jer 31:15; Matt 2:18). She proposes that the figure of Rachel offers readers the opportunity to begin to contemplate the reality and effects of reproductive loss. However, to do so one needs help to imagine that which is not voiced in the biblical text itself. In conversation with the courageous representation of reproductive loss in the 2012 novel,

The Light Between Oceans, by M. L. Stedman, this chapter seeks to explore the hidden trauma of reproductive loss. Trauma narratives that voice the pain of reproductive loss, and do not shy away from exploring the complexities associated with dealing with the profound grief associated with infertility, miscarriage, and stillbirth are important as they create a safe space for women and men to begin to voice their own experiences of grief and loss. Moreover, trauma narratives, both ancient and contemporary, offer readers the opportunity to imagine, as Serene Jones has said so well, "new narratives that enable the return of a future and the possibility of grace to take hold of those traumatized by loss."[7]

Charlene van der Walt, in "'The Bra is Wearing a Skirt!': Queering Joseph in the Quest to Enhance Contextual Ethical Gender and Sexuality Engagements," argues that when considering the role of religion as it pertains to contextual embodied issues within the landscape of sexual reproductive health and rights, the common perception is often that faith speaks with a singular, predominantly negative voice and that God's will is deducible from the sacred Scriptures. In the pursuit of sexual and reproductive justice, as proposed by Catriona Macleod and others, faith actors are often deemed obstructionist or counter the ideals of a reproductive justice approach. This approach draws on a social justice framework and emphasizes systemic or holistic analyses, seeking to illuminate the complex array of social, economic, cultural, and healthcare possibilities and challenges that serve to either enhance or hinder women's reproductive freedoms and the rights of those identifying within the spectrum of sexual fluidly. Issues within the contextual embodied intersection of gender, sexuality, and religion such as GBV, family planning, abortion, female genital mutilation, and sexual diversity often pose great ethical challenges to those within the faith landscape; especially those who primarily draw from the interpretation of sacred Scriptures in the process of ethical decisionmaking. At the heart of this chapter is a concern for the integrity and soul of the process of biblical hermeneutics, as much of the debate around SRHR issues in general and sexual diversity, in particular, boils down to divergent understandings of the role and nature of Scripture and a violent clash in the epistemological underpinnings foundational to conflicting methods of interpretation. Beyond a general reflection on the role of the Bible in the process of ethical reflection about contextual issues relating to gender and sexuality, the essay offers a queer engagement with Joseph's character as he is embedded within the Genesis narrative. Drawing on queer biblical hermeneutics' insights, the essay aims to destabilize the normative notions of gender and sexuality often assumed

7. Jones, *Trauma and Grace*, 150.

as stable and unquestionably associated with central biblical characters, and those who are deemed worthy of emulating by contemporary Bible readers in their poses of ethical reflection.

Ntozakhe Cezula discusses "Theology on Gender Reformation for the (South) African Reconstruction Process: Perceptions from Exodus 21:7 and Deuteronomy 15:12, 17." The advent of a democratic dispensation in South Africa in 1994 supposedly ordained a sincere and honest reconstruction of society. Sexual and gender reformation cannot be more relevant than in this phenomenon of social reconstruction. Since theology has played a role that cannot be undermined in pigmenting social relations in the past, it is just as well for it to play a role in informing reconstruction; specifically, gender reformation as the discussion in this chapter focuses thereon. Against this background, this chapter intends to vigorously engage with the nature of the Bible (specifically the Old Testament) and some of the theologies that transpire from it concerning gender. According to Cezula, the Bible advocates both liberative and oppressive theologies. It therefore cannot be argued that there is a singular biblical theology on gender. What we find, instead, are different theological perspectives on gender; both liberative and oppressive. The Bible reader is thus confronted with theologies that can serve reconstruction in (South) Africa either positively or negatively, and subsequently one must take responsibility for a choice for oppressive or liberative theological perspectives. To demonstrate this point, this chapter takes a closer look at Exodus 21:7 and Deuteronomy 15:12 and 15:17. Dealing with the same issue of women slaves, these two texts differ on the legal status of women slaves. Exodus 21:7 lacks the legal status of women slaves, while Deuteronomy 15:12 and 15:17 extend the legal status to women slaves as well. The Bible reader can pick any of these two positions of these verses to argue for or against the equality of men and women. However, readers must also acknowledge that they prefer one standpoint over the other.

In "Paul on Sex: Viable Proposition, Impossible Conundrum, or Simply Queer?" Jeremy Punt notes that, not unlike other aspects of his writings, Paul's stance on gender and sexuality often meets with lofty praise or harsh criticism. His position on sex, in particular, has elicited criticism to an extent that it is matched only by dogmatic discussions deemed critical for certain Christian groups. In First Corinthians, Paul's view on sexuality and sex appears to move from and eventually oscillate between his unwillingness to accept and affirm human sex on the one hand, and on the other hand, his eagerness to construe sex as self-fulfilling, necessary, and unrestricted in contexts such as marriage. Moving away from the conventional dichotomized readings of Paul, and framed by queer inquiry's non-essentialist, post-conventional, binary-resisting, social constructionist view of gender and sexuality, Paul's approach to human sexuality can be described as queer.

Finally, in "How Far Does God's Violence Go?: John's Jezebel in Conversation with Rape Culture," Nina Müller van Velden argues that the South African society is a profoundly violent society, with an extremely high prevalence of domestic violence, gender-based violence, sexual violence, and rape. It is a society marked by rape culture, where such acts of violence are the tip of the proverbial iceberg underscored by sexist, patriarchal, and heteronormative attitudes and language. It is also a deeply religious society, with the vast majority of its members indicating that they affiliate with the Christian faith tradition. Central to the Christian religion is its foundational source document, the Bible—a document which also includes graphic, sexually violent imagery and narratives. This chapter attempts to engage the depiction of Godself as violent in Revelation 2:18–29 (with a focus on verses 20 to 23) from a literary perspective: a scene in which the narrator describes how Jezebel and her children will be violently punished by the deity character, the Son of God. She suggests that such a description is not merely violent, but specifically sexually violent, given the actions performed by the Son of God. Furthermore, she asks how such a sexually violent narration dialogues with a contemporary context of sexual violence, such as the South African society, and suggests that these types of biblical texts could be helpful for critical engagement about the role of religion in sustaining and even supporting rape culture.

The third and final section of this volume has as focus practical, pastoral and ethical concerns on the notions of sexual reformation.

Tanya van Wyk, in "Revisiting the Church's Moral Authority on Sexual Ethics: Reform or Retreat?" notes that for a very long time, the Christian church has regarded and conducted itself as a moral authority, enabling itself to make claims about human sexuality. This "sexual ethics" practiced by the church can be traced through a long history of philosophical and theological interpretations. In this way, the church appropriated for itself a "legal" voice on matters pertaining to the nature of people's relationships, gender roles, their sexuality, and sex itself. A core aspect of this ethics is that it operates as a binary framework of absolutes. During the last part of the twentieth century and the first part of the twenty-first century, the Christian church has increasingly been named in relation to sexual abuse, misconduct, and oppression related to gender distinctions. Members of the church are increasingly turning to legal justice systems for moral guidance in "church matters." Therefore, revisiting the church's moral authority on matters of human sexuality has become an urgent endeavor. In this chapter, the nature of the church in the twenty-first century, its identity and conduct, specifically with regard to the church-mark of "holiness" will be considered. It will be investigated if it is possible and necessary for the church, amidst personal conflicts and cultural controversies, to rethink its "sexual ethics," or if the church has lost the right/ability to be an authoritative voice in this regard.

In "Swipe Right for Love: Social Media and the Born-Free Generation," Ashwin Thyssen argues that the generation of millennials are presently navigating the complex landscape of adulthood (a process termed "adulting"). There can be no doubt that social media is an important contender for this generation's attention. More pointedly, this generation is the first to experience the digital age as a default fact of life. As such, a study is warranted as to how social media (a product of the digital age) impacts millennial's experience of sexuality and theologizing. The world is witnessing the democratization of information, via the worldwide web. For young millennials, it may thus not have been strange to do a Google search about the LGBTIQA+ community. This access to information has allowed this generation to be rather articulate in their conceptualization of sexuality. Moreover, the continued rise of dating platforms (the likes of Tinder and Grindr) requires theological interrogation. Creating a space for networking and "matching," these applications have garnered a strong following by the generation of millennials. The millennial generation in South Africa also forms part of what has been termed the "born-frees" (or those born post-1994). Their articulation of their sexuality, via social media, also relates to the complexities of what it means to be in South Africa—given its divided history. This chapter, then, attempts to grapple with how social media plays a definitive role in our society. Further, it seeks to consider how millennials (also born-frees) construct their sexuality using social media. Fundamentally, it challenges faith communities and the theological academy to recognize the realities of the digital age and how it is related to sexualities.

Natalia Strydom, in "A Practical-Theological Consideration of Infertility," describes from her experience in pastoral settings the realities for couples dealing with infertility. Proceeding from the reality of infertility as a "silent matter" in the denomination where she holds office (the Dutch Reformed Church), she describes the journey of not only women, but specifically couples suffering from the emotional crisis and trauma of infertility. In an effort to equip ministers and pastoral counselors as well as congregants, the second part offers valuable practical advice for three church settings: congregational services and the pulpit, pastoral situations in the counseling office, and the broader life of the congregation as a whole.

In "Transforming Masculinities in the Reformed Church in Zambia? An Ethnographic Sketch," Mias van Jaarsveld provides an overview of observations made in the preliminary stages of a larger research project on the transforming masculinities in the Reformed Church in Zambia (RCZ). Following an ethnographic approach, and entering the field as a participant-observer, he describes the context in which this project was conducted by first providing a brief history of the RCZ, as well as observations made and insights gained while doing fieldwork. This becomes the backdrop for the rest of the study, which has a strong narrative component and focuses on the contents of the formal, face-to-face, semi-structured interviews conducted during official visits to Zambia's capitol, Lusaka. Interviews were conducted with both male and female respondents and concerns their views on masculinity and manhood in the RCZ. It is noticeable that what the hegemonic masculine members of the RCZ proclaim and maintain does not only exclude and marginalize women, but also a considerable number of men in Zambia. A theological response follows, with a particular emphasis on the person of Jesus Christ, who most likely also did not live up to the hegemonic standards of his time. The cross, vulnerability, wounds, unconditional love, and the giving up of power could be considered as important Christological markers when rethinking masculinities in the RCZ.

The section concludes with "Invisible No Longer: In Search of the Lived Experiences of Transgender People in African Independent Churches," by Sizwe Sithole. He notes that transgender people experience incongruence between their gender identity and sex assigned at birth. In South Africa, the transgender population has remained largely an invisible population until the development of organizations such as Gender Dynamix, who lobby for the rights and the visibility of transgender and intersex people in Africa. In line with this aim of greater visibility and understanding of trans people, he draws from his own experience as a transman and those of other trans people in African Independent Churches (AICs) in the Midlands area of KwaZulu-Natal. First, he reflects on the religio-cultural concepts used to negotiate and engage transgender individuals located within the landscape of African Independent Churches. Second, (and more importantly) he reflects on the experiences of transgender people in the development of their gender identity, and how faith features in this process of negotiation. Questions informing this part of the study is among others: How is the transgender identity embodied in the Zion churches? Furthermore, how do transgender individuals respond to an embodiment of their identity in these churches? The reflection is structured around three key central themes that form an important part in the development of the transgender identity; namely: naming, body, and cultural identity. He draws on the insights of feminist, queer, and transgender theorists in order to engage the lived experiences of transgender individuals. As part of the argument, he highlights how transgender participants identified between the gender categories of feminine and masculine, which was different from their sex category assigned to them at birth and in the process challenged the essentialist view of understanding gender in relation to sex. Moreover, he illustrates that the Zion churches lack vocabulary and theories to engage transgender people as the identity of transgender people is often mistaken for those who identify as gay or lesbian; consequently, the church adopts derogatory Zulu names such as Inkonkoni/Isitabane to refer to transgender people. Central to the argument is, however, the notion of body and how body relates to identity and gender expressions.

As is clear from the above, the chapters in this volume include a diverse range of perspectives from several theological disciplines and represent a variety of academic views and denominations, including a substantial number of women's voices. It is our hope that this volume will contribute to scholarly discussion and deeper theological and Christian ethical reflection on human sexuality through offering new and novel lines of inquiry, new topics for discussion, and new insights into established research. At the same time, we are acutely aware that the theme of human sexuality is much broader than can be presented in one volume. The task of theological and biblical interpretation is always contextual, persistent, and provisional. It is therefore our hope that this volume may play some small part in the larger conversations on human sexuality.

BIBLIOGRAPHY

Cornwall, Susannah. *Theology and Sexuality*. London: SCM, 2013.

Grenz, Stanely. *The Social God and the Relational Self: A Trinitarian Theology of the Imago Dei*. Louisville: Westminster John Knox, 2001.

Kotzé, Manitza, et al., eds. *Reconceiving Reproductive Health: Theological and Christian Ethical Reflections*. Reformed Theology in Africa Series Volume 1. Cape Town: AOSIS, 2019.

Loughlin, Gerald. "Sex After Natural Law." In *The Sexual Theologian. Essays on Sex, God, and Politics*, edited by Marcella Althaus-Reid and Lisa Isherwood, 86–98. London: T&T Clark, 2004.

Nelson, James B. *Body Theology*. Louisville: Westminster John Knox, 1992.

SECTION 1

Systematic Theological Reflections

2

Sacramentum Matrimonii?

Sexuality, Human Flourishing, and the Grammar of Grace[1]

Nadia Marais

INTRODUCTION

> How I dread preaching on the estate of marriage! I am reluctant
> to do it because I am afraid if I once get really involved in the
> subject it will make a lot of work for me and for others. . . I
> would much prefer neither to look into the matter nor to hear
> of it. But timidity is no help in an emergency; I must proceed.
> I must try to instruct poor bewildered consciences and take up
> the matter boldly.

With these words Martin Luther introduces his well-known treatise on marriage.[2] He was, by this time, under both papal ban (since 1520) and imperial
ban (since 1521); and returned out of necessity to Wittenberg after hiding

---

1. This chapter is a reworked version of a paper presented at the Reformation
Conference of the Faculty of Theology, Stellenbosch University, from 11 to 13 October
2017. The theme of the conference was "Crying for Life?: Reformation Today."

2. Luther, "Estate of Marriage," 11–50; see 17, in particular.

out in Wartburg.[3] What makes this treatise all the more remarkable is that Luther is, at the time of composing this treatise, a 39-year-old bachelor, with no prospect of marrying Katharina von Bora as of yet. She is still a nun in a Cistercian convent; and would not meet Luther until the next year (after fleeing the convent in 1523).[4] They would get married three years after this treatise was published (in 1525).[5]

A crucial theological question that continues to haunt church debates and ecumenical discussions on marriage matters has to do with theological interpretation of the form and function of marriage.[6] Is marriage a

---

3. Luther, "Estate of Marriage," 13.

4. Luther, "Estate of Marriage," 27, n. 22.

5. Luther, "Estate of Marriage," 27, n. 22.

6. Witte, *From Sacrament to Contract*. John Witte explains that Catholic, Lutheran, Calvinist, Anglican, and Enlightenment thinkers have worked out at least five "systematic models of marriage" in their efforts to interpret the form and function of marriage, and in particular "competing claims of ultimate authority over the form and function of marriage"—including "claims by the state, by family members, and by God and nature." As such, "[t]he Western Christian Church has, from its apostolic beginnings, offered four perspectives on marriage": (1) a religious perspective (shaped by the church community and subject to the church's "creeds, cults, and canons" as religious sanction), (2) a social perspective (shaped by the local community and subject to the laws of the community—such as state laws—as communal legitimation), (3) a contractual perspective (shaped by the couple and their family and subject to their "voluntary association" as voluntary formation), and (4) a naturalist perspective (shaped by reason and conscience and subject to natural law and natural theology as natural origin). These perspectives would be integrated in different ways, argues Witte, and be complementary to a large extent. Yet these perspectives would also "come to stand in considerable tension"—and ultimately lead to the rethinking and reinterpretation of marriage at crucial historical moments, exactly because this tension would create the impetus for examining some of "the deepest fault lines" in the historical formations and transformations of marriage. (Witte, *From Sacrament to Contract*, 2).

sacrament,[7] an estate,[8] a covenant,[9] a commonwealth,[10] or a contract[11]? We

7. The Catholic sacramental model of marriage arose during the twelfth century, and herein a number of strands—namely, (1) natural, (2) contractual, and (3) religious elements—held the sacramental portrayal of marriage together. Marriage herein "rose to the dignity of a sacrament," in that "[t]he temporal union of body, soul, and mind within the marital estate symbolized the eternal union between Christ and His Church, and brought sanctifying grace to the couple, the church, and the community" (Witte, *From Sacrament to Contract*, 2–4). See in particular the chapter on this model, entitled "Marriage as Sacrament in the Roman Catholic Tradition," in *From Sacrament to Contract*, 16–41.

8. The Lutheran social model of marriage was developed in the sixteenth century, and herein a number of strands—namely, (1) natural, (2) contractual, and (3) social elements—were reinterpreted in response to the Roman Catholic sacramental model of marriage, by recasting marriage into a two kingdoms theology and allocating marriage not to the heavenly kingdom (which makes of marriage "a sacred estate"), but to the earthly kingdom (which makes of marriage a "social estate"). Marriage also has theological and pedagogical uses in this model, which includes a soteriological rhetoric that speaks of marriage as "remedy" and "gift of God." Marriage herein is "a natural and social estate" within "the earthly kingdom" ("the natural order of creation") instead of "the heavenly kingdom" ("the spiritual order of redemption"). As such, "marriage was subject to the state" and governed by "civil law"; and not to the church and "canon law" (Witte, *From Sacrament to Contract*, 2–5). See in particular the chapter on this model, entitled "Marriage as Social Estate in the Lutheran Reformation," in *From Sacrament to Contract*, 42–73.

9. The Calvinist covenantal model of marriage was established in the sixteenth century (in Geneva), and herein a number of strands—namely, (1) natural, (2) contractual, and (3) religious elements—were reformulated in confirmation of Lutheran theological and legal reforms, but recast marriage into a covenantal theology. Marriage was, however, not only an agreement between two parties—but a "triparty agreement" wherein God is the "third-party witness, participant, and judge." Moreover, "[b]y superimposing the doctrine of covenant on the two kingdoms framework . . . added a spiritual dimension to marriage life in the earthly kingdom, [and] a marital obligation to spiritual life in the heavenly kingdom" (Witte, *From Sacrament to Contract*, 7–8). See also John Witte's chapter on this model, entitled "Marriage as Covenant in the Calvinist Tradition," in Witte, *From Sacrament to Contract*, 74–129.

10. The Anglican commonwealth model of marriage was worked out in the sixteenth and seventeenth centuries (in England), and herein a number of strands—namely, (1) natural, (2) contractual, (3) social, and (4) religious elements—shaped the view that marriage (or the family) was "a little commonwealth" which reflected the "tradition of stability" that underlie the political concept of England as "great commonwealth." Marriage as "little commonwealth" was subordinate to "the great commonwealth," but a crucial institution within the commonwealth "hierarchy of social institutions." This model was "thus used to integrate a whole network of parallel domestic and political duties rooted in the Bible and English tradition" (Witte, *From Sacrament to Contract*, 8–10). See also John Witte's chapter on this model, entitled "Marriage as Commonwealth in the Anglican Tradition," in Witte, *From Sacrament to Contract*, 130–193.

11. The Enlightenment contractarian model of marriage emerged in the eighteenth century, and herein a number of strands—namely (1) natural, (2) contractual, and (3) social—played into the development of marriage as "the voluntary bargain struck between

will not progress in any of our debates if we do not deal with such questions theologically; yet neither are we today the first to ask serious questions about marriage. The sixteenth-century Protestant Reformation would become a "watershed" in the history of marriage[12]—and Martin Luther would stand "at the forefront of this reformation of marriage."[13] It is therefore well worth remembering that marriage was a reformation concern; also, to Luther, "reformer of marriage" and "married reformer."[14]

REFORMING MARRIAGE—A REFORMATION CONCERN?

Already from the very beginnings of the Reformation, questions of marriage would preoccupy Protestant theologians and jurists.[15] John Witte points out that this preoccupation with marriage was driven by the Reformers' theology, jurisprudence, and politics.[16] Their theological focus fell to "[t]he

---

two parties who wanted to come together into an intimate association." Yet the terms of such agreements were set by the parties involved, and "in accordance with general rules of contract formation and general norms of a civil society" (Witte, *From Sacrament to Contract*, 10). See also John Witte's chapter on this model, entitled "Marriage as Contract in the Enlightenment Tradition," in Witte, *From Sacrament to Contract*, 94–215.

12. Witte, *From Sacrament to Contract*, 40.

13. Hendrix, "Luther on Marriage," 335–50; see 335, in particular.

14. Hendrix, "Luther on Marriage," 335–50. In anticipation of 2017, the Lutheran publication house Fortress Press has published a new series on Martin Luther's life and work for the five-hundredth anniversary of Luther's *95 Theses*, with the title *The Annotated Luther Series*. The series provides a new English translation of Luther's work, by following a thematic (rather than a chronological) approach to Luther's writing (Hillerbrand et al., "Series Introduction," vii). The volumes within this series include the following titles: *The Roots of Reform* (vol. 1, edited by Timothy Wengert; 2015), *Word and Faith* (vol. 2, edited by Kirsi Stjerna; 2015), *Church and Sacraments* (vol. 3, edited by Paul Robinson; 2016), *Pastoral Writings* (vol. 4, edited by Mary Jane Haemig; 2016), *Christian Life in the World* (vol. 5, edited by Hans Hillerbrand; 2017), and *The Interpretation of Scripture* (vol. 6, edited by Euan Cameron; 2017) (Hillerbrand et al., "Series Introduction, viii). These volumes rely on the Weimar edition of Martin Luther's works, the *Weimarer Ausgabe* (WA) (1983–1973), which is a complete edition of Luther's writings; and the American edition *Luther's Works* (LW) (1955–1986), which provides the basis for this volume's English translations (Hillerbrand et al., *Roots of Reform*, vii–viii).

15. Witte, *From Sacrament to Contract*, 42.

16. Witte, *From Sacrament to Contract*, 42. See also Witte, "'The Mother of All Earthly Laws,'" 111–25. Priests, nuns and monastics who converted to Protestantism had forsaken their vows (including celibacy vows)—and, as "[o]ne of the important symbolic acts of solidarity with the new Protestant cause"—married (and even sometimes married, divorced, and remarried) "in open violation of canon law rules." For this reason, many "early leaders of the Reformation faced aggressive prosecution by the Catholic

Catholic sacramental concept of marriage" which raised "deep questions of sacramental theology";[17] and if we listen carefully, we might hear the echoes of their own debates on marriage, which would come to shape the Reformed tradition in definitive ways. Of the many Protestant theologians who wrote about marriage—including John Calvin, Philip Melanchthon, Martin Bucer, and Thomas Cranmer[18]—Martin Luther himself had strong opinions and advice to give on marriage matters; perhaps surprisingly so, for a man who only married at 41 years of age![19] Some would go as far as

---

Church and its political allies for violation of the canon law of marriage," being "ex-priests and ex-monastics." As John Witte notes, "[s]uch acts of deliberate disobedience were quite common in the early years of the Reformation" (Witte, *From Sacrament to Contract*, 42–43; see also Luther, "Judgment of Martin Luther," 243–400).

17. John Witte explains "[m]any of the core issues of the Protestant Reformation were implicated by the Roman Catholic theology and canon law of marriage that prevailed throughout much of the West on the eve of the Reformation. The Catholic Church's jurisdiction over marriage was, for the reformers, a particularly flagrant example of the Church's usurpation of the magistrate's authority . . . [In short, i]ssues of marriage doctrine and law thus implicated and epitomized some of the cardinal theological issues of the Protestant Reformation" (Witte, *From Sacrament to Contract*, 42).

18. Witte, *From Sacrament to Contract*, 42.

19. He is, moreover, thoroughly aware of this fact; for he addresses this in his treatise on the estate of marriage: "I will not mention the other advantages and delights implicit in a marriage that goes well—that husband and wife cherish one another, become one, serve one another, and other attendant blessings—lest somebody shut me up by saying that I am speaking about something I have not experiences, and that there is more gall than honey in marriage. I base my remarks in Scripture, which to me is surer than all experience and cannot lie to me. He who finds still other good things in marriage profits all the more and should give thanks to God" (Luther, "The Estate of Marriage," 43). With this, he has had his say and does not let his unmarried state deter him from interpreting biblical texts that he associates with marriage, or criticizing the pope for the way in which the church deals with marriage matters, or freely giving his advice on such matters. Toward his later writings, such as *On Marriage Matters* (1530), he does become more defensive about his advice than he would be in his sermon (1519) and treatise (1522) on marriage, but still does not withhold what he really thinks and believes: "I will not withhold my opinion from you. Yet I give it with this condition . . . that I want to do this not as a judge, official, or regent, but by way of advice, such as I would in good conscience give as a special service to my good friends. So, if anyone wishes to follow this advice of mine, let him do so on his own responsibility; if he does not know how to carry it out, let him not seek shelter or refuge with me, or complain to me about it. I do not wish to place myself under the restraint of any authority or court, and since I am under none now, I do not wish to be under any in the future. Let whoever is supposed to rule or wants to rule be the ruler; I want to instruct and console consciences and advise them as much as I can. Whoever wishes to or can comply, let him do so; whoever will not or cannot, let him refrain. This has been my position up to now, and I intend to adhere to it in the future" (Luther, "On Marriage Matters," 259–320; see 267, in particular).

describing Luther as "the reformer of marriage"[20]; others would view Luther as a "German revolutionary" who "disparaged marriage."[21]

Arguably, his definitive work in this regard is his sermon (1519) and treatise (1522) on the estate of marriage, but his reflections on marriage are varied—in pastoral intent, rhetorical strategy, practical examples, and theological analyses—and spread throughout much of his written work.[22] As such, I can provide nothing more than a glimpse into the rich tradition from which Luther himself drew; a tradition which Luther would also help form. Three documents provide the contours for this glimpse, namely (1) his *Sermon on the Estate of Marriage* (1519),[23] (2) his book on *The Babylonian Captivity of the Church* (1520),[24] and (3) his *Treatise on the Estate of Marriage* (1522).[25] This glimpse is a small glimpse, for it focuses on a mere three years in Luther's life, but these three years would be crucial to the formation of his theology of marriage.

In his sermon on marriage, on the wedding of Cana (John 2:1–11), Martin Luther would develop the first impulses of his theology of

20. Hendrix, "Luther on Marriage," 336–42.

21. *Correctio Filialis De Haeresibus Propagatis*; see 15, in particular.

22. The sermon on marriage is available in WA 2:166–171 ("Ein Sermon von dem ehelichen Stand") and LW 44:3–14; and the treatise on marriage is available in WA 10.2:275–304 ("Vom ehelichen Leben") and LW 45:13–49. There are also substantial reflections on marriage in a number of his other published works, including *Babylonian Captivity of the Church* (1520; cf. WA 6:497–573 and LW 3611–126), *To the Christian Nobility of the German Nation concerning the Reform of the Christian Estate* (1520; cf. WA 6:404–469 and LW 44:123–217), *Of Monastic Vows* (1521; cf. WA 8, 573–669 and LW 44, 243–400), and *On Marriage Matters* (1530; cf. WA 30.3, 205–248 and LW 46, 265–320).

23. Luther, "Sermon on the Estate of Marriage," 3–14.

24. Luther, "Babylonian Captivity of the Church," 9–130.

25. Luther, "Estate of Marriage," 11–50.

marriage,[26] including thoughts on companionship,[27] desire,[28] and love.[29] He examines three theological portrayals of marriage, as was provided by the church's theologians of the time, namely: (1) marriage as sacrament,

26. Brandt, *Luther's Works*, 14.

27. It is interesting to note that although Luther preaches on the wedding of Cana (John 2:1–11), which was the Gospel text for the second Sunday after Epiphany (16 January 1519) (Luther, "Sermon on the Estate of Marriage," 5), Luther begins his sermon with an exegesis of the creation accounts in Genesis 1 and 2. He is particularly interested in the creation of Eve, perhaps because he is interested in marriage and how marriage fits into the created world. He argues that God created Adam and all the animals, but that Adam could find no suitable companion among them—and since "Adam found no marriageable partner for himself," God intervenes—and gives Adam the gift of a partner, Eve (Luther, "Sermon on the Estate of Marriage," 7–8).

28. The woman is created to be the man's "helpmeet"—not only by managing the sin of lust, by channeling sexual desire into the marital relationship, but also by bearing children. Luther's remarks on desire are particularly interesting to examine. On the one hand, he does not shy away from using the language of desire; in this sermon, he says that "the desire of the man for the woman, and vice versa, is sought not only for companionship and children . . . but also for the pursuance of wicked lust." Now, he is admittedly very pessimistic about sexual desire, but it is nonetheless remarkable that he is willing to speak about desire at all. He writes about the desire of a bride for her husband, which "glows like a fire" and which leads the bride to say to her husband: "It is you I want, not what is yours: I want neither your silver nor your gold; I want neither. I want only you. I want you in your entirety, or not at all." If it was not for the fall, Luther argues, this desire would have been admirable; expressive of "the loveliest thing," namely the love between a bride and groom. On the other hand, he consistently describes "lust" as "wicked." Luther cautions that Adam's fall has disordered our desires forevermore, and that desire after the fall cannot avoid becoming corrupted and sinful. He argues that "although a married partner desires to have the other" this desiring is intrinsically selfish, in that "each seeks to satisfy his desire with the other." Marriage is an indispensable channel for desire; "the means of which the sin of lust which flows beneath the surface is counteracted and ceases to be a cause of damnation." He maintains this ambiguity about desire throughout his writings on marriage. However, James Atkinson remarks in a footnote that it would not be until 1523 that Luther would complement this view of marriage—namely, "marriage as a remedy against sin"—with the view that marriage is also "an estate of faith" (Luther, "Sermon on the Estate of Marriage," 8–9; cf. Atkinson, *Luther's Works*, 9, n. 1).

29. There are three kinds of love, argues Luther; namely, (1) false love, (2) natural love, and (3) married love. False love, firstly, "seeks its own"—like "a man [who] loves money, possessions, honor, and women taken outside of marriage and against God's command." Natural love, secondly, is familial love—the kind of love found "between father and child, brother and sister, friend and relative, and similar relationships." Married love, thirdly, is the best of all loves—for "[a]ll other kinds of love seek something other than the loved one: this kind wants only to have the beloved's own self completely." Yet Luther cautions that even this kind of love would not remain pure after the fall, but becomes corrupted when the desire for the other is disordered and selfish (Luther, "Sermon on the Estate of Marriage," 9).

(2) marriage as covenant,[30] and (3) marriage as family.[31] Of these it is this last description, with its implications for children and future generations, that matters most to Luther.[32]

Much can be said and much has been written about these various descriptions of marriage; yet there is an important detail here that ought not be missed: namely, that the Martin Luther of 1519 still regarded marriage as a sacrament, as he had been taught.[33] He describes marriage as a sacrament himself; by which he means "a sacred sign of something spiritual, holy, heavenly, and eternal."[34] Herein Luther leans heavily on the church father

30. In his portrayal of marriage as a covenant, Martin Luther means that "[t]he whole basis and essence of marriage is that each gives himself or herself to the other, and they promise to remain faithful to each other." This involves husband and wife "binding" and "surrendering" themselves to one another, as each other's only companions. It is within this covenant of fidelity that desire is contained and children are begotten. As such, marriage takes the form of a promise, a vow, or a commitment to remain in a relationship with only this person (Luther, "Sermon on the Estate of Marriage," 10–11).

31. In his portrayal of marriage as a family, Martin Luther means that "marriage produces offspring." This is "the end and chief purpose of marriage," argues Luther, namely, not only that children are born or heirs are sought, but that parents teach their children to serve, praise, and honor God. This is not only parents' "appointed work," but also "their shortest road to heaven" (although Luther adds, in the following paragraph, that "hell is no more easily earned than with respect to one's own children"!) (Luther, "Sermon on the Estate of Marriage," 12–13).

32. This last description of marriage is "the most important of all," as well as "the most useful," because of the utmost seriousness with which Martin Luther regards children and young people. His many urgings about the education of children makes this very clear, for a child is "an eternal treasure": "[T]his all married people should know. They can do no better work and do nothing more valuable either for God, for Christendom, for all the world, for themselves, and for their children to bring up their children well . . . [I]f you want to atone for all your sins, if you want to obtain the fullest remission of them on earth as well as in heaven, if you want to see many generations of your children, then look but at this . . . point with all the seriousness that you can muster and bring up your children properly. If you cannot do so, seek out other people who can and ask them to do it. Spare yourself neither money nor expense, neither trouble nor effort, for your children are churches, the altar, the testament, the vigils and masses for the dead for which you make provision in your will [*ablasz*; this is the same word that Luther uses to refer to indulgences]. It is they who will lighten you in your hour of death, and to your journey's end" (Luther, "Sermon on the Estate of Marriage," 12, 14). Indeed, for Luther children are "the greatest good in married life, that which makes all suffering and labor worthwhile" for it is "God [who] grants offspring and commands that they be brought up to worship and serve him. In all the world this is the noblest and most precious work, because to God there can be nothing dearer than the salvation of souls" (Luther, "The Estate of Marriage," 46).

33. Hendrix, "Luther on Marriage," 336.

34. Luther, "Sermon on the Estate of Marriage," 10.

Augustine,[35] whose thoughts on marriage were systematized by canon law-yers in the twelfth and thirteenth centuries[36] and formalized by the Council of Trent (1545–1563).[37] Although Augustine would not himself use the term *sacramentum matrimonii* in meaning the "inpouring" of sanctifying grace, Augustine would underscore "symbolic stability" in his language of sacrament.[38] And Augustine is important, because Luther was Augustin-ian—and never discarded this tradition completely.[39]

35. Hendrix, "Luther on Marriage," 336; Witte, *From Sacrament to Contract*, 22.

36. Witte, *From Sacrament to Contract*, 22.

37. Witte, *From Sacrament to Contract*, 36. John Witte outlines the development of what he calls "the robust sacramental model of the High Middle Ages" and Augustine's role therein. He points out that Augustine did not describe marriage as a sacrament in the manner in which it would be understood in the Middle Ages (namely, "as an instru-ment or cause of grace instituted by Christ for the purpose of sanctification"); nor did Augustine "draw out many of the legal and theological implications of his theory." In-stead, "sacrament" referred to "symbolic stability" in Augustine's work—argues Witte; so that marriage was a sacrament because it was permanent. In the thought of later Catholic theologians, this relationship was exactly the other way around: namely, that marriage was permanent because it was a sacrament. Marriage was "a sacred bond" for Augustine, in that "it could not be dissolved except by the death of a spouse." Augustine's intention in describing marriage as sacrament is perhaps also important here, for "[h]is main goal was to distinguish Christian marriage from prevailing pagan marriages and from the attacks on the institution by Gnostic, Manichean, and other heresies." Augustine, in short, "sought to show that Christian marriage was a stable and permanent union" (Witte, *From Sacrament to Contract*, 22; and Hendrix, "Luther on Marriage," 336; see also Clark, *St. Augustine on Marriage and Sexuality;* Bennet, *Water Is Thicker Than Blood*).

38. Witte, *From Sacrament to Contract*, 22. Martin Luther understood this very well. It is exactly because he understands this point that he invokes the sacrament of baptism in his theological reflection on the sacrament of marriage, for it provides the theologi-cal analogy for describing the "inpouring" of grace into a person (Luther, "Sermon on the Estate of Marriage," 10). "In the same way the estate of marriage is a sacrament. It is an outward and spiritual sign of the greatest, holiest, worthiest, and noblest thing that has ever existed or ever will exist: the union of the divine and human natures in Christ" (Luther, "Sermon on the Estate of Marriage," 10). Later Luther would hold that only baptism and eucharist (and, for the early Luther, perhaps penance) could be signs of God's gifts, signs, and promises of grace (Witte, "The Mother of All Earthly Laws," 121).

39. Martin Luther was, after all, a monk in the Augustinian order. The Augustinian Hermits were a leading mendicant order in Martin Luther's time (together with the Franciscan Minorites and the Dominican Brothers) and were founded in the thirteenth century when two popes, Innocent IV and Alexander IV, "united several small hermit societies under the so-called Augustinian *Rule*" (Atkinson, *Luther's Works*, 172, n. 143). Luther's sermon on marriage (1519) refers to this self-description explicitly, already in the title of this sermon—wherein he describes himself as an "Augustinian at Wit-tenberg" (as does *Babylonian Captivity* (1520), wherein he again describes himself as an "Augustinian") (Luther, "Sermon on the Estate of Marriage," 1; Luther, "Babylonian Captivity of the Church," 13). Augustine is right there, not only in the very theological

In this early sermon on marriage, Luther concludes that the sacrament of marriage "is indeed a wonderful sacrament."[40] This is a remarkable description for someone who—three years later, by the time that his treatise on marriage would be published (1522)—would charge that the inclusion of marriage among the sacraments is an insult to the sacraments![41] But here, in 1519, Luther does not appear to have changed his mind—*yet*. He even calls upon the apostle Paul (Eph 5:32) for theological support in bolstering his argument that the marital union between man and woman signifies a greater reality: namely, the union of God and human beings in the one person of Jesus Christ, as well as the union between Christ and the church.[42] This matter—of marriage being a sacrament—must be considered "with the respect it deserves," argues this Luther, for "the union of man and woman signifies such a great *mystery*" (my emphasis—NM).[43]

A year later he would have changed his mind on exactly this point, and the Martin Luther of 1520 would replace sacrament—as "a chief feature of marriage"—with love.[44] Yet Luther reconsidered not only his thoughts on marriage as a sacrament—he reconsidered *all* sacraments.[45] In *The Babylonian Captivity of the Church* (1520) Luther rejects the sacramental interpretation of marriage. In this work Luther reminds his readers of an earlier argument that he worked out in his discussions of the sacraments of baptism, the eucharist, and penance—namely, that "in every sacrament there is a word of divine promise."[46] Here Luther again echoes Augustine, for it is Augustine that describes sacraments as sacred signs (in *City of God*,

---

rhetoric that Luther employs, but in Luther's own theology of marriage—initially in agreement with Augustine, and later in protest against a sacramental theology of marriage. Indeed, as Scott Hendrix points out, "Luther knew the Augustinian view of marriage well" and even cites Augustine's three benefits of marriage in his Genesis lectures (1535–1545). In his 1522 treatise on marriage, he also refers specifically to Augustine, albeit by employing Monica—Augustine's mother—as an example for the possibilities of marriage between Christians and non-Christians. In short, "Luther never discarded all of this Augustinian heritage" (Hendrix, "Luther on Marriage," 348, 336). Later, Luther would again appeal to Augustine in a dispute on justification and sacramentality. See Lohse, *Martin Luther's Theology*, 114–5. See also the latest report of the bilateral Catholic-Reformed Dialogue (2011–2015), entitled *Justification and Sacramentality: The Christian community as an agent for justice* (2017).

40. Luther, "Sermon on the Estate of Marriage," 10.

41. Witte, "Mother of All Earthly Laws," 121; Hendrix, "Luther on Marriage," 337.

42. Luther, "Sermon on the Estate of Marriage," 10.

43. Luther, "Sermon on the Estate of Marriage," 10.

44. Hendrix, "Luther on Marriage," 337, 348.

45. Hendrix, "Luther on Marriage," 337.

46. Luther, "Babylonian Captivity of the Church," 96; see also Lohse, *Martin Luther's Theology*, 57–59, 78–80.

book 10); the "visible signs of the invisible God."[47] But by now Luther has serious reservations about the sacralization of marriage; for even if marriage is a sign of grace, signs are not sacraments.[48] He argues that "[n]owhere in all of the Holy Scriptures is this word *sacramentum* employed in the sense in which we use the term."[49] A sign of "a sacred thing" is not "the sacred, secret, hidden thing itself."[50] This collapse of meaning would confuse consciences. Moreover, having been busy with his translation of the New Testament, Luther also disputes that we "read anywhere that marriage was instituted by God to be a sign of anything."[51]

So where did the interpretation of marriage as sacrament come from?

Martin Luther explains that the association of marriage with sacramentality—and thereby the basis of the Catholic church's "entire sacramental theology and canon law of marriage"[52]—came from a misunderstanding of one biblical verse: Eph 5:32 (the exact same verse that *he* quotes when describing marriage as a sacrament, a year earlier!).[53] This misunderstanding arose partly because of "a careless and thoughtless reading of Scripture,"[54] and partly due to a mistranslation of the Greek *mysterion* into the Latin *sacramentum* (in the Vulgate).[55] Here the power of rhetoric becomes cru-

---

47. Augustine, *City of God*, 275.

48. Luther, "Babylonian Captivity of the Church," 96. He uses the example of the marriages of non-Christians to illustrate his point: "[S]ince marriage existed from the beginning of the world and is still found among unbelievers, there is no reason why it should be called a sacrament . . . of the church alone. The marriages of the ancients were no less sacred than are ours, nor are those of unbelievers less true marriages than those of believers, and yet they are not regarded as sacraments. Besides, even among believers there are married folk who are wicked and worse than any heathen; why should marriage be called a sacrament in their case and not among the heathen? Or are we going to talk the same sort of nonsense about baptism and the church and say that marriage is a sacrament only in the church, just as some make the mad claim that temporal power exists only in the church? That is childish and foolish talk, by which we expose our ignorance and foolhardiness" (Luther, "Babylonian Captivity of the Church," 96–97).

49. Luther, "Babylonian Captivity of the Church," 97.

50. Luther, "Babylonian Captivity of the Church," 97.

51. Luther, "Babylonian Captivity of the Church," 96.

52. Witte, "Mother of All Earthly Laws," 121. Erik Herrmann explains that it was the scholastic theologian Peter Lombard (1096–1160), among others, who listed "marriage as one of the seven sacraments" (even though marriage was no "helping grace," but "only a remedy against sin"). The Second Lateran Council (1139) assigned marriage—together with baptism and the eucharist—as "a priestly act," and at the Council of Verona (1184) "marriage was designated a sacrament" (Robinson, *Church and Sacraments*, 96, n. 206).

53. Luther, "Babylonian Captivity of the Church," 96–97; see in particular n. 206.

54. Luther, "Babylonian Captivity of the Church," 97.

55. Luther, "Babylonian Captivity of the Church," 98. John Witte explains Luther's

cial.[56] Luther does not altogether refute the association of "sacrament" with "mystery" (1520a:98–99), but he is very interested in the antecedent of Eph 5:32. Is the sacrament that this verse refers to applied to Christ and the church (as in Paul), or applied to a man and woman (as in scholastic theology)?[57] That, for Luther, is the question.[58] At most, marriage is an al-

---

position as follows: "The Greek term *mysterion* in this passage means 'mystery,' not 'sacrament.' St. Jerome had just gotten it wrong a millennium before when he translated the Greek word *mysterion* as the Latin word *sacramentum* and included that in his Latin translation of the Bible, the Vulgate. The Catholic Church has gotten it wrong ever since. In this famous Ephesians passage, Luther argued, St. Paul is simply describing the loving and sacrificial union of a Christian husband and wife as a reflection, an echo, a foretaste of the perfect mysterious union of Christ and his church. But that analogy does not make marriage a sacrament that confers sanctifying grace . . . Ephesians 5 is not giving a new sacrament here, Luther insisted, but driving home a lesson about marital love that much of the chapter has just explicated" (Witte, "Mother of All Earthly Laws," 121).

56. Erik Herrmann notes that, already in his Romans lectures (1515–1516), "Luther began to realize certain incompatibilities with the way the Scholastic tradition used and defined theological word and the manner in which Paul used them . . . In his 1522 translation of the New Testament, he included in his preface to Romans a list of biblical vocabulary that had been misinterpreted by the Scholastics, providing his own definitions for such key words as *law, sin, grace, faith, righteousness, flesh, and spirit*" (Robinson, *Church and Sacraments*, 98, n. 211). In his interpretation of Eph 5:32, Luther applies the translation of the Greek *mysterion* into the Latin *sacramentum* to 1 Tim 3:16's reference to Christ and points out that this would make of Christ a sacrament. "Why have they not drawn out of this passage an eighth sacrament of the New Law, since they have the clear authority of Paul?" asks Luther. He comes to the conclusion that "it was their ignorance of both words and things that betrayed them. They clung to the mere sounds of the words, indeed, to their own fancies. For, having once arbitrarily taken the word *sacramentum* to mean a sign, they immediately, without thought or scruple, made a 'sign' of it every time they came upon it in the Holy Scriptures." This is a cause for deep concern, argues Luther, for it means that "[t]hey have transformed the Scriptures according to their own dreams, making anything out of any passage whatsoever. Thus they continually chatter nonsense about the terms: good work, evil work, sin, grace, righteousness, virtue, and almost all the fundamental words and things. For they employ them all after their own arbitrary judgment, learned from the writings of men, to the detriment of both the truth of God and of our salvation" (Luther, "Babylonian Captivity of the Church," 98).

57. Luther, "Babylonian Captivity of the Church," 99.

58. But not only for Luther—also for contemporary theologians who write about marriage, such as Mark Jordan. In his book *Blessing Same-Sex Unions: The Perils of Queer Romance and the Confusions of Christian Marriage*, Jordan points out that Eph 5:22–33 remains crucially importance within debates about marriage today, exactly because it in we find "the New Testament's most Christocentric passage on marriage." Yet he shares Luther's reservations about the interpretation of the analogy presented here. He argues that "[t]he analogy has force because marriage is presumed to be familiar already to the readers and hearers as not specifically Christian in its essence. Christ's relation to the church can be illuminated by marriage only if marriage is not already conceived in Christocentric terms. Once the analogy is established, it can be reversed so that Christ's love for the church adds a further ideal to the relation of husband and

legory for Christ and the church, which is a mystery: "a great and secret thing."[59] Yet marriage cannot be called a sacrament just because it is used allegorically, argues Luther;[60] and *he* is convinced that this verse refers to Christ, not to marriage, anyway. The implications of this insight would be far reaching, for it would ultimately lead Luther to the conclusion that marriage "is not a divinely instituted sacrament."[61]

---

wife. Still the marriage must already exist before the analogy can begin. Marriage is not created out of Christ, however much it can be raised up through his example" (Jordan, *Blessing Same-Sex Unions*, 103). Again it is the analogical reversal that causes rhetorical confusion here: Is husband and wife analogous to Christ and church, or is Christ and church analogous to husband and wife?

59. Luther, "Babylonian Captivity of the Church," 99.

60. Luther, "Babylonian Captivity of the Church," 99.

61. Luther, "Babylonian Captivity of the Church," 100. This, of course, does not mean that Luther did not believe that marriage as such was "divinely instituted." Marriage is very much instituted by God, according to Luther; for marriage is "a work or estate which God has commanded and placed under worldly authority" (Luther, "On Marriage Matters," 314). In his treatise on marriage, it is made very clear that marriage is an initiative of God; that "God himself instituted it, brought husband and wife together, and ordained that they should beget children and care for them" (Luther, "On Marriage Matters," 38). Yet, in his later writing, he also holds to the position that marriage is a worldly matter: "No one can deny that marriage is an external, worldly matter, like clothing and food, house and property, subject to temporal authority, as the many imperial laws on the subject prove. Neither do I find any example in the New Testament where Christ or the apostles concerned themselves with such matters, except where they touched upon consciences" (here Luther cites Paul's writing in 1 Cor 7:1—24 as an example). Indeed, "what use would it be if we Christians set up a lot of laws and decisions, as long as the world is not subject to us and we have no authority over it?" (Luther, "On Marriage Matters," 265). For "[a]s soon as we begin to act as judges in marriage matters, the teeth of the millwheel will have snatched us by the sleeve and will carry us away to the point where we must decide the penalty. Once we have to decide the penalty, then we must also render judgment about the body and goods, and by this time we are down under the wheel and drowned in the water of worldly affairs." It is therefore of the utmost importance to Luther, particularly in marriage matters, that "the two authorities or realms, the temporal and the spiritual, are kept distinct and separate from each other"; and "that each is specifically instructed and restricted to its own task." The rationale for this is "the example of the pope," argues Luther, "who was the first to get mixed up in this business and has seized such worldly matters as his own to the point where he has become nothing but a worldly lord over emperors and kings." Indeed, this is exactly what Luther is trying to avoid, namely that "[t]he papacy [of his day] has so jumbled these two together and confused them with each other that neither one has kept to its power or force or rights and no one can disentangle them again." Luther "dreads" making the same mistake (Luther, "On Marriage Matters," 266). For this reason, Luther also argues that papal or canon law should yield to imperial or temporal law; not only because "papal laws often run counter to public ordinances, reason, and good sense" but also because "we are bound to obey the temporal law" in all worldly matters (Luther, "On Marriage Matters," 268).

In his treatise on marriage (1522) the groundwork for his theology of marriage has been laid[62]—even if he would in later work expand on some parts of his argument.[63] A major part of his treatise relies on the argument just explained, as it is outlined in *The Babylonian Captivity of the Church* (1520). The treatise on marriage consists of three parts: (1) impediments (who may we marry?),[64] (2) divorce (when can we divorce?),[65] and (3) salvation (how do we live a good life?).[66] Each of these parts are rich in rhetoric, sometimes quite funny, somewhat problematic (such as the reliance on creation orders and natural theology), and deeply concerned with human flourishing; within marriage, but also outside of marriage. Marriage makes for human flourishing; it is "delight," "love," "joy"—"without end," Luther argues.[67] Marriage is "pleasing to God" and "precious to God"—and therein gives "real happiness."[68] However, it is in Luther's surprising reinterpretation

---

62. Hendrix, "Luther on Marriage," 342.

63. For instance, in tracing the implications for interpreting marriage by way of his doctrine of two kingdoms. Herein marriage is governed by the jurisdiction of worldly commandments, as "an outward, bodily thing, like any other worldly undertaking" (Luther, "The Estate of Marriage," 31, 25). Martin Luther distinguishes here between "two types of government" that has been established by "the law of Moses"; namely, spiritual commandments and worldly commandments. Spiritual commandments teach "righteousness in the sight of God, such as love and obedience"; while world commandments are drawn up to limit misbehavior and "prevent [those who do not live up to the spiritual commandments] . . . from doing worse" (Luther, "Estate of Marriage," 31). Therefore, the many enforced impediments to marriage that Luther reviews and corrects in his treatise on marriage must be seriously considered in the light of biblical commandments—including the impediment against marrying a non-Christian, for "[j]ust as I may eat, drink, sleep, walk, ride with, buy from, speak to, and deal with a heathen, Jew, Turk, or heretic, so I may also marry and continue in wedlock to him. Pay no attention to the precepts of those fools who forbid it. You will find plenty of Christians—and indeed the greater part of them—who are worse in their secret unbelief than any Jew, heathen, Turk, or heretic. A heathen is just as much a man or a woman—God's good creation—as St. Peter, St. Paul, and St. Lucy" (Luther, "Estate of Marriage," 25). Scott Hendrix describes this specific declaration by Luther a "famous declaration about the secular nature of marriage" (Hendrix, "Luther on Marriage," 339).

64. Luther, "Estate of Marriage," 22–30.

65. Luther, "Estate of Marriage," 30–35.

66. Luther, "Estate of Marriage," 35–49. See also Hendrix, "Luther on Marriage," 339.

67. Luther, "Estate of Marriage," 38.

68. Luther, "Estate of Marriage," 42–3. That does not mean that marriage is sinless, or that Luther romanticized marriage—"[o]n the contrary, I say that flesh and blood, corrupted through Adam, is conceived and born in sin . . ." Sex is "never without sin," writes Luther; but "God excuses it by his grace because the estate of marriage is his work, and he preserves in and through the sin all that good which he has implanted and blessed in marriage" (Luther, "Estate of Marriage," 49). Herein, Luther follows the

of 1 Corinthians 7—an interpretation that some call "revolutionary"[69]—that he provides a robust theological alternative to marriage as sacrament; a change in hermeneutical key, so to speak, from Ephesians 5 to 1 Corinthians 7. His proposal is that we view both marriage and celibacy as gifts from God. God gives God's gifts; human beings can only receive these gifts and thank God for them. As such, both celibacy and marriage are gifts.[70] Herein he redefines both marriage and celibacy[71] and subverts the relationship between marriage and celibacy—but he also introduces the soteriological language of gift-giving into his theology of marriage.[72] The rhetoric of

---

theologian of the order in which he had been a monk, Augustine, who associated sex with the sin of lust and described sex outside of marriage as "a mortal sin" (Hendrix, "Luther on Marriage," 336). Augustine admits that we cannot assume that Adam and Eve "felt that lust which caused them afterward to blush and hide their nakedness, or that by its means they should have fulfilled the benediction of God" to increase and multiply (Gen 1:28). Yet he does argue that "it was after sin that lust began"; and thus, that children are begotten in sin, because "children could no more . . . be begotten without lust, which, after sin, was kindled, observed, blushed for, and covered; and even that children could not have been born in Paradise, but only outside of it, as in fact it turned out. For it was after they were expelled from it [Adam and Even from Paradise] that they came together to beget children, and begot them" (Augustine, *City of God,* 423). Children are thereby inevitably born into sin. It was only within the sacramental scope of the marital union that sex came to be tempered by sanctifying grace, and thereby "rendered inoffensive in marriage" (Hendrix, "Luther on Marriage," 336).

69. Hendrix, "Luther on Marriage," 338.

70. Luther, "Estate of Marriage," 49. Martin Luther makes provision for those who have received the gift of celibacy—although he warns that "celibacy is given to very few," calling upon Christ's words in Matt 19:11–12 and Paul's words in 1 Cor 7:7 (1520b, 175) (Martin Luther, "To the Christian Nobility," 113–219; see 175, in particular, in this regard). Celibacy is impossible "without special grace from God"—which is why, argues Luther, neither the apostles nor Christ himself made celibacy "a matter of obligation" (Luther, "Sermon on the Estate of Marriage," 9). Instead, he remarks cheekily, "if you would like to take a wise vow, then vow not to bite off your own nose; you can keep that vow" (Luther, "Estate of Marriage," 27). At the same time, he is honest about the reality of what he calls "human frailty"; he says that it is "only the strength of angels and the power of heaven" that makes it possible to live a celibate life. As such, ministers "should be given liberty by a Christian council to marry to avoid temptation and sin"; and nobody is allowed to "bind them" to celibacy, whether these be "the pope" or "an angel from heaven." What, then, stands a church to do? "I say that where they are so minded and live together, they should appeal anew to their conscience. Let the priest take and keep her as his lawful wedded wife, and live honestly with her as her husband, whether the pope likes it or not, whether it be against canon or human law. The salvation of your soul is more important than the observance of tyrannical, arbitrary, and wanton laws which are not necessary to salvation or commanded by God." Luther, "To the Christian Nobility," 177).

71. Hendrix, "Luther on Marriage," 338.

72. See Hendrix, "Luther on Marriage," 342. Although Martin Luther does not view marriage as belonging to the realm of redemption, he is also particularly concerned

"gifts given by God" fulfils a function that that none of his other arguments against marriage as sacrament could, for it is a rhetoric that is incompatible with ranking marriage above celibacy, or celibacy above marriage (as was the case in Luther's time). As such, celibacy is neither more[73] nor less[74] a gift from God than marriage.

---

about a kind of "marriage which will be conducive toward the soul's salvation" (Hendrix, "Luther on Marriage," 340; Luther, "Estate of Marriage," 35). Remarkably, the language of gift giving—and particularly, marriage as gift—and the grammar of grace would also find its way into Pope Francis in his reflections on marriage and the family (all references below come from his apostolic exhortation, *Amoris Laetitia*). See Francis, *Amoris Laetitia*. Here the pope portrays marriage as a gift from God that the church needs to safeguard—and "[t]his divine gift includes sexuality" (Francis, *Amoris Laetitia*, 61, 48–9). Marriage is a response to God's grace (35, 26), that requires "openness to grace" (37, 27) and being touched by "the power of grace" (38, 28). Indeed, the church should be "offering the healing power of grace" and not "lead people to feel judged and abandoned by the very Mother called to show them God's mercy" (49, 39).

73. Those who would therefore think Luther pessimistic about marriage, based on his argument against marriage as sacrament, are wrong. Luther is quite concerned about the public reputation of marriage; and while still unmarried himself, he laments "the fact that the estate of marriage has universally fallen into such awful disrepute" (Luther, "Estate of Marriage," 36). He criticizes "all those who criticize and censure marriage," including parents who "deter their children from marriage" (37). Marriage is "God's good will and work," proclaims Luther; and as such, marriage "does not set well with the devil" (37). However, it is not enough simply to marry—we must also do the work of *recognizing* marriage. Those who *do not* recognize the estate of marriage are prone to continue in wedlock "[with] bitterness, drudgery and anguish," or even "complaint" and "blasphemy." Those who *do* recognize the estate of marriage "will find therein delight, love, and joy without end." According to Luther, those who recognize the estate of marriage are those that believe (a) that marriage is instituted by God, (b) that it is God who brings husbands and wives together, (c) that couples should have children and care for the children (38). The most difficult of all, however, is in not making the mistaking of judging marriage "according to our own feelings . . . [and] own desires." When we judge marriage by our desires, writes Luther, we become unable to recognize God's work—including the good and pleasant work of marriage (39). In short, marriage is an estate "which God has ordained," and which is therefore holy, godly, honorable, and precious (41). It is clear that Luther takes marriage very seriously and describes marriage as "a weighty matter in the sight of God." Yet at the same time he likens marriage to "a hospital for incurables which prevents inmates from falling into graver sin" (Luther, "Sermon on the Estate of Marriage," 8–9). Perhaps it is therefore no surprise that he concludes his sermon on marriage as follows: "O what a truly noble, important, and blessed condition the estate of marriage is if it is properly regarded! O what a truly pitiable, horrible, and dangerous condition it is if it is not properly regarded!" (13–4).

74. An argument *for* marriage is, however, also not an argument *against* celibacy. It would again be a profound misunderstanding of Luther to think of him as against celibacy and virginity. "I do not wish to disparage virginity, or entice anyone away from virginity to marriage," writes Luther, for each person should "act as he able, and as he feels it has been given to him by God" (Luther, "Estate of Marriage," 46). He explains that celibacy was a practice among the early church fathers in order to live a contemplative

His resistance against compulsory clerical celibacy was an important impetus for his rethinking of marriage.[75] Yet not *only* resistance, but care, comfort, consolation—for Luther reminds his readers, time and again, that he is writing with pastoral intent, and that his primary concern is not upholding church laws, but comforting consciences. "It is my heartfelt wish," writes Luther in *The Babylonian Captivity of the Church*,[76] "for everybody to be helped." For this reason, in the church, the law must always yield to caring for consciences; for burdened and troubled consciences must be consoled and comforted.[77] It is the pastor Martin Luther that we encounter here; who

life, and that "there were many holy fathers who voluntarily abstained from matrimony that they might better devote themselves to study and be prepared at any moment for death or battle" (Luther, "To the Christian Nobility," 176). He regards such a spirituality as something completely different to mandatory celibacy enforced by church laws and vows of chastity—and indeed, "[i]n a worldly sense celibacy is probably better, since it has fewer cares and anxieties. This is true, however, not for its own sake but in order that the celibate may better be able to preach and care for God's word . . . It is God's word and the preaching which make celibacy—such as that of Christ and of Paul—better than the estate of marriage" (Luther, "Estate of Marriage," 46–7). Yet there is no hierarchy proposed here, where either estate of marriage is regarded as more important than the estate of celibacy, or the estate of celibacy is regarded as more important than the estate of marriage; for Luther's intention with this argument is that he "simply wanted to check those scandalmongers who place marriage so far beneath virginity that they dare to say . . . celibacy would still be better" (46–7).

75. Hendrix, "Luther on Marriage," 227. Those who could not forgo marriage were not worthy of the church's holy orders and offices," writes John Witte. In the sacramental model of marriage "[c]lerics, monastics, and other servants of the church were thus to forgo marriage as a condition for ecclesiastical service" (Witte, *From Sacrament to Contract*, 4). If we listen carefully enough, we will hear the serious reservations that the reformers had with such requirements. Marriage would not only be a political and theological matter for them, but also have serious practical and pastoral implications—particularly for "all priests, monks, and nuns who had vowed to live a celibate life and then decided to leave that life and take a spouse" (Hendrix, "Luther on Marriage," 335). Yet marriage would also be a deeply personal issue for Martin Luther, as an ex-monk who would himself live a celibate life for many years, and who therefore understands—in a way in which John Calvin, for instance, could not— what celibacy requirements do to ministers (335). Luther does not play around when he gives his view of church commandments which forbid ministers to marry: "[S]o much misery has arisen from this . . . What, then, shall we do about it? My advice is, restore freedom to everybody and leave every man free to marry or not to marry. . . I advise henceforth being ordained a priest or anything else that he in no wise vow to the bishop that he will remain celibate. On the contrary, he should tell the bishop that he has no right whatsoever to require such a vow, and that it is a devilish tyranny to make such a demand" (Luther, "To the Christian Nobility," 176–77).

76. Luther, "Babylonian Captivity of the Church," 175.

77. Luther writes that whenever difficult cases or unusual matters in the church arises, which "cannot be decided on the basis of some writing or book, then one should seek the advice and opinion of one or two good, pious men"—even if their advice "may not always

is deeply concerned about the salvation and flourishing of all, even when he writes about some of the most difficult theological matters of his time.

REDEEMING MARRIAGE—A GRAMMAR OF GRACE?

These are also among some of the most difficult theological matters of our time. Some recent titles of theological books that deal with marriage, sexuality, and desire include *A Time to Embrace*,[78] *Saving Desire*,[79] *Liberating Sex*,[80]

---

meet with the strictest demands"—for "it is better at last to have peace and quiet with this drawback and less justice than to have to keep on seeking the most pointed and severe justice with endless discord and unrest" (Luther, "On Marriage Matters," 287). Moreover, should "these pious men . . . err a little in such confused cases, God will be satisfied with their error, because their intentions are sincere and true, and they are not seeking advantage for themselves or knowingly speaking against the established laws." Any error that may arise will be "buried" in the Lord's Prayer, writes Luther; in the words "[f]orgive us our trespasses." Herein Luther does not want to be misunderstood: "no tyrant or villain is to understand this to mean that I am allowing him the freedom to render an opinion in any matter according to his own pleasure or fancy and contrary to public law and truth." Here Luther is speaking only about "pious men," and only as "obscure, confused cases [arise] which cannot be decided by means of indisputable pubic laws." His intent remains pastoral: the church is to "satisfy people in their consciences and not leave them forever dangling in doubt" (288). It is then that he establishes the principle of peace to which the law must yield. He writes that "peace is certainly worth more than all law and peace is not made for the sake of the law; rather, the law is made for the sake of peace. Therefore, if one must yield, then the law ought to yield to peace and not peace to the law. Now if we can have peace without legal squabbling, then let the quarrelsome law go, and the error will do no harm to the law, but rather will it be the great virtue of peace" (288–89). Later, he would make use of this same argument—but replace "peace" with "conscience": we are to "respect the conscience more than the law. And if conscience or law has to yield and give way, then it is the law which is to yield and give way, so that the conscience may be clear and free. The law is a temporal thing which must ultimately perish, but the conscience is an eternal thing which never dies." Whenever ministers and theologians have to do with confused consciences (*perplexis conscientiis*), this is the direct result of a "commingling" of "spiritual and temporal law" (318). Moreover, confused consciences are also a sign of incompetence on the part of theologians, argues Luther!—for "[o]ne is not well learned in the law . . . if one confuses consciences by them; laws are supposed to instill fear and punish, prevent and forbid, not to confuse and ensnare." His advice is that "if you find that a confusion of conscience is about to arise over the law, then tear through the law confidently like a millstone through a spiderweb, and act as if this law had never been born. And if you cannot tear it up outwardly before the world, then let it go and tear it up in your conscience . . . [W]hoever wishes to restore the law . . . so that he would rather let consciences choke on it before he would omit one bit of the law—he is the biggest fool on earth. . . To learn or know laws is no great art, but to use those laws correctly and keep them within their goals and province requires that one use restraint, and that is an art" (319).

78. Johnson, *A Time to Embrace*.

79. Schultz and Henriksen, *Saving Desire*.

80. Thatcher, *Liberating Sex*.

and *Blessing Same-Sex Unions*.[81] What is striking about these book titles is the soteriological rhetoric employed therein: "embrace," "save," "liberate," "bless." Those who would read contemporary theological works dealing with marriage may therefore also have to deal with salvation. Redeeming marriage in a time of considerable debate about the nature and function of marriage—in various church traditions, and on an array of topics, including same sex marriage, divorce, and ecclesiastical sex scandals[82]—may require paying closer attention to soteriology, particularly if the church wants to have anything to do with human flourishing, including the cries for life from LGBTIQA+ faith communities.[83]

Yet what does marriage have to do with salvation? Should we speak of a "gospel of marriage?"[84] Is marriage the good news that the church pro-

81. See Jordan, *Blessing Same-Sex Unions*.

82. See Coakley, "Ecclesiastical Sex Scandals," 29–54; Witte, "The Perils of Celibacy," 107–19.

83. Celibacy has been regaining popularity through church debates on sexuality. Whereas a number of churches admit that sexual orientation cannot be changed, celibacy has been resurrected within a number of Reformed churches as a compromise that may hold two groups together: namely, those who argue for full recognition and ordination of homosexual ministers, and those who argue that homosexuality is a sin that bars ministry candidates from ordination. Celibacy became a practical solution to this dilemma: homosexual ministers and theology students may be ordained, but must remain celibate. Celibacy becomes an additional requirement, a new promise, that only homosexual candidates for ministry must make—and thereby a punishment for something which none of us choose; namely, our sexual orientation. As such, our debates on marriage require of us not only to speak about sexual ethics or biblical texts that appear to condemn homosexuality, but also raises the question of the theological fabric or texture of our theologies of marriage.

84. In the apostolic exhortation *Amoris Laetitia*, Pope Francis speaks of "the Gospel of marriage and the family" (Francis, *Amoris Laetitia* 89, 71). He explains that marriage itself has "been redeemed by Christ" (here Eph 5:21–32 is referenced explicitly) and "restored in the image of the Holy Trinity, the mystery from which all true love flows" (63, 49). Yet marriage itself also becomes soteriological in that it makes for human flourishing, for "the flowering of the good qualities present in each person"—but more than this, "[e]ach marriage is [also] a kind of 'salvation history'" (221, 167). Here marriage itself becomes of soteriological significance *because* it is a sacrament, for "[t]he sacrament is a gift given for the sanctification and salvation of the spouses" (72, 55). Married couples are "witnesses of salvation" and "a permanent reminder for the Church of what took place on the cross" (72, 55). Herein it is also made clear what the sacrament of marriage is *not* (72–73, 55–6): (a) not a social convention, (b) not an empty ritual, (c) not an outward sign of commitment, (d) not a "thing," and (e) not a "power." In the sacrament of marriage Christ is encountered (73, 56), in that the sacrament of marriage (74, 58) "flows from the incarnation and paschal mystery whereby God showed the fullness of his love for humanity by becoming one with us." Significantly, marriage as covenant further strengthens this soteriological interpretation of marriage as sacrament, for the "spousal covenant" is "revealed in the history of salvation" and

claims? Are we those "saved by marriage?" Should we *not* worry about marriage? Is marriage only a contract—or even just a piece of paper?

In a book by this title *Marriage—Just a Piece of Paper?*[85] John Witte responds to this question by arguing that marriage *is* just a piece of paper, but that it is not *only* just a piece of paper. It is also, he argues,[86] what this paper signifies or represents—including "a bundle of rights, responsibilities, privileges, and immunities" that "are quite unique to the institution." This includes, argues Mark Jordan, not only a legal change in status but also a theological change of status—from being single to being married—which is expressed by the image of a bond between two persons.[87]

Two theological images have been particularly influential in imaging this marital bond, namely "sacrament" and "covenant"—both of which are deeply soteriological metaphors that assumes God's gracious intervention in human lives and have played no small part in our debates on marriage.[88]

"takes on its full meaning in Christ and his Church" (63, 50). Christ the Lord is made present and remains present with spouses in the sacrament of marriage (67, 52).

85. Anderson et al., *Marriage—Just a Piece of Paper?*

86. Witte, "Just a Piece of Paper?," 410.

87. Jordan, *Blessing Same-Sex Unions,* 124. "Marriage has been understood, for theological and legal reasons, as a decisive change of status. It is the change from being single to being married. The change has been equated both culturally and theologically with entry into maturity, loss of sexual innocence, and putting on a set of new duties, both in the city and in the church . . . Christian theologies describe the change of status in marriage with dozens of images. The most enduring is the image of the bond that unites the two married partners" (Jordan, *Blessing Same-Sex Unions,* 124).

88. And indeed, in the wake of Martin Luther's rejection of marriage as a sacrament, Protestant theologians would have to grapple with the deep tradition of sacramental theology and the challenge of proposing alternative theological models to the Catholic sacramental model of marriage. The Lutheran, Calvinist, and Anglican traditions would consequently "give birth" to three Protestant models of marriage: (a) marriage as social estate (Lutheran), (b) marriage as covenant (Calvinist), and (c) marriage as commonwealth (Anglican) (Witte, *From Sacrament to Contract,* 4–9). John Witte writes that "[a] Protestant social model rooted in Calvinist covenant theology" also found its way to South Africa (Witte, "Church, State, and Marriage," 40–47; see in particular 47). Yet this is by no means a singular theological argument (namely, marriage as covenant), for Don Browning and others have also employed the metaphor of covenant to work out what they call "a natural law theory of marriage," and attempts therein—particularly from Emil Brunner's theology of marriage—to "thereby discern some of the rhythms of our natural human sexuality and other natural needs that then anticipate and incline us toward covenanted life-long monogamy (Browning, "Don Browning's Christian Humanism," 733–60; in particular, 734–53). This would become particularly complicated within the Dutch Reformed tradition, which would in its church law and polity be "Catholic in origins and Calvinist in orientation" (Witte, "Catholic Origins," 328–51). Theologians such as Don Browning (in "Don Browning's Christian Humanism") and Sarah Coakley (in her as-yet-unpublished Gifford Lectures at the University of Aberdeen in 2012,

Yet I find it curious that Martin Luther's insights on gift-giving have not played a more prominent role in our theologies of marriage. Of the various models for marriage that we have encountered so far—in following John Witte's portrayal of marriage as sacrament, social estate, covenant, commonwealth, and contract[89]—sanctification, and sanctifying grace, has played a central role in articulating theological portrayals of marriage. But what has happened to the doctrine of justification?

Simon Peura writes that justification is expressed in Luther's theology by the concepts grace (*gratia* or *favor*) and gift (*donum*).[90] Christ himself is this grace and gift; and already in his *Lecture on Romans* (1515–1516) these two concepts—of grace and gift—would belong together, argues Peura.[91]

which included a lecture on "Reconceiving Natural Theology: Meaning, Sacrifice and God") do raise questions as to the role that natural theologies or natural law could and should play in theologies of marriage. However—at least in my mind—there is also an important question that remains regarding the social fabric or texture of our theologies of marriage, particularly in the theological and rhetorical relationship between the metaphors "sacrament" and "covenant," for how we position or describe sacramentality and covenantality in our views of marriage has serious implications for our discussions on what marriage is. For instance, this may require asking such questions: What is the relationship between marriage as sacrament and marriage as covenant? Is "covenant" a better alternative to "sacrament"—or perhaps even an alternative at all, seeing as this presupposes a choice between "sacrament" and "covenant"? Martin Luther himself did not juxtapose marriage as covenant to marriage as sacrament; and—as John Witte has pointed out—even the Calvinist covenantal model of marriage "mediated" and "confirmed" "the sacred and sanctifying qualities of marriage" (Witte, *From Sacrament to Contract*, 8). Does the covenantal model or marriage not rely upon an inner sacramentality; and the sacramental model on an outer covenantality? If marriage as sacrament is, after all, intended to signify Christ's covenantal relationship with the church, and marriage as covenant signifies Christ's relationship with the church as well—what are the important nuances to consider in such theological frameworks of reference? Do such frames of reference, wherein the theological antecedent that lends meaning to both the sacramental and covenantal models of marriage, is Christ's relationship to the church—not require more careful rhetorical distinction, lest sacrament and covenant may come to be collapsed into one another?

89. Cf. Witte, *From Sacrament to Contract*; Witte, "Church, State, and Marriage."

90. Peura, "Christ as Favor and Gift (donum)," 42–69; see in particular 42.

91. Peura, "Christ as Favor and Gift (donum)," 43. Simon Peura notes that "[t]he conceptions of grace and gift rest on Romans 5:15 (*gratia Dei et donum et gratia*), wherein Luther understands that both grace and gift are given to a Christian through Christ." For Luther, "grace and gift together constitute the donated righteousness of a Christian"; and "grace and gift are given not only through Christ, but in Christ and with Christ" (Peura, "Christ as Favor and Gift (donum)," 42–3). In the foreword to his translation of Romans into German (1522), "Luther points out that grace and gift are in Christ and they become ours when Christ is 'poured' into us." In short, for Luther grace and gift are the two goods of the gospel (43). Yet Luther also distinguishes between "grace" and "gift," argues Peura, for whereas grace "is the external good that opposes

Scott Hendrix has noted that Luther's insight that marriage and celibacy are among the gifts given by God, is a "revolutionary" insight that would may have equally profound implications as Luther's insight that all believers are called to be priests.[92] The language of gift-giving is, however, also embedded in Luther's view of God's self-giving wherein "the triune God proves to be the real God when he donates his own being to humanity."[93] But the relationship between grace and gift may also be of theological and rhetorical importance, for there is a "mutual conditioning of grace and gift" in Luther's thinking.[94] In short, "grace is the necessary condition of gift,"[95] so that the language of gift-giving requires a grammar of grace. After all,

> [N]o Christian should either trust in himself (sic) or steal the gifts that belong to God and make them his (sic) own. A Christian must always be aware that salvation is based in Christ. The Christian's own righteousness is sufficient for salvation only when it is linked to the righteousness of Christ and flows as a continuous stream from it.[96]

Martin Luther can "be a common teacher for Lutherans, Catholics, and other Christians," argues Simon Peura,[97] because "[t]he content of Luther's theology [of the real presence of Christ] makes him a Catholic teacher in the primary sense of the word and not a denominational one." And so perhaps Luther may yet teach us something after all. We need not speak the language of impediments, commandments, and compulsion; we need not speak the language of power, which watches us, seeks out our mistakes, and punishes us for them; and we need not speak the violent language that forces, silences, and shames people—particularly with

---

the greater evil"—namely, God's wrath—gift is "the Christian's internal good, and it opposes his internal evil," namely, sin. The good deeds that Christians do are themselves the "fruits" or consequences of "receiving the gift," whereas grace is nothing less than "God's mercy (*misericordia Dei*) and favor (*favor Dei*)." These two goods of the gospel belong together, for Luther, and therefore "a Christian must have both grace and gift" (44). Moreover, "Luther's interpretation of the relation between grace and gift becomes understandable only from the point of view that a Christian is in Christ and one with Christ. It is the idea of *unio cum Christo* that secures for Luther the principle of *sola gratia* in his doctrine of salvation . . . This means that the presence of Christ is the permanent condition of the Christian's effective righteousness" (59).

92. Hendrix, "Luther on Marriage," 338.

93. Peura, "Christ as Favor and Gift (donum)," 50.

94. Peura, "Christ as Favor and Gift (donum)," 56.

95. Peura, "Christ as Favor and Gift (donum)," 57.

96. Peura, "Christ as Favor and Gift (donum)," 59.

97. Peura, "Christ as Favor and Gift (donum)," 68.

regards to sexuality. We can speak this language, but we need not. We are the people that can also speak the language of human flourishing; we can speak a language that is good news, that tells of salvation, redemption, reconciliation; and we can speak a lifegiving, gift giving language that heals, helps, and blesses—particularly those most discriminated against in the church.

RESACRALIZING MARRIAGE—A TALE OF TWO DECLARATIONS?

> This is the grand movement of Western marriage law in the course of the past millennium. . . [namely,] a movement "from sacrament to contract"—from a sacramental model that prioritizes canonical norms and ecclesiastical structures to a contractarian model that prioritizes private choice and contractual strictures. . . This is a movement not so much of incremental secularization as of intermittent resacralization of Western marriage.

The story that John Witte describes is a story of resacralizing marriage.[98] This story is "a rich resource for the lore and law of modern marriage that is too little known and too little used today," he argues.[99] It is exactly for this reason that contemporary Christian churches should be doing the work of translating its deep and diverse theological heritage of marriage, for "[t]hese ancient sources ultimately hold the theological genetic code that has defined the contemporary family for what it is—and what it can be."[100] The debate about marriage as sacrament is therefore of much greater significance than merely being "a recurring theological quarrel,"[101] for it represents countless efforts—by many different traditions—to work out a theology of "marriage after modernity."[102] The danger of working with grammatical patterns is that the connections between theological words can be ignored or misunderstood.[103] The story of resacralizing marriage

98. Witte, *From Sacrament to Contract*, 13.

99. Witte, *From Sacrament to Contract*, 15.

100. Witte, *From Sacrament to Contract*, 15.

101. Cf. Jordan, *Blessing Same-Sex Unions*, 106.

102. Thatcher, *Marriage after Modernity*.

103. Jordan, *Blessing Same-Sex Unions*, 107. For exactly this reason Mark Jordan is wary of "[e]fforts to find a core teaching about marriage that never changes" because it will inevitably lead to interpretive dissonance: "Cutting a few formulas from one theologian in order to equate them with formulas from others, quite distant, is like

is also such a story: namely, a story that grapples with grammar, rhetoric, doctrines, and landscapes of faith.[104]

I offer two small examples of the rhetorical negotiation that continually takes place within this story of marriage. Theological disputes and debates about marriage, within various church traditions, are neither new nor surprising—and little of what is being said has not been said before. Yet recently there have been two significant doctrinal corrections issued with regards to theological portrayals of marriage in two major church traditions—namely a Catholic declaration called a *Correctio Filialis* (issued July 16, 2017);[105] and an Evangelical declaration called the Nashville Statement (issued August 29, 2017).[106] In both of these documents, marriage—and the theological portrayal thereof —stands at the very center of the respective disputes; and in both of these documents there are attempts to rectify not only what is considered to be doctrinal error, but also the deliberate, intentional, and measured use of rhetoric to persuade or steer the readers thereof toward a particular theological view of marriage.

In the Nashville Statement, written in response to the "secular spirit of our age," American Evangelical theologians and church leaders—in large part from Baptist churches and seminaries—offer fourteen articles of faith by way of affirmation and denial.[107] Three articles have to do with marriage (namely the first, second and ninth articles). The very first article deals with their theological understanding of marriage: they affirm that marriage is a covenant and deny that marriage is (only) a (human) contract.[108] Following on this, their second article deals with their theological

---

trying to prove the unity of all painting by cutting out little patches of the 'same' blue from Michelangelo's frescoes and Matisse's canvasses. A string of (translated) words on marriage in Augustine is not equal to the string of the 'same' words in John Paul II— unless one already accepts what the comparison is trying to prove, namely that there are invariant core meanings. Theological traditions have often been built by collage, but most influential collages have acknowledged their newness. A medieval disputed question collects earlier statements around newly controversial topics, but it does so in candid awareness that it is advancing the topic. The meaning of marriage in particular is liable to be missed—or grossly misunderstood—unless it is read against the other arrangements that surround it" (107).

104. Mark Jordan includes, among these, an attempt at "standardizing" within the church and theology: "The motley history of Christian weddings is united by the effort to sacralize existing civil rites—followed, of course, by efforts to desacralize or resacralize them differently. For generations, part of sacralizing has been standardizing within both church law and moral theology" (Jordan, *Blessing Same-Sex Unions,* 142).

105. *Correctio Filialis,* 2017.

106. Coalition for Biblical Sexuality, *Nashville Statement,* 2017.

107. Coalition for Biblical Sexuality, *Nashville Statement,* 1.

108. Coalition for Biblical Sexuality, *Nashville Statement,* 1. More specifically, they

understanding of celibacy: they affirm "chastity outside of marriage" and "fidelity within marriage."[109] Their ninth article focuses on sexual immorality, which they attribute to sin—which "distorts sexual desires."[110]

In the *Correctio Filialis*, written in response to Pope Francis's *Amoris Laetitia*,[111] Pope Francis is accused of propagating seven heretical propositions.[112] Of these, three propositions have to do with marriage (namely the second, fifth and seventh propositions); and one proposition refers directly to marriage as sacrament.[113] Serious issue is taken with the pope's perceived sympathy for Martin Luther, particularly with regards to marriage.[114] The complainants are concerned that the pope is not upholding and

---

affirm that "God has designed marriage to be a covenantal, sexual, procreative, lifelong union of one man and one woman, as husband and wife, and is meant to signify the covenant love between Christ and his bride the church" (*Nashville Statement*, 1); and they deny that "God has designed marriage to be a homosexual, polygamous, or polyamorous relationship" (*Nashville Statement*, 1).

109. Coalition for Biblical Sexuality, *Nashville Statement*, 1.

110. Coalition for Biblical Sexuality, *Nashville Statement*, 3. A number of declarations were issued in response to the Nashville Statement—including a Lutheran response by Nadia Bolz Weber and the House for All Sinners and Saints, called the Denver Statement. This declaration, written in the form of a filial correction, adds an article to the original fourteen articles. The fifteenth article rejects all forms of violence against the LGBTQIA+ community and individuals. Significantly, it also provides its own theological portrayal of marriage in the first article: namely that marriage is a gift and characterized by love. Other statements that would respond to the Nashville Statement is the Liturgists Statement and the Chicago Statement (Huppke, "Anti-LGBT 'Nashville Statement'").

111. Francis, *Amoris Laetitia*, 2016.

112. It should be mentioned that the writers distinguish between what they call "heretical propositions" and "heresy" (*Correctio Filialis*, 12). They accuse Pope Francis of "heretical propositions propagated by the words, deeds and omissions of Your Holiness"; which—according to them, at least—does not mean that they "have the competence or the intention to address the canonical issue of heresy." As such, their descriptions and accusations pertain only to "the personal sin of heresy" and not to "the canonical crime of heresy" (12).

113. Cf. *Correctio Filialis*, 8–9, 17–9.

114. *Correctio Filialis*, 12–6. "[W]e feel compelled by conscience to advert to Your Holiness's unprecedented sympathy for Martin Luther, and to the affinity between Luther's ideas on law, justification, and marriage, and those taught or favored by Your Holiness in *Amoris Laetitia* and elsewhere . . . Surprisingly we notice here, as in several other parts of this Apostolic Exhortation, a close relationship with Luther's disparagement of marriage" (*Correctio Filialis*, 12–5). They proceed by explaining Luther's position on marriage, namely that marriage is not a sacrament—particularly as it is outlined in *The Babylonian Captivity of the Church* (1520). They then continue to describe their complaint: "How can we not see here a close similarity with what has been suggested by Your Holiness in *Amoris Laetitia*?" (*Correctio Filialis*, 15). It appears to be the pope's pastoral leniency, particularly regarding divorce

defending marriage as a sacrament, but allowing space for Martin Luther's "heresy"—that marriage is not a sacrament, which by implication allows for divorce[115]—to thrive.

As John Witte notes, "[the] ancient battles over clerical and monastic celibacy and marriage are a world away from our. . . experience today"— but inevitably, "they are [also] the stuff of the very latest headlines."[116] In these more recent debates in church and state "over the forms and norms of marriage," there appears to be a renewed interest in the "long history of Christian marriage"—particularly "as proponents and opponents of marital change seek to prove the vintage and veracity of their arguments."[117] The Reformation itself, he notes, would gather several fragments and streams of "classical and Catholic legal ideas and institutions"—and therefore remain deeply embedded in such traditions—but would also "remix" and "revise" these in an attempt to provide contours for new theologies of marriage.[118] This is the kind of theological work that continues—and that needs to continue—in our day too, if we are serious about the power of traditions, and all that they do to shape us. Our rethinking and reinterpretation of marriage and sexuality may require reforming marriage, or redeeming marriage, or resacralizing marriage—or perhaps something altogether differently, such as a contemporary theology of desire.[119]

In 2017 Jürgen Moltmann offered a "clarion call" to the world-wide church, on the eve of the 500th commemoration of the Protestant

---

and remarriage, that is at issue here for the complainants; apparently, the pope is *too* gracious, and the pope's exhortation *too* pastoral—for it has led to the spread of "heresies" and "error" through the church by the pope's lack of "rebuke" (1). Instead, Pope Francis is to "defend the divinely held truths about marriage, the moral law, and the reception of the sacraments"—as some bishops and cardinals have continued to do, according to the writers—and to "guard" three things: "natural law," "the law of Christ," and "the law of the Church" (1).

115. Yet—as Scott Hendrix points out—Luther himself was not a firm advocate of divorce at all but remained uncertain about whether or not divorce should be allowed on any other grounds than the death of a spouse or adultery. His rejection of the "marriage as sacrament" was not a rejection of marriage; nor was it meant to condone the abuse of marriage. He argues, in a sermon from 1532, that divorce "is still a question for debate whether it is allowable. For my part, I so greatly detest divorce that I should prefer bigamy to it; but whether it is allowable, I do not venture to decide" (Hendrix, "Luther on Marriage," 337).

116. Witte, "Perils of Celibacy," 7.

117. Witte, "Church, State, and Marriage," 40.

118. Witte, "Church, State, and Marriage," 40.

119. Cf. Coakley, *God, Sexuality, and the Self*; Coakley, "Ecclesiastical Sex Scandals"; Jenson, *God, Desire, and a Theology of Human Sexuality*.

Reformation, to continue "the unfinished Reformation."[120] The 16th century Reformation centered on faith, he argues, and herein it remains unfinished, for it was *only* a reformation of faith.[121] What the churches of the Reformation, and the entire world, needs is a continuation of this reformation—namely, a reformation of hope.[122] A "reformation of hope" must follow a "reformation of faith," he argues[123]—but, curiously, his argument stops here. Surely, the reformations of faith and hope will remain hopelessly unfinished if it is unaccompanied by a reformation of love? For these three remain—faith, hope, and love—but the greatest of these is love?

An important implication of admitting that the Reformation is indeed unfinished is that we would have to admit that we are not done dealing with Martin Luther, and in particular the theological ramifications of his rejection of marriage as sacrament. What would follow is far more dramatic than what perhaps even Luther himself could have imagined; for it would impact countless relationships between spouses, children, parents, families—in different times and different contexts.

CONCLUSION

Tradition is the living faith of the dead; traditionalism is the dead faith of the living.

Reflecting on just more than 500 years since the Reformation, Jaroslav Pelikan's well-known description of "tradition" is helpful,[124] for—as John Witte's magisterial work on marriage[125] illustrates—traditions shape and reshape our theologies of marriage. Inevitably these traditions play in on how we view marriage, and shape the rules and regulations, the liturgies and language, the metaphors and message, of our theologies of marriage.

---

120. Moltmann and Lösel, "The Unfinished Reformation," 10–21; see in particular 10.

121. Moltmann and Lösel, "The Unfinished Reformation," 19–20.

122. Moltmann and Lösel, "The Unfinished Reformation," 19–20.

123. Moltmann and Lösel, "The Unfinished Reformation," 19–20.

124. Pelikan, *Vindication of Tradition*, 65.

125. Cf. Witte, *From Sacrament to Contract* (with the important subtitle *Marriage, Religion, and Law in the Western Tradition*). Scott Hendrix is critical of John Witte's explanation of the Lutheran reformers' portrayal of marriage, because it "places too much emphasis . . . upon the social and secular nature of marriage" (Hendrix, "Luther on Marriage," 349, n. 51). Martin Luther "is not trying to secularize marriage in the sense of separating it from God or religion," argues Hendrix (340; see also Althouse, *Ethics of Martin Luther*, 89–90).

Yet these traditions are not only "socially embedded," but also "historically extended."[126]

In three short years, Martin Luther changed his mind about marriage. Just more than five hundred years ago it was possible for theologians to rethink and reinterpret the meaning of marriage, and to reconsider whether marriage is indeed a sacrament. In our day, when we too grapple with the sacramentality of marriage—often falling just short of describing marriage itself as sacrament, but extending our theological descriptions of marriage to include such sacramental characteristics as "holy" and "God-instituted"—Luther himself could take us beyond Luther.[127] However, in order to open ourselves up to the possibility of thinking differently about marriage we need to be willing and able to reconsider our theologies of marriage, and the very real possibility that we might have to change our minds about who can and may marry whom.

And if Martin Luther could change his mind about marriage, so can we.

BIBLIOGRAPHY

Althouse, Peter. *The Ethics of Martin Luther*. Translated by R. C. Schultz. Philadelphia: Fortress, 1972.

Anderson, Katherine, Don Browning, and Brian Boyer, eds. *Marriage: Just a Piece of Paper?* Grand Rapids: William B. Eerdmans, 2002.

Augustine. *The City of God*. Translated by M. Dods. Massachusetts: Hendrickson, 2016.

Atkinson, James, ed. *Luther's Works*. Vol. 44, *The Christian in Society I*. Philadelphia: Fortress, 1966.

Bennet, Jane M. *Water Is Thicker than Blood: An Augustinian Theology of Marriage and Singlehood*. Oxford: Oxford University Press, 2008.

Brandt, W. I., ed. *Luther's Works*. Vol. 45, *The Christian in Society II*. Philadelphia: Fortress, 1962.

Browning, Don. "Don Browning's Christian Humanism: A Natural Law Theory of Marriage." *Zygon* 46:3 (2011) 733–60.

Cameron, Euan, ed. *The Annotated Luther*. Vol. 6, *The Interpretation of Scripture*. Minneapolis: Fortress, 2017.

Clark, Elizabeth, ed. *St. Augustine on Marriage and Sexuality*. Washington, DC: Catholic University of America Press, 1996.

---

126. MacIntyre, *After Virtue*.

127. It is worth quoting Lutheran theologian Kirsi Stjerna in greater length here: "Today we know too much to just keep holding on to the old assumptions of what Christian theology says about human sexuality and marriage. We can be Luthers in our day and dare to reinterpret our central concepts and experiences, such as maleness and femaleness, sexuality and sexual/gendered realities . . . in his footsteps, so can we" (Stjerna, "Luther on Marriage," 126–43; see 136, in particular).

Coakley, Sarah. "Ecclesiastical Sex Scandals: The Lack of a Contemporary Theology of Desire." In *The New Asceticism: Sexuality, Gender and the Quest for God,* 29–54. Oxford: Bloomsbury, 2015.

———.*God, Sexuality, and the Self: An Essay "On the Trinity."* Cambridge: Cambridge University Press, 2013.

Coalition for Biblical Sexuality. *Nashville Statement.* Nashville: Council on Biblical Manhood and Womanhood, 2017.

Correctio Filialis De Haeresibus Propagatis. August 11, 2017. http://www.correctiofilialis. org/wp-content/uploads/2017/08/Correctio-filialis_English_1.pdf.

Francis. *Amoris Laetitia.* Rome: Vatican, 2016.

Haemig, Mary Jane, ed. *The Annotated Luther.* Vol. 4, *Pastoral Writings.* Minneapolis: Fortress, 2016.

Hendrix, Scott. "Luther on Marriage." *Lutheran Quarterly* 14 (2000) 335–50.

Hillerbrand, Hans J. *The Annotated Luther.* Vol. 5, *Christian Life in the World.* Minneapolis: Fortress, 2017.

Hillerbrand, Hans J., et al., eds. "Series Introduction." In *The Annotated Luther,* Vol. 1: *The Roots of Reform,* edited by Timothy J. Wengert, vii–x. Minneapolis: Fortress, 2015.

Huppke, Rex. "Anti-LGBT 'Nashville Statement' meets a more loving 'Chicago Statement.'" *Chicago Tribune,* August 30, 2017. https://www.chicagotribune.com/ columns/rex-huppke/ct-nashville-statement-lgbt-huppke-20170830-story.html.

Jensen, David H. *God, Desire, and a Theology of Human Sexuality.* Louisville: Westminster John Knox, 2013.

Johnson, William Stacey. *A Time to Embrace: Same Sex Relationships in Religion, Law, and Politics.* 2nd ed. Grand Rapids: William B. Eerdmans, 2012.

Jordan, Mark D. *Blessing Same-Sex Unions: The Perils of Queer Romance and the Confusions of Christian Marriage.* Chicago: University of Chicago Press, 2005.

Justification and Sacramentality: The Christian Community as an Agent for Justice (2017). Report of the International Conversation between the Catholic Church and the World Communion of Reformed Churches. http://www.vatican. va/roman_curia/pontifical_councils/chrstuni/alliance-reform-docs/rc_pc_ chrstuni_doc_20171130_fourth-phase-dialogue-en.html.

Lohse, Brian. *Martin Luther's Theology: Its Historical and Systematic Development.* Translated by R. A. Harrisville. Minneapolis: Fortress, 2011.

Luther, Martin. "A Sermon on the Estate of Marriage." In *Luther's Works,* Vol. 44: *The Christian in Society I,* edited by James Atkinson, 3–14. Translated by James Atkinson. Philadelphia: Fortress, 1966.

———."On Marriage Matters." In *Luther's Works,* Vol. 46: *The Christian in Society III,* edited by R.C. Schultz, 259–320. Translated by F. C. Ahrens. Philadelphia: Fortress, 1966.

———."The Babylonian Captivity of the Church." In *Annotated Luther,* Vol. 3: *Church and Sacraments,* edited by Paul W. Robinson, 9–130. Translated by E. H. Herrmann. Minneapolis: Fortress, 2006.

———."The Estate of Marriage." In *Luther's Works,* Vol. 45: *The Christian in Society II,* edited by W.I. Brandt, 11–50. Philadelphia: Fortress, 1962.

———."The Judgment of Martin Luther on Monastic Vows." In *Luther's Works,* Vol. 44: *The Christian in Society I,* edited by James Atkinson, 243–400. Philadelphia: Fortress, 1966.

————.“To the Christian nobility of the German nation concerning the reform of the Christian Estate.” In *Luther's Works*, Vol. 44: *The Christian in Society I*, edited by James Atkinson, 113–219. Translated by C. M. Jacobs. Philadelphia: Fortress, 1966.

MacIntyre, Alasdair. *After Virtue: A Study in Moral Theory*. Notre Dame: University of Notre Dame Press, 1981.

Moltmann, Jürgen, and Steffen Lösel. “The Unfinished Reformation.” *Theology Today* 74.1 (2017) 10–21.

Pelikan, Jaroslav. *The Vindication of Tradition*. New Haven: Yale University Press, 1984.

Peura, Simon. “Christ as Favor and Gift (donum): The Challenge of Luther's Understanding of Justification.” In *Union with Christ: The New Finnish Interpretation of Luther*, edited by Carl E. Braaten and Robert W. Jenson, 42–69. Grand Rapids: William B. Eerdmans, 1998.

Robinson, P. W. *The Annotated Luther*. Vol. 3, *Church and Sacraments*. Minneapolis: Fortress, 2016.

Shultz, F. Leron, and Jan-Olav Henriksen, eds. *Saving Desire: The Seduction of Christian Theology*. Grand Rapids: William B. Eerdmans, 2011.

Schultz, R. C., ed. *Luther's Works*. Vol. 46, *The Christian in Society III*. Philadelphia: Fortress, 1967.

Stjerna, Kirsi I. “Luther on Marriage, for Gay and Straight.” In *Encounters with Luther: New Directions for Critical Studies*, edited by Kirsi I. Stjerna and B. Schramm, 126–143. Louisville: Westminster John Knox, 2016.

————.*The Annotated Luther*. Vol. 2, *Word and Faith*. Minneapolis: Fortress, 2015.

Thatcher, Adrian. *Liberating Sex: A Christian Sexual Theology*. London: SPCK, 1993.

————.*Marriage after Modernity: Christian Marriage in Postmodern Times*. New York: New York University Press, 1999.

Weber, Nadia Bolz. “The Denver Statement.” *Sarcastic Lutheran*, August 30, 2017. https://www.patheos.com/blogs/nadiabolzweber/2017/08/the-denver-statement/.

Wengert, Timothy I., ed. *he Annotated Luther*. Vol. 1, *The Roots of Reform*. Minneapolis: Fortress, 2015.

Witte, John. “Church, State, and Marriage: Three Reformation Models.” *Word and World* 23.1 (2003) 40–7.

————. *From Sacrament to Contract: Marriage, Religion, and Law in the Western Tradition*. Louisville: Westminster John Knox, 1997.

————.“Just a Piece of Paper?” In *Marriage: Just a Piece of Paper?*, edited by Katherine Anderson et al., 410. Grand Rapids: William B. Eerdmans, 2002.

————.“The Catholic Origins and Calvinist Orientation of Dutch Reformed Church Law.” *Calvin Theological Journal* 28 (1993) 328–51.

————.“‘The Mother of All Earthly Laws’: The Lutheran Reformation of Marriage.” In *Encounters with Luther: New Directions for Critical Studies*, edited by Kirsi I. Stjerna and B. Schramm, 111–25. Louisville: Westminster John Knox, 2016.

————.“The Perils of Celibacy: Clerical Celibacy and Marriage in Early Protestant Perspective.” In *Sexuality in the Catholic Tradition*, edited by L. Cahill and J. Garvey, 107–119. Lexington: Crossroad Publishers, 2006.

3

The Crisis of the Sexual Abuse
Scandal as Catalyst for Reform
in the Catholic Church

Nontando Hadebe

INTRODUCTION

> The Catholic Church has reached a crossroads. Its leaders can
> either change, become open and accountable, or maintain the
> status quo: an institution lacking transparency, wrapped in se-
> crecy and beholden to a clerical culture that is at the heart of the
> institution's problems.[1]

The significance of the above statement is that it is the voice of a survivor of
sexual abuse in the Catholic Church, Marie Collins who recently resigned
from the *Pontifical Commission for the protection of minors*. Her incisive
observations about the root cause of sexual abuse of minors in the Catholic
Church are shared by survivors, laity, theologians and significantly Pope
Francis who has consistently implicated clericalism as the root cause of
the crisis. There are other perspectives that also focus on a single issue
cause for the crisis, for example celibacy or lack of adherence to orthodoxy.

1. Roberts, "US Tour."

Others seek a more integrated approach that combine the "elephants in the room," that include power, sexuality, institutional culture, clericalism and patriarchy. The proliferation of different and varied responses to the sexual abuse crisis, however, has polarized the issue and deepened existing divisions within the church. The proposed call for reformation in the Catholic Church driven by the sexual abuse crisis is an attempt to build a thesis based on the integration of salient points from each perspective in relation to the elephants in the room, using the methodological framework of *Laudato Si*. No attempt will be made to provide definitive answers as the purpose is to propose a methodology that would open up the discourse in ways that *Laudato Si* did in making the environmental crisis the responsibility of all persons and institutions, an issue of global justice that required theological and spiritual renewal. The rest of the essay will elaborate further on these topics beginning with a summary of the sexual abuse scandal in the Catholic Church.

SUMMARY OF THE SEXUAL ABUSE SCANDAL IN THE CATHOLIC CHURCH

The sexual abuse of minors was brought to the notice of the public in the USA and globally through the investigative work of the *Boston Globe Newspaper* in 2002. The widespread appeal of their findings was, according to Jan Henley (2010), the extensive documentary evidence that substantiated the allegations which included "material relating to more than 100 priests," correspondence from parents and church documents that exposed the mechanisms of concealment, and protection of perpetrators by moving them around to different parishes without notifying these of cases of abuse associated with the priest—thus deliberately concealing their crime.[2] Initially the crisis was thought to be uniquely American, but more revelations of sexual abuse and concealment emerged across the world and it soon became clear that this was a global crisis in the church. The numbers involved are staggering. A BBC article entitled "Catholic Church sexual abuse scandal" quoted a church commission report in 2004 (US) that put the figure at more than 4000 priests guilty of sexual abuse of more than 10 000 minors (mostly boys), over a period of 50 years.[3] Similar reports from Australia and Ireland exposed widespread abuse of minors in schools, orphanages and churches. More allegations surfaced in Europe, Latin America, Asia and

2. Henley, "How the Boston Globe exposed the abuse scandal that rocked the Catholic Church."

3. See "Catholic Church Sexual Abuse Scandal."

Africa. The crisis was global and could no longer be reduced to being either an exclusively western phenomenon, or the result of anti-Catholic media reporting. There were differences among bishops in their responses and treatment of perpetrators and victims, but there were also common features which included concealment, secrecy, non-reporting of the crime to civil authorities, and protection of perpetrators. According to the preliminary report issued by the Child Rights International Network entitled *Clerical Abuse and the Holy See: The need for accountability, justice and reform,* the sexual abuse crisis is global:

> Victims all around the world have reported cases of child sexual abuse by Catholic clerics. From Ireland to Kenya, from Colombia to Poland, from the United States to the Philippines—no matter where one turns, it is hard to find a country which has a significant Catholic population and where there have not been serious allegations. And the pattern keeps repeating itself: Catholic priests who misuse their position of authority and regular contact with children.[4]

The report described the common response by bishops to cases of priests found guilty of abuse of minors as the "geographical cure" which was meant to,

> . . . relocate, forget, sweep under the rug cases of child abuse in order to protect the institution. Some bishops chose this method of ridding themselves and their parishes of abusive priests instead of forcing them to retire, removing them permanently from the priesthood—and contact with children—or reporting allegations to the civil authorities, including the police.[5]

Victims were often "intimidated, bought off, sworn to secrecy and confidentiality. They were destined to live with their guilt, shame and emotional scars."[6] However, some resisted and turned to courts for justice. It is estimated that the court cases and settlement in the USA cost around $2 billion! These huge sums of money cannot compensate fully the damage to the lives of so many and the breakdown of trust in the church. According to research done by Clair Gecewitcz (2019) of Pew Foundation, it was found that 79% of Catholics believed that the sexual abuse reflected "ongoing problems" within the church, compared to 12% who thought that the problems were of the past and actions taken by parishioners were less

4. Child Rights International Network, *Clerical Abuse and the Holy See.*
5. Child Rights International Network, *Clerical Abuse and the Holy See.*
6. Bausch, *Breaking Trust,* 5.

attendance of mass (27%) and reducing giving (26%).[7] In some countries, there was a sizable exodus from the church, for example according to *The Tablet* 216 078 Catholics in Germany left the church in 2018—a 29% increase from 2017. These different responses to the crisis are what Bartunek refers to as "sense making" in cases where there is incongruence or dissonance between fact and reality. In this case there is a "a large gulf between church officials' actions and the ways they had portrayed themselves and had been perceived."[8] However in countries and continents where there has been less reporting of sexual abuse of minors, as is the case in Africa, the Catholic Church has experienced considerable growth. Despite geographical differences, this article will argue that the core issues driving the sexual abuse of minors that include clericalism, sexuality, institutional culture and patriarchy are universal, and therefore the scandal provides a catalyst for reformation of the global church. The next section will explore further these themes through a discussion on two examples of responses to the crisis, namely one dimensional, and multi-dimensional.

ONE-DIMENSIONAL RESPONSES TO SEXUAL ABUSE OF MINORS IN THE CATHOLIC CHURCH

The one-dimensional perspectives focus on one issue as the primary cause of the crisis of sexual abuse of minors in the Catholic Church. Two of the most popular views will be briefly discussed, namely clericalism and celibacy.

Clericalism

> The clerical sexual abuse scandal has laid bare crimes and complicity within the Catholic Church. Not only has the extent of the abuse been concealed, so too has its handling by bishops and their superiors. This deeply ingrained instinct for institutional survival has dominated the hierarchy's mentality and approach to this scandal.[9]

The above quotation locates the root cause of the crisis within the church and implicates its leaders. There are several reasons for this and one of these is the culture of clericalism. In his *Letter to the People of God* (2018),

---

7. Gecewitcz, "Key Takeaways."
8. Bartunek, "Sexual Abuse Scandal," 17.
9. Sullivan, "Clerical Abuse," 18.

Pope Francis unequivocally laid the blame of the sexual abuse of minors on clericalism. "To say 'no' to abuse is to say an emphatic 'no' to all forms of clericalism."[10] Clericalism can be defined as "an expectation, leading to abuses of power, that ordained ministers are better than and should be over everyone else among the People of God." According to Daly, clericalism forms an integral part of the formation of priests and bishops:

> In other words: clerics (bishops and priests) are often trained to think they are set apart from and set above everyone else in the church. Their word is not to be questioned. Their behavior is not to be questioned. Their lifestyle is not to be questioned. They rule over the church as if they were feudal lords in a feudal society.[11]

Similarly, lay persons are socialized to accept and perpetuate clericalism through as explained by Daly "always deferring to 'Father' and putting 'Father' on a pedestal." Summarizing the impact of clericalism on the relationship between the clergy and laity, Blakely explains as follows:

> In an overly clericalized church, priests are not in open, equal, vulnerable human relationships with their flock. Instead, they are isolated by their own moral and spiritual status. Rather than a laity that might know its priests as human beings (and thereby see warning signs and intervene when abuse is suspected), parishioners see the priest as a shaman or a guru.[12]

Clericalism evolved over centuries creating an institutional culture characterized by unequal power relationships between clergy and laity, deference, and silence—which provided fertile ground for abuse, silencing of victims, and concealment to occur. The sexual abuse crisis seen through the lens of clericalism is primarily not about sex, but abuse of power. Consequently, Pope Francis has made dismantling and replacing the culture of clericalism an urgent priority in responding to the crisis:

> Looking ahead to the future, no effort must be spared to create a culture able to prevent such situations from happening, but also to prevent the possibility of their being covered up and perpetuated.[13]

---

10. Francis, *Letter*.
11. Daly, "Tackle Clericalism First."
12. Blakely, "Sexual Abuse."
13. Francis, *Letter*.

Celibacy

Mandatory celibacy is a requirement for priesthood in the Catholic Church according to Canon Law, Code 277:

> Can. 277 §1. Clerics are obliged to observe perfect and per-
> petual continence for the sake of the kingdom of heaven and
> therefore are bound to celibacy which is a special gift of God by
> which sacred ministers can adhere more easily to Christ with an
> undivided heart and are able to dedicate themselves more freely
> to the service of God and humanity. §2. Clerics are to behave
> with due prudence towards persons whose company can endan-
> ger their obligation to observe continence or give rise to scandal
> among the faithful.[14]

The reasons given for mandatory celibacy include dedication to Christ in undivided dedication to the church and humanity. Although scholars differ on the history of mandatory celibacy in the Catholic Church, there is some consensus that it was a gradual development formalized in 1123 at the first Lateral Council:[15]

> We absolutely forbid priests, deacons, subdeacons and monks
> to have concubines or to contract marriages. We adjudge, as the
> sacred canons have laid down, that a marriage contract between
> such persons should be made void and the persons ought to
> undergo penance.

This implies that there was a time when priests, bishops and popes were either married or had concubines. Celibacy separated the clergy from laity and consolidated their power. The history of mandatory celibacy in the church is beyond the scope of this essay, which will be limited to con-temporary views advocating for the abolition of mandatory celibacy as a response to sexual abuse crisis. In her research, Keenan disputes the link between celibacy and sexual abuse, but argues for the link between manda-tory celibacy and abuse:

> Some researchers and commentators have suggested that there
> is a positive link between celibacy and sex abuse. I am not con-
> vinced by this argument. Many men and women successfully
> live the celibate commitment without ever abusing anyone. On
> the contrary they enhance many peoples' lives. My own research
> is suggestive of a relationship however between the compulsory

14. Holy See, "Title III, Sacred Ministers or Clerics," cann. 232–93.
15. Daly, "Tackle Clericalism First," 24.

nature of celibacy and sexual abuse in many forms, including child sex abuse.[16]

Thus, for Keenan and others, mandatory celibacy is the core issue and needs to be replaced with optional celibacy. Therefore, Dorr calls for a delinking of celibacy from priesthood: "If the Church authorities were to loosen the present rigid link between celibacy and priestly ministry, it would open the way for a freer choice of celibacy by those who are really willing to take it on."[17] Thus celibacy per se is not the issue; rather it is the imposition of celibacy on priests. Similarly, many reform organizations led by laity are calling for optional celibacy, for example *Change.org* is running a campaign for abolition of mandatory celibacy.[18]

MULTI-DIMENSIONAL RESPONSES TO THE SEXUAL ABUSE SCANDAL IN THE CATHOLIC CHURCH

> Sexual abuse, however private its exercise, is never entirely personal. Nor is abuse an isolated incidence. Whether it occurs within a family, or within an institution, sexual abuse occurs within both a concrete social context and specific patterns of relationship.[19]

Multidimensional responses incorporate the intersection of different variables as causes of the sexual abuse scandal. Intersectionality is a characteristic of feminist and liberation theologies, which argue that no single factor can explain injustice and abuse of power. The former intersects variables such as patriarchy, power, class, race, culture, and coloniality, while the latter class and capitalism. The limitations of some of the one-dimensional perspectives on the causes of sexual abuse—as evident in the cases of clericalism and celibacy—is that they (as Keenan argues) do not address institutional authority and power:

> Since child sexual abuse is by definition an abuse of power involving dishonest and secretive sexual agendas, and made up of a mixture of sexuality, anger and opportunity then the issues

---

16. Keenan, "Institution and the Individual," 6.
17. Dorr, "Celibacy," 144.
18. See the website, www.change.org.
19. Ranson, "Climate of Sexual Abuse," 388.

of power/powerlessness, secrecy/ honesty and authority/subjec-
tion are important themes to be considered.[20]

Similarly, Ranson frames these issues as intersecting dysfunctions of
theology, psychology and social context. Dysfunctional theologies produce
"attitudes and behaviors that follow a particular theological framework."[21]
For example, inadequate concepts of God as father emphasize power and
control. As a consequence, relationships based on such a theology produce
relationships that normalize dominance and power which characterize
most relationships between clergy and their superiors and clergy and laity,
as seen in clericalism. In contrast, a Trinitarian theology of God that emphasizes relationality—"community, collaboration, participation, reconciliation and empowerment"[22]—yields egalitarian, transparent and vulnerable
relationships that are essential to overcome. As discussed earlier, the culture
of clericalism is at the root of the sexual abuse scandal.

Dysfunctional applications of psychology emphasize individualism
and fails to "recognize sexual abuse and pedophilia as complex psychological realities that are beyond simple moral appeal to the will or spiritualization that masks psychic conflict into a safe and respectable zone."[23] There is
an underlying inability to deal with "*eros* in a life-giving way as an impulse
for life in life to life" and a "source of connection between people, an affirmation of creation." This failure is associated with the fear of *eros* and the
negation of the feminine which has resulted in the "over-development of
masculine ethos" at the root of clericalism.[24]

Lastly, social dysfunction "colludes with the other two social structures" to create "dependency and illusory sexual institutionalization" that
has produced an institutional relationship characterized by abuse of power,
lack of accountability and transparency.[25] The three dysfunctions do not
operate in isolation from each other. Together they provide a more nuanced
explanation of the intersection of multifaceted factors that have contributed
to the sexual abuse of minors by clergy.

Some lay organizations adopting a multidimensional approach advocate for concrete practical action. One such example is FutureChurch:

---

20. Keenan, "Institution and the Individual," 7.

21. Ranson, "Climate of Sexual Abuse," 389.

22. Ranson, "Climate of Sexual Abuse," 389.

23. Ranson, "Climate of Sexual Abuse," 392.

24. Ranson, "Climate of Sexual Abuse," 392.

25. Ranson, "Climate of Sexual Abuse," 395.

> For over 28 years, FutureChurch activists have been commit-
> ted to dismantling the structural patriarchy and clericalism that
> has excluded married men from the priesthood, barred women
> from ordained ministry and governance, closed parishes, and
> created an elite culture of privilege that has produced far too
> many predator priests and bishops.[26]

Thus, multi-dimensional perspectives can be found in theological circles as well as lay organizations—advocating for justice and change as critical in confronting and eradicating the institutional context that has allowed
sexual abuse to occur. As mentioned in the introduction, there is often little
dialogue among the different perspectives, which has contributed to public
confusion and internal fragmentation in the responses to the crisis. Hence
the focus will be on a method that could provide a platform for dialogue
within and outside the church, because the sexual abuse of minors is found
in all religions and societies and therefore constitutes a global challenge that
requires a global response that will create a safer world for children and
vulnerable adults. Much has already been written on the subject; therefore,
the proposal of this essay will be on a methodology that can achieve these
objectives of globalizing the abuse of minors. The methodology of *Laudato
Si* will be proposed, as it managed to contribute to the globalizing of the
ecological crisis based on multidisciplinary analysis and critique of theologies that contributed to the crisis and advocated for participation of all in
resolving the crisis.

PROPOSED METHODOLOGY FROM *LAUDATO SI*

Laudato Si—as mentioned earlier—provides a framework for globalizing
the sexual abuse scandal as an issue of global injustice; one that requires a
multidisciplinary approach and participation of all institutions in the common struggle for a world that is safe for children, and a transformed church
that plays a role in this. Before discussing these issues, first a brief introduction of *Laudato Si*.

Laudato Si

Laudato Si literally means "Praise be to you" and is the title of an encyclical written by Pope Francis to address the global environmental crisis.
An encyclical represents the teaching of the Pope and is authoritative for

26. FutureChurch, "Faithful Catholics."

Catholics, second only to the Gospels and church councils like Vatican II. However, in *Laudato Si*, Pope Francis extends his appeal to all persons because environmental issues affect everyone: "In this encyclical I would like to enter into dialogue with all people about our common home."[27] The encyclical is a comprehensive overview of the environmental crisis drawing from multiple sources including science, environmental groups, global summits and Catholic contributions from Popes, Catholic Social Teaching and bishop conferences from different parts of the world. It implicates social systems of injustice (economic and political), consumerist lifestyles and anthropocentric theologies based on misinterpretation of scripture in the environmental crisis, and advocates for theologies, spiritual practices as well as global dialogues to facilitate change and transformation. Its fundamental message is the relatedness of all of creation and the ecological crisis as an injustice that affects the most vulnerable: "the cry of the earth is the cry of the poor."[28] In what follows, I propose a methodology based on *Laudato Si* as a framework for addressing the crisis of sexual abuse globally and in the Catholic Church.

The Four Principles from *Laudato Si* as Methodology for Addressing the Crisis of the Sexual Abuse of Minors

The four principles from *Laudato Si* that will be appropriated as the framework for a methodology that has the potential to address comprehensively both the crisis of sexual abuse of minors globally, and serve as a catalyst of change in the Catholic Church, are (a) the framing of the problem of sexual abuse of minors as a global issue of injustice and violence that demands accountability and responsibility from every person; (b) an integrated interdisciplinary approach that addresses the causes of sexual abuse; (c) a theological response that addresses underlying issues including sexuality, power, clericalism and patriarchy; and (d) a spirituality that will sustain a counter cultural context of safety for children and all persons. As mentioned in the introduction, the purpose is not to generate information but to pose questions within this methodology that can be a catalyst for dialogue that will produce change globally and in the Catholic Church.

First, as noted in the previous section, *Laudato Si* consistently describes the ecological crisis in global terms that include every person and nation. Further, the global nature of the crisis is reinforced by values such as interconnectedness, relatedness, justice, and human agency. Interconnectedness

27. Francis, *Laudate Si*, 4.
28. Francis, *Laudate Si*, 49.

and relatedness bridge the often perceived gap between the ecological crisis and social context: "A true ecological approach always becomes a social approach; it must integrate questions of justice in debates on the environment, so as to hear both the cry of the earth and the cry of the poor."[29] Human agency is implicated in both crises through what Rakoczy describes as "social sin" that is "embedded in social structures through the decisions of human beings which take on a life of their own," hence "the continuing ecological destruction of creation is the result of human action and inaction."[30] However, transformation is driven by human agency: "Yet not all is lost. Human beings, while capable of the worst, are also capable of rising above themselves, choosing again what is good, and making a new start, despite their mental and social conditioning."[31] This brief analysis of examples of core values used in *Laudato Si* serves to illustrate how these can be applied in response to the sexual abuse crisis in the Catholic Church. These values will be contextualized in order to generate questions that seek to contribute to the ongoing analysis of the crisis. The values of interconnectedness and relatedness are defining characteristics of the Catholic Church as the Body of Christ where all the baptized (clergy and laity) are joined together as one: "For in the one Spirit we were all baptized into one body" (1 Cor 12:12 NRSV), so that "(i)f one member suffers, all suffer together with it" (1 Cor 12:26 NRSV).[32]

Some of the questions that arise are:

- How does this intrinsic and ontological oneness of the Church frame the discourse on the sexual abuse crisis, considering it is no longer tenable to confine the abuse to either a private matter between the abuser and victim or ecclesial as the church, clergy and victims; it is a matter that includes every member of the Church without exception?

- How do issues of power, inequality, vulnerability, silence express themselves in the sexual relationships, beliefs and practices of all members of the Church including the clergy?

- How is the relationship of dominance, inequality and power between the abusing clergy and minor reflected in the hierarchical relationships in the church, home and society? What models of relationships within the church—for example between priest and bishop, among priests, priests and laity—reflect the dynamics of the relationships between clergy and minors that made the abuse possible?

29. Francis, *Laudato Si*, 49.

30. Rakoczy, "Conclusion," 170.

31. Rakoczy, "Conclusion," 205.

32. Also refer to Paul VI, *Lumen Gentium*.

The injustice and criminality of the abuse and concealment by church officials makes a fundamental connection between sexuality and justice: the cry of the abused minors is the cry for justice.

Second, *Laudato Si* draws on multiple resources, including scientists and environmental activists. in developing a comprehensive understanding of the ecological crisis: "A very solid scientific consensus indicates that we are presently witnessing a disturbing warming of the climatic system."[33] Environmental groups are also commended for their contributions: "Thanks to their efforts environmental questions have increasingly found their place on public agendas and encouraged more far-sighted approaches."[34] The broad-based approach of *Laudato Si* provides a conceptual framework for a similar multi-resourced response to the sexual abuse of minors' crisis. However, despite its claim of inclusion, the exclusion of feminist and women scholars who have written extensively on the same themes, such as linkages between exploitation of the environment and exploitation of the poorest of the poor being women are glaring; sexuality, patriarchy, inequality and power compromises the global claims of *Laudato Si*. Rakoczy noted that the "major lacuna in the encyclical is the silence on the relation between gender and ecojustice for it is women, especially poor women, who experience most seriously the ravages of the earth."[35] Chigoroma concurs and states that "the encyclical would have been richer if it had embraced the massive contribution of eco-feminists and acknowledged the interconnectedness between the global ecological crisis and the subjugation and exploitation of women."[36] Consequently, questions of inclusion and exclusion are critical for the discourse on the sexual abuse of minors crisis: whose voices, contributions and scholarship are prioritized and given authority and which groups or persons are excluded, subsumed or mentioned in passing? Are homosexual persons (since homosexuality is implicated in the crisis), women, children, victims, their families, laity, and all members of churches across the globe included? In the current highly polarized state in the Catholic Church, the danger is selective scholarship, research and sources that are used to prove beliefs, rather than to search for truth. These challenges require vigilance and commitment to inclusion and justice.

Third, *Laudato Si* challenged interpretations of the bible that have been used to justify exploitation of the environment. One of the most

---

33. Francis, *Laudato Si*, 23.

34. Francis, *Laudato Si*, 166.

35. Rakoczy, "Conclusion," 170.

36. Chigoroma, "Eco-Feminism," 153.

misinterpreted texts is the command in Genesis 1:28 to "subdue and have dominion":

> We are not God. The earth was here before us and it has been given to us. This allows us to respond to the charge that Judaeo-Christian thinking, on the basis of the Genesis account which grants man "dominion" over the earth (cf. Gen 1:28), has encouraged the unbridled exploitation of nature by painting him as domineering and destructive by nature. This is not a correct interpretation of the Bible as understood by the Church. Although it is true that we Christians have at times incorrectly interpreted the Scriptures, nowadays we must forcefully reject the notion that our being created in God's image and given dominion over the earth justifies absolute domination over other creatures.[37]

This confession of misinterpreting the bible starts with an acknowledgement that human beings are not equal to God and therefore can err in their interpretations of the bible with disastrous consequences, as evidenced in the ecological crisis. The crises of sexual abuse of minors requires a similar interrogation of misinterpretations of the bible that have culminated in the destruction of the lives as well as the faith of victims, their families, laity, clergy and the world. Some of the questions that need to be asked begin with which texts in the bible have been misinterpreted, resulting in the following destructive consequences:

- endowing unaccountable and absolute power to authority figures in the Church and family;

- creation of servile obedience among those subjected to such power in church and family—particularly subordinates, laity, women and children;

- definition and practice of power as dominance (power over);

- justification of criminality, silence, secrecy and violence; and

- normalization of gender inequality and hierarchical relations.

As noted earlier by Ranson, dysfunctional theologies are responsible for actions, behaviors and relationships that contribute to the sexual abuse crisis. Therefore, re-interpretation of these texts is critical for transformative responses to the sexual abuse of minors' crisis.

---

37. Francis, *Laudato Si*, 67.

Last, *Laudato Si* concludes on a hopeful note of human agency as catalyst for change. Among the proposals given for change is the call for "ecological conversion" for everyone:

> This conversion calls for a number of attitudes which together foster a spirit of generous care, full of tenderness. First, it entails gratitude and gratuitousness, a recognition that the world is God's loving gift, and that we are called quietly to imitate his generosity in self-sacrifice and good works. [. . .] By developing our individual, God-given capacities, an ecological conversion can inspire us to greater creativity and enthusiasm in resolving the world's problems and in offering ourselves to God "as a living sacrifice, holy and acceptable."[38]

Through this call for transformation, sustained by daily practices of virtues and sacrificial self-giving for the common good, a new culture is envisaged that will contribute to resolving the ecological and social crises. This affirmation of change and transformation through human agency makes possible accountability and responsibility at personal and social levels making it more sustainable than government or international interventions. Sexuality and relationships are universal experiences; hence the abuse of minors is a social injustice and violation that affects everyone. As proposed in *Laudato Si*, there is need for a conversion at a personal and social level that is infused by values which are essential in addressing the fundamental underlying causes of the sexual abuse of minors' crisis. Therefore, we need to ask questions such as: what kind of conversion is needed that responds directly to the cluster of issues at work in the abuse of minors such as power, sexuality, violence, secrecy, clericalism and institutional culture? What virtues are necessary to produce persons and institutions that normalize equality, non-harm, accountability, justice, accountability, safety where violence and domination are not options? How can these practices be a catalyst for change in the Catholic Church?

CONCLUSION

The sexual abuse scandal in the Catholic Church has opened up discussions on subjects that were taboo such as power of clergy, institutional culture, patriarchy and celibacy. The different responses witness to the vibrant and often divisive dialogues that create confusion for those within and outside the church. The goal of this essay was to unpack these issues and propose

---

38. Francis, *Laudato Si*, 220.

the methodology of *Laudato Si* as a starting point for bringing these perspectives in dialogue within the church and also outside because sexual abuse of minors is found in all religions, cultures and institutions. Just as the environmental crisis is a global issue brought about by human agency, so too is the abuse crisis. The lessons from *Laudato Si* provide a road map for a global response, as well as a church response, that can be a catalyst for reformation and change.

BIBLIOGRAPHY

Bartunek, J. M. "The Sexual Abuse Scandal as Social Drama." In *Church Ethics and its Organizational Context: Learning from the Sex Abuse Scandal in the Catholic Church*, edited by J.M. Bartunek, M.A. Hinsdale and J.F. Keenan, 17–29. Sheed and Ward: Lanham, 2006.

Bausch, William. *Breaking Trust. A Priest Looks At The Scandal Of Sexual Abuse.* Mystick: Twenty Third, 2002.

Blakely, Jason. "Sexual abuse and the culture of clericalism." https://www.america magazine.org/faith/2018/08/23/sexual-abuse-and-culture-clericalism.

"Catholic Church Sexual Abuse Scandal." *BBC*, October 5, 2021. https://www.bbc.com/news/world-44209971.

Change.org, "Help Us Abolish the Mandatory Celibacy Law in the Catholic Church-We Want Optional Celibacy." https://www.change.org/p/we-want-optional-celibacy.

Chigoroma, S. "Eco-Feminism and Gender Justice: The Missing Link in Laudato Si." *Journal of Theology for Southern Africa* 157 (2017) 147–53.

Child Rights International Network. "Clerical Abuse and the Holy See: The need for accountability, justice and reform." https://archive.crin.org/sites/default/files/CRIN_Holy%20See%20Report_WEB_0.pdf.

Daly, Fr. Peter. "Tackle clericalism first when attempting priesthood reform." https://www.ncronline.org/print/news/opinion/priestly-diary/tackle-clericalism-first-when-attempting-priesthood-reform.

Dorr, Donald. "Celibacy," *The Furrow* 55/3 (2004) 138–44.

FutureChurch. "Faithful Catholics Engender Significant #MeToo, #CatholicToo Moment with Decades Long Work to Dismantle Clericalism and Hold Those in Authority Accountable for Clergy Sex Abuse." https://www.futurechurch.org/press-releases/faithful-catholics-engender-significant-metoo-catholictoo-moment-with-decades-long.

Gecewitcz, Claire. "Key takeaways about how Americans view the sexual abuse scandal in the Catholic church." https://www.pewresearch.org/fact-tank/2019/06/11/key-takeaways-about-how-americans-view-the-sexual-abuse-scandal-in-the-catholic-church/.

Henley, Jon. "How the Boston Globe exposed the abuse scandal that rocked the Catholic Church." https://www.theguardian.com/world/2010/apr/21/boston-globe-abuse-scandal-catholic.

Keenan, Marie. "The Institution and the Individual: Child Sexual Abuse by Clergy." *The Furrow* 57/1 (2006) 3–8.

Pope Francis. *Laudato Si.* http://w2.vatican.va/content/francesco/en/encyclicals/docu
　　ments/papa-francesco_20150524_enciclica-laudato-si.html.

———. *Letter of His Holiness Pope Francis to the People of God.* http://w2.vatican.
　　va/content/francesco/en/letters/2018/documents/papa-francesco_20180820_
　　lettera-popolo-didio.html.

Pope Paul VI. *Lumen Gentium-Dogmatic Constitution of the Church by Pope Paul VI
　　1984.* http://www.vatican.va/archive/hist_councils/ii_vatican_council/documents
　　/vat-ii_const_19641121_lumen-gentium_en.html.

Rakoczy, S. "Conclusion." *Journal of Theology for Southern Africa* 157 (2017) 170–71.

Ranson, David. "The Climate of Sexual Abuse." *The Furrow* 53 (7/8) (2002) 387–97.

Roberts, Tom. "In US Tour, Marie Collins exposes clerical culture behind abuse cover
　　up." https://www.ncronline.org/print/news/accountability/us-tour-marie-collins-
　　exposes-clerical-culture-behind-abuse-cover.

Sullivan, Francis. 2018. "Clerical Abuse." In Joshua McElwee and Cindy Wooden, *A
　　Pope Francis Lexicon. Essays by Over 50 Noted Bishops Theologians and Journalists.*
　　18–20. Collegeville, Minnesota: Liturgical Press, 2018.

The Holy See, "Title III, Sacred Ministers or Clerics (Cann. 232–293)." http://www.
　　vatican.va/archive/cod-iuris-canonici/eng/documents/cic_lib2-cann208–329_
　　en.html#TITLE_III.

4

On Bodies and Theologies

The Aftermath of the Sexual Revolution

Jacob Meiring

INTRODUCTION

How relevant is it to refer to the sexual revolution when doing theology? It seems it still is. On 11 April 2019, BBC News published an article, "Ex-Pope Benedict XVI blames 1960s revolution for sex abuse." He had published a 5500-word letter in the German Catholic magazine *Klerusblatt*, divided into three parts, first exploring the "wider social context of the question," how the period of the sexual revolution affected the "dissolution of the Christian concept of morality," especially in Catholic educational institutions and then concludes by advocating a return to faith. Pope Emeritus Benedict XVI laments the 1960s as a time when previously normative standards regarding sexuality collapsed entirely. He blames sexual films, images of nudity and "the clothing of that time" leading to "mental collapse" and violence and argues that at the time of the sexual revolution that "Catholic moral theology suffered a collapse that rendered the Church defenseless against these changes in society." The sexual revolution led to pedophilia being "diagnosed as allowed and appropriate" and amongst others, also advocated "a new, modern Catholicism" which allowed the formation of "homosexual cliques" in seminaries.[1]

How is it possible that one cultural movement could cause so much discontent? This letter by the former Pope also opens up other questions: how relevant is it to still refer to the sexual revolution when talking about human theologies and human bodies? Who were the human bodies that wrote about theology and the body and why is it necessary to know that?

THEOLOGICAL RESPONSES TO
THE SEXUAL REVOLUTION

The sexual revolution of the 1960s to the early 1980s had a deep impact on how the church and theology viewed the bodies of believers. There were two major theological reactions in the late 1970s and early 1980s which culminated in two diverse theologies of the body—the one was a theology of the body of the Roman Catholic Church, which culminated in Pope John Paul II's book, *Man and Woman He Created Them* (published in English in 2006). The other reaction was the liberal Protestant body theology of James B Nelson, for many decades a sole voice in the desert. His first book, *Embodiment: An Approach to Sexuality and Christian Theology* (1978) was followed by *Body Theology* (1992) and ended in his last book, *Thirst: God and the Alcoholic Experience* (2004). His work was deeply influenced by liberation and black theology and in turn had an impact on queer theory and feminist theology. What is clear is that the body became a contentious topic in the church of the twentieth and twenty-first centuries in the wake of the sexual revolution. This revolution reached its culmination in the early 1980s when its momentum was stumped by social, economic and political factors—the HIV/AIDS epidemic being one of them.

THEOLOGY OF THE BODY AS REACTION
TO THE SEXUAL REVOLUTION

It would be good to remember that Pope Emeritus Benedict XVI served as the Prefect of the Sacred Congregation for the Doctrine of the Faith (the historical Roman Inquisition) from 1981 until 2005 when he was still Cardinal Joseph Ratzinger and a close confidant of Pope John II, who drafted his theology of the body when the latter was still a cardinal in Poland. Before Cardinal Wojtyla was inaugurated as Pope John Paul II, he finished the

---

1. See "Ex-Pope Benedict XVI."

typescript in Polish for a book titled *Man and Women He created them*, and he brought this manuscript from Krakow to Rome soon after his election. This pre-papal work was published in Polish in 1986 as a theology of the body and a copy of the original typescript served as a basis for the Pope's Wednesday catechesis which was given over a period of five years. The first of the 129 catechesis was delivered on 5 September 1979, and the last on 28 November 1984.[2] The Pope himself described the catechesis as "reflections on the theology of the body." The John Paul Institute published this catechesis one by one in Italian; an Italian one-volume edition appeared in 1985.[3] The 2006 English edition endeavored to research all the data supplied directly by the Pope, as well as the Polish text that served as basis for the catechesis.[4]

Michael Waldstein opens his extensive introduction to *Man and Woman He Created Them: A Theology of the Body* (2006) with a reference to the sexual revolution, which "was heralded by its advocates as a breakthrough for human development, for the freedom and happiness of the person."[5] He refers to the influence of Wilhelm Reich, a student of Sigmund Freud who initiated this revolution with his book published in 1936 and believed that "the free availability of sexual pleasure beyond the limits imposed by the patriarchal Christian family would lead to health and happiness" and even prevent war, insanity and mysticism. Waldstein asks whether the sexual revolution really brought happiness or merely transformed people into "users" and "consumers."[6] In contrast to this, the Pope's book puts forward "sexual politics of the radical gift of self of man and woman to each other, profoundly different from mere use and consumption."

In the preface to the 2006 English edition of the Pope's book *Man and Woman He Created Them: A Theology of the Body*, Christopher West writes that the theology of the body of Pope John Paul II is a response to the sexual revolution, to modern rationalism, to super-spiritualism, to Cartesian dualism and to all disembodied anthropologies.[7] West describes the world as "reaping a bitter suffering from the lies of the sexual revolution" and as "a mission field ready to soak up the good news of the 'redemption of the body' that he proclaimed."[8]

2. Waldstein, "Introduction," 4.
3. Waldstein, "Introduction," 5.
4. Waldstein, "Introduction," 11.
5. Waldstein, "Introduction," 1.
6. Waldstein, "Introduction," 2.
7. West, "Preface," xxvii.
8. West, "Preface," xxix.

The Pope's book was, however, not merely a knee-jerk reaction to the sexual revolution, but also a defense against Descartes's attack on the body, with the Pope stating that the body can never be reduced to mere matter and affirming that "the richest source of knowledge of the body, is the Word made flesh."[9] The incarnation indicates that the body has a spousal meaning: the body was created in Christ and for him and "Christ's gift of self is thus the goal that most deeply explains God's original intention in creating the body."[10] It is also an important response to the Cartesian-Kantian-Schelerian form of subjectivity and a defense against a scientific-technological attack from scientific rationalism which holds a narrow mechanist image of nature, especially from the viewpoint of biology. The Pope views the body as profoundly meaningful with an inseparable unitive and procreative meaning, which reveals the true focus of his theology of the body—a defense of the *Humanae Vitae*: the unitive and procreative meaning of the conjugal act.[11] *Humanae Vitae*, an encyclical written by Pope Paul VI, was issued on 25 July 1968 and reaffirms the traditional position of the Roman Catholic Church with regard to love in marriage, responsible parenthood and birth control. *Humanae Vitae* is a response against the control of matter by technology (for example contraception), and a call to the duty of man (sic.) to humanize nature. Waldstein writes that the opponents of *Humanae Vitae* do not criticize it because of its failure to grapple with modern issues, but because it is "an act of treason against the newly established alliance between Catholicism and modernity."[12] With technology man (sic.) wants to extend his domination over the totality of life, which includes the body and soul and the transmission of life.

Pope John Paul II develops his understanding of the body and personhood on the Boethius's definition of the person as an individual substance of a rational nature, which in turn has its grounding in the ontology of a human being by Thomas Aquinas as "a being composed of body and soul, the rational soul being the form of the body."[13] His book, *Love and Responsibility* (2013) builds upon this Thomistic account of the intellectual powers of the soul and the richness of a person's consciousness, with the claim that love should be formed by rational power, will and reason. Only then love can be love, with the body expressing the person in relationship to truth.[14]

9. Waldstein, "Introduction," 96.

10. Waldstein, "Introduction," 97.

11. Waldstein, "Introduction," 99.

12. Waldstein, "Introduction," 101.

13. Reimers, "Christian Personalism," 128.

14. Reimers, "Christian Personalism," 134.

The implicit dimension of love is the desire for a union between a man and a woman, not only physical, but also moral and spiritual.[15] A person's heart is a metaphor for this love, sensing the meaning of the human body, being both spousal and generative.[16] The body of a woman is made for motherhood complimented by that of a man, and when the heart is contaminated by erotic desire, it does not reflect the spousal meaning of the body. Pope John Paul II contends that the "deepest and fullest human love is spousal love."[17]

The question posed in the introduction now becomes more acute: who were the human bodies that wrote about theology and the body, and why is it necessary to know that? The feminist theologian, Katie Grimes compliments this inquiry, by asking: "Theology of whose body?" She argues that the theology of the body of John Paul II and his theory of sexual complementarity contradicts itself.[18] She emphatically states that "the irruption of the intersex person into history further undermines John Paul II's understanding of the human body."[19] Intersex human beings derail the Pope's understanding of a female body, demonstrating that God did not exclusively create humans as only male or female. His understanding of personhood and sexuality does not make space for the Other bodies, "for all of the human beings God created."[20]

THE ENIGMATIC WILHELM REICH

To understand the reaction of these two popes, we need to go back to the 1930s and the enigmatic Wilhelm Reich, sometimes called the godfather of the sexual revolution[21] and a sexual evangelist.[22] Reich was born in Austria in 1897, initially studied law, switched to study medicine as a veteran of World War I, and became one of Sigmund Freud's star pupils. He encountered psychoanalysis in a seminar on sexology and at age twenty-one Freud gave him permission to take on analyses and he then became very active in the Vienna Psychoanalytical Association, presenting numerous papers.[23] Then Freud and Reich had a fallout about the significance of desire and orgasms in psychoanalysis. Freud regarded the libido as an unruly beast and

15. Reimers, "Christian Personalism," 139.

16. Reimers, "Christian Personalism," 142.

17. Reimers, "Christian Personalism," 143.

18. Grimes, "Theology of Whose Body," 75.

19. Grimes, "Theology of Whose Body," 76.

20. Grimes, "Theology of Whose Body," 84.

21. Bramwell, "Godfather of the Sexual Revolution," 84.

22. Turner, "Wilhelm Reich," 1.

23. Bennett, "Wilhelm Reich's Self-Censorship," 242.

rejected any connection between sexual repression and violence. Reich on the other hand regarded war and aggression as a psychological death wish and as "humanity's innate drive towards destruction."[24] The persecution of Reich as a revolutionary thinker, began according to Bennett in 1927 when he published *Die Funktion des Orgasmus* ("The function of the Orgasm") in the journal of the International Psychoanalytical Association, the same year he witnessed the shooting of striking workers in Vienna.[25] This urged him to join the Communist Party, but forever associated his reputation with sexual liberation and radical politics, although he became a militant anti-Communist in the later part of his life—the dangerous mixture of politics, sex and psychoanalysis, which became a great concern to Freud and his daughter Anna.[26] He was eventually expelled by the Communist party in 1933.

Where Freud focused on the treatment of individual neuroses, Reich wanted to treat sexual mass neuroses, resisting attempts to do away with "the psychoanalytical theory of sex and to evade its social consequences."[27] He published two books in 1933, *Character Analysis*, which is still being used in psychoanalytical therapy and *Mass Psychology of Fascism*. Reich believed that the rise of fascism in Europe in the 1920s and 1930s was as a direct result of repressed sexual desire, "sublimated into hatred and war."[28] Impotence, like a lack of sexual pleasure or the inability to have an orgasm, were all symptoms of ill health which needed to be treated. A sexual revolution could liberate people from the brutal authoritarianism of politics and state.

Reich coined the phrase "sexual revolution" in his early work. He was a key organizer of the Sex-Pol movement of Austria and Germany in the late 1920s and 1930s, advocating sexual liberation.[29] He believed that a real political revolution can only be possible when sexual repression was overthrown. That was the main obstacle which had ruined the efforts of the Bolsheviks. Reich declared that "a sexual revolution is in progress and no power on earth will stop it."[30]

Many Jewish psychoanalysts emigrated from Austria and Germany under the Nazis from 1933 until 1939 and it was no wonder that Reich also became a target for the Gestapo with his anti-Nazi stance in *The Mass*

24. Bramwell, "Godfather of the Sexual Revolution," 84.

25. Bennett, "Persecution of Dr. Wilhelm Reich," 51.

26. Bennett, "Wilhelm Reich's Self-Censorship," 345.

27. Reich, cited in Lothane, "Wilhem Reich Revisited," 105.

28. Bramwell, "Godfather of the Sexual Revolution," 84.

29. Matviyenko, "Wilhem Reich's Machines," 120.

30. Turner, "Wilhelm Reich," 1.

Psychology of Fascism (1933).[31] In it he conducted a political and psycho-analytical analyses of the Third Reich, its genocide of European Jewry, and its culturecide (the destruction of East European Jewish culture). He was concerned about the Jewish denial of the Nazi menace and the growing anti-Jewish persecution, and for many years he was the only psychoanalyst who openly confronted the Nazi regime.[32] Having relocated to Berlin in 1930, Reich escaped certain death a few years later when the Gestapo were ordered to burn his books and shoot him. He disguised himself as a tourist and left for Denmark under a false name. In Denmark his promotion of abortion and ideas around teenage sex were as controversial and he moved to Sweden, then Norway.[33] Here he was the target of a smear campaign in the Left Labor periodical focusing on his biological work (his theory on orgone energy) and the Fascist press attacked him as a "Jewish pornographer of the worse kind."[34] He left for the USA in August 1939 where he hoped his radical ideas would be more acceptable.

He was wrong. Within months the Federal Bureau of Investigation (FBI) opened a file on him as an "alien enemy" and although he was natu-ralized in 1946, the Immigration and Naturalization Service (INS) started an eight-year process to denaturalize and deport him.[35] The Food and Drug Administration (FDA) began a campaign in 1947 to discredit Reich's work, branding him as a medical fraud involved in some kind of sex racket. They investigated his claims about orgone energy and his notorious "orgone accu-mulator." Reich refused to appear in court, the complaint became an injunc-tion banning the interstate selling of his orgone accumulators, his book and journals were restricted from circulation, and his journals were destroyed. He was found guilty and received a two-year prison sentence and a huge penalty. Wilhelm Reich died on 3 November 1957 at the age of sixty, just be-fore his parole hearing. Bennett sums up the irony of this persecution as "a singularity in US history: the large-scale burning of a world-famous think-er's books and journals ordered by a branch of the Federal government."[36] In America he was portrayed by right-wing Christian moralists in the same way as in Nazi Germany and Norway—the "dirty Commie Jew." The FBI

---

31. Lothane, "Wilhem Reich Revisited," 104.
32. Lothane, "Wilhem Reich Revisited," 104.
33. Bramwell, "Godfather of the Sexual Revolution," 86.
34. Bennett, "Persecution of Dr. Wilhelm Reich," 52.
35. Bennett, "Persecution of Dr. Wilhelm Reich," 52.
36. Bennett, "Persecution of Dr. Wilhelm Reich," 52.

and INS were more concerned with his ideas on sexuality and politics than in his so-called medical fraud.[37]

While in Norway, Reich taught at the University of Oslo and was able to use a laboratory. Here he began experiments in exploring the connection between sexuality and anxiety and its bioelectrical function. He named it the "orgone energy field" and by connecting a body to a machine, he believed he could measure it. This energy field was the basis for sexual desire. He viewed the human body as a "complicated electric machine" and by wiring the body to a machine he could increase the body's bio-electric charge.[38] Reich's body-orientated therapy was an enlargement of psychoanalysis and his experiments were based on Ferenczi's bio-analysis and genital theory, which endeavored to ground psychoanalysis in biological sciences.[39]

In America Reich gathered physical evidence of orgone energy. He believed that a person's orgone levels reflected their vitality which in turn was an indication of the level of pleasure derived from orgasm. He founded the Orgone Institute in 1942, and by this time he was convinced that he could measure the orgone energy in a human with a voltmeter when he or she was going through "intense emotional release." To increase the level of orgone energy, he invented the "orgone accumulator," an upright rectangular box made of different layers of wood and metal. Sitting upright inside this box, it was able to amplify the "orgone energy." He also claimed that it could boost the immune system and eliminate cancer cells.[40] Reich became the figurehead of a new sexual movement that was spreading across the country and his "orgone accumulator" was used by such countercultural figures such as Norman Mailer, JD Salinger, Saul Bellow, Paul Goodman, Allen Ginsberg, Jack Kerouac, Dwight Macdonald, and William S Burroughs.[41]

In 1947, Harper's magazine portrayed Reich to Americans as the leader of "a new cult of sex and anarchy" that was thriving along the west coast. Turner argues that Reich inspired post-World War II radicals to "view their promiscuity as political activism and justify their retreat from traditional politics" by crafting a morality out of pleasure.[42] The campaign against Reich was connected to the libertarian ideas of the biologist and zoologist, Alfred Kinsey, who in 1953 published his notorious report "Sexual Behavior in the Human Female." The American Medical Association accused Kinsey

37. Bennett, "Persecution of Dr. Wilhelm Reich," 53.
38. Matviyenko, "Wilhem Reich's Machines," 122.
39. Bennett, "Wilhelm Reich's Self-Censorship," 346.
40. Bramwell, "Godfather of the Sexual Revolution," 86.
41. Turner, "Wilhelm Reich," 2.
42. Turner, "Wilhelm Reich," 3.

of sparking a "wave of sexual hysteria." The same association encouraged the FDA to persecute Reich, perhaps reasoning that persecuting Reich, will stem the tide of libertarianism that Kinsey's report unleashed. Kinsey and Reich were fused in popular media as part of a communist plot to bring down America.[43] The FDA spent approximately $2 million in the investigation and prosecution of Wilhelm Reich. Seven years after his death, Time magazine in January 1964 professed that "Dr Wilhelm Reich may have been a prophet. For now, it sometimes seems that all America is one big orgone box."[44] The magazine described this new "sex-affirming culture" as the "second sexual revolution" with the youth of the 1960s "adrift in a sea of permissiveness." Inspired by Reich's experiments and philosophy, the belief spread that repression was the great evil and not promiscuity. During the 1968 student protests, students in Berlin threw copies of *The Mass Psychology of Fascism* at the police and at the University of Frankfurt, students were advised to "Read Reich and Act Accordingly!"[45]

Matviyenko views Reich as a "representative man," similar to the way in which the artist Kafka "communicate(s) the century to us."[46] A "non-canonical" artist pushes the boundaries of a genre by challenging norms and pushing imagination forward often "by means of magnificent failure." A "non-canonical" scientist in contrast finds him- or herself on the border of pseudoscience as a temporary or permanent no-man's land.

BODY THEOLOGY AS A FULLER RESPONSE TO THE SEXUAL REVOLUTION

In contrast to the Theology of the Body as advocated by Pope John Paul II and other Roman Catholic theologians, the Christian ethicist, James B. Nelson had a completely different reaction to the influences of the sexual revolution. He was not afraid of the body and like Reich did in psychoanalysis, put the body and its experiences in the center of theology. This was apparent from the start in his first book, *Embodiment: An Approach to Sexuality and Christian Theology* (1978). In many ways he can be considered as the father of body theology or a theology that takes the experiences lived through and as the body seriously—and for this also found himself in no-man's land. Similar to the ideas of Wilhelm Reich in the late 1920s and 1930s, Nelson is of the opinion that when sexuality gets trivialized, one fails to recognize the

43. Turner, "Wilhelm Reich," 4.
44. Turner, "Wilhelm Reich," 5.
45. Turner, "Wilhelm Reich," 5.
46. Matviyenko, "Wilhem Reich's Machines," 124.

"intricate, subtle, and far-reaching ways in which it permeates current social issues."[47] He pleads for a holistic vision of sexuality that can lead the church to see more clearly and respond more effectively to important sexual dimensions in vast social issues, for example social violence, racism, and ecology.[48] He wrote about "embodiment in sexual theology," but also emphatically stated that "sexual theology is body theology."[49] He considered liberation theology as a source of body theology, which is indicative at the time of writing the book, of the era of sexual and political liberation between the 1960s and the 1980s, and his personal involvement in the cause of LGBTIQA+ persons.

When I read the following words of James Nelson in the early 1990s from his second book, it completely changed my way of doing theology:

> . . . body theology begins with the concrete and not with doctrines or creeds or problems in tradition. It begins with the concrete and the fleshly experience of life—with our hungers and our passions, our bodily aliveness and deadness. . . with the bodyself making love with the beloved and lovemaking with the earth, even though these bodily experiences are filtered through an interpretive web of meanings. . .[50]

Nelson considers "lived experience" (and in his last book the lived experience of addiction and recovery) to be the most neglected in theology. For this reason, oppression and poverty are considered to be one of the most essential aspects of God's activity and a cardinal principle in liberation theology.[51] Economic hardships as well as the insights from marginalized groups like African Americans, white women, and LGBTIQA+ persons have contributed to the formation of liberation theologies.

Nelson significantly held that for many, theology is a "second moment" and that the first moment is "life itself," that "theology comes afterward, attempting to understand and serve life."[52] There are no universal theologies, but only theologies as "attempts by believers to make sense of life's challenges and to respond to them in faith." He argues that "theology as 'second moment' involves understanding our 'first moment' experience, as fully as we can." Liberation theology reminds us that "all theologies are bound to specific histories and life experiences" and that theology is, in its core, a social enterprise. It is not primarily an intellectual task of an individual person, but

47. Nelson, *Embodiment*, 261.

48. Nelson, *Embodiment*, 263.

49. Nelson, *Embodiment*, 20.

50. Nelson, *Body Theology*, 43.

51. Nelson, *Thirst*, 11.

52. Nelson, *Thirst*, 13.

an authentic "outgrowth of life in community."[53] Additional sources for his insider theological perspective in this book include the theological insights from Scripture and tradition, which he views as insights "about God in the human experience;" the contemporary wisdom from "novelists, playwrights and poets;" disciplines, such as psychology, sociology, anthropology; and medical theory and practice.[54]

Feminist theologians Lisa Isherwood and Elizabeth Stuart emphasize the place of experience in theology, "not the experience of the ruling males but of the individual believer."[55] The total person is taken seriously and "the body in its entirety is the site of experience."[56] This entails that we should learn to trust and value our own experience and put experience at the center of theology. They follow in Nelson's footsteps by stating that "the concrete stuff of people's lives" is at the beginning of theological reflection and not "some lofty contemplation of an Almighty Absolute." This is a theology from below which contemplates the incarnate God in the "stuff of the world." Body theology makes room for the body and its experiences to be "a site of revelation."[57] They do admit that by giving supremacy to the body and the experiences of the body, one can fall into total relativism, but write that "understood in the right way experiential/embodied knowing is neither self-indulgent nor narrow." All experiences can be expanding and also limiting, but they are of the opinion that history of experience has shown that "experiences do change people who in turn change society."[58]

A BETTER HOME FOR THE BODY IN THEOLOGICAL ANTHROPOLOGY?

The dilemma for me is that the reactions of Pope John Paul II and James Nelson to the influences of the sexual revolution, were located in Christian ethics or moral theology. Why is that a problem? The limitation of body theology and theology of the body is that it primarily remains focused on issues of human sexuality and confines their profound insights to Christian ethics or moral theology—a theology about the body and not a theology from the body. Isherwood and Stuart argue that body theology aims to

---

53. Nelson, *Thirst*, 12.

54. Nelson, *Thirst*, 11.

55. Isherwood and Stuart, *Introducing Body Theology*, 38.

56. Isherwood and Stuart, *Introducing Body Theology*, 39.

57. Isherwood and Stuart, *Introducing Body Theology*, 40.

58. Isherwood and Stuart, *Introducing Body Theology*, 40.

construct a new anthropology centered on embodiment.[59] Such an anthropology should incorporate notions of the relational self, the natural solidarity and social togetherness of human beings, the cosmic nature of human embodiment ("all bodies, cosmic, animal and human have an effect upon one another, and that effect can reach across space and time") and recognize the social and communal character of humans. They conclude that it is astounding that conservative theologians (like Pope John Paul II) and queer and feminist theologians can agree that "the flesh is the hinge of salvation" and that it is crucial to guard against the vanishing of "the real, lived, laughing, suffering, birthing and dying body underneath the philosophical and theological meaning it is called to bear."[60]

LeRon Shults, for example, introduces his relational theological anthropology, writing that "the search for self-understanding in relation to the divine 'Other' cannot be divorced from a trembling fascination with the human 'other.'"[61] He holds the opinion that modern theological anthropology should explore the social and psychological relations we have with other persons within the "physical and cultural relations that compose the matrices within which our lives are dynamically embedded."[62] He continues that people struggle to be wise, good and free within their communal relations and advocates a reforming and reformative theological anthropology where each generation has the task to interpret the power of the gospel through dialogue with "contemporary philosophical and scientific interpretations of the world within the living, dynamic biblical tradition."[63]

David Kelsey indicates that his contemporary theological anthropology is the reflective practice of "primary theology" and "secondary theology" which forms part of the common life of Christian communities.[64] He continues that primary theology is analytical, but also very concrete, and that Christian communities employ primary theology often in very "unselfconscious ways" when they disagree or reflect together on the "faithfulness" of received ways, often expressed in some kind of communal practice such as education, prayer, liturgies, ethical analysis, moral judgment-making, and a variety of other expressions. Secondary theology is about the critical reflection on these received authoritative theological formulations and endeavors to put new formulations of theological themes forward to primary theology

---

59. Isherwood and Stuart, *Introducing Body Theology*, 51.

60. Isherwood and Stuart, *Introducing Body Theology*, 51.

61. Shults, *Reforming Theological Anthropology*, 1.

62. Shults, *Reforming Theological Anthropology*, 2.

63. Shults, *Reforming Theological Anthropology*, 5.

64. Kelsey, "Response to the Symposium," 85.

and then concedes that his theological anthropology as exposed in *Eccentric Existence* is "perhaps relentlessly, an exercise in secondary theology."[65] A transition should be made from primary theology to secondary theology, and this is where theological anthropology provides a wider and deeper conceptual basis for inquiries and reflections on the body in theology. It is wide open to interdisciplinary research about the body, as well as the different voices from the history of Christianity and concrete life-worlds. I can but only agree with Kelsey's assessment that theological anthropology is "the point at which Christian and secular thought most easily and immediately engage each other in the service and also practices within the common life of pluralistic culture," with the most direct bearing on practical life.[66]

In my own research, I have relocated the interpretation of bodies in theological anthropology with a very practical exploration through body-mapping, widening the focus on the body and not merely on sexuality or what people do with their genitals. My research centers around the body as the main site of interpretation, resistance and meaning making, and the experiences of the body as the first moment of theology. A contemporary theological anthropology with a sentiment of the flesh and a sensitivity to the textures of life, functions within the intricate and complex connection of the living body, language, and experiencing in a concrete lifeworld. In line with this, I have proposed a model for theological anthropology as the embodied sensing of meaning.[67] It is about the sensing (feeling, thinking, meaning making) of words about God (Scripture, doctrines and tradition), and how it resonates with a lived body in a concrete situation, and how the experiencing of that body in its lifeworld in turn informs the speaking of words about God (interpretation of Scripture and tradition in doctrines). It is an ongoing process of embodying theology and theologizing (from) the body in the process of making inquiries within theological anthropology about the embodied existence of human and nonhuman creatures before God.[68]

A far cry from the theological anthropologies of former Pope Benedict XVI and Pope John Paul II, are the words on 21 October 2020 of Pope Francis in a new documentary. He gave his clear support for the rights of same-sex couples, saying that "they're children of God and have a right to a family."[69] It is a clear break from the official teaching of the Roman Catholic Church, with previous Popes calling same-sex unions "deviant" and by

---

65. Kelsey, "Response to the Symposium," 86.

66. Kelsey, *Eccentric Existence*, 7.

67. Meiring, "Theology in the Flesh," 3.

68. Meiring, "Theology in the Flesh," 6.

69. Harlan et al., "Pope Francis."

default calling the body of the Other, abnormal. It is a Pope listening to the lived experiences of Other bodies in their life-worlds, embodying his theology and theologizing from the body.

The sexual revolution is not yet over.

BIBLIOGRAPHY

BBC. "Ex-Pope Benedict XVI blames 1960s revolution for sex abuse." April 11, 2019. https://www.bbc.com/news/world-europe-47898562.

Bennett, Philip W. "The Persecution of dr. Wilhelm Reich by the Government of the United States." *International Forum of Psychoanalysis* 19 (2010) 51–65.

———."Wilhelm Reich's Self-Censorship after his Arrest as an Enemy Alien: The Chilling Effect of an Illegal Imprisonment." *The International Journal of Psychoanalysis* 95 (2014) 341–64.

Bramwell, David. "The Godfather of the Sexual Revolution?." *The Psychologist* 31 (2018) 84–7.

Grimes, Kathleen M. "Theology of Whose Body? Sexual Complementarity, Intersex Conditions and La Virgen de Guadalupe." *Journal of Feminist Studies in Religion* 32/1 (2016) 75–93.

Harlan, Chico et al. "Pope Francis calls for civil union laws for same-sex couples." https://www.washingtonpost.com/world/europe/pope-francis-civil-unions/2020/10/21/805a601c-139e-11eb-a258-614acf2b906d_story.html.

Isherwood, Lisa and Elizabeth Stuart. *Introducing Body Theology*. Cleveland: Pilgrim, 1998.

Kelsey, David H. *Eccentric Existence: A Theological Anthropology*. 2 vols. Louisville: Westminster John Knox, 2009.

———."Response to the Symposium on Eccentric Existence." *Modern Theology* 27/1 (2011) 72–86.

Lothane, Henry Z. "Wilhelm Reich Revisited: The Role of Ideology in Character Analysis of the Individual versus Character Analysis of the Masses and the Holocaust." *International Forum of Psychoanalysis* 28/2 (2019) 104–14.

Matviyenko, Svitlana. "Wilhelm Reich's Machines of Sexual Revolution." *Emotions, Space and Society* 31 (2019) 120–25.

Meiring, Jacob. "Theology in the Flesh—A Model for Theological Anthropology as Embodied Sensing." *HTS Teologiese Studies/Theological Studies* 71(3), Art. #2858 (2015) 8 pages.

Nelson, James B. *Embodiment: An Approach to Sexuality and Christian Theology*. Augsburg: Minnesota, 1978.

———.*Body Theology*. Louisville: Westminster John Knox, 1992.

———.*Thirst: God and the Alcoholic Experience*. Louisville: Westminster John Knox, 2004.

Reimers, A. J. "The Christian Personalism of John Paul II." *Journal for Interdisciplinary Studies* 29/1/2 (2017) 125–48.

Shults, F. LeRon. *Reforming Theological Anthropology: After the Philosophical Turn to Relationality*. Grand Rapids: Eerdmans, 2003.

Turner, Christopher. "Wilhelm Reich: the man who invented free love." https://www.theguardian.com/books/2011/jul/08/wilhelm-reich-free-love-orgasmatron.

Waldstein, Michael. "Introduction." In *Man and Woman He Created Them: A Theology of the Body*, John Paul II, 1–24. Boston: Pauline Books and Media, 2006.

West, Christopher. "Preface." In *Man and Woman He Created Them: A Theology of the Body*, John Paul II, xxvii–xxx. Boston: Pauline Books and Media, 2006.

5

Reproductive Technology, Sexuality, and Reproduction
Theological and Ethical Reflection

Manitza Kotzé

INTRODUCTION

There have been numerous advances in reproductive technology, offering couples and individuals the opportunity to become parents who would otherwise be unable to biologically, whether it is because they are unable to conceive naturally or choose not to for various reasons. This includes couples and individuals struggling with various forms of infertility, women past menopause, or nontraditional parents such as same-sex partners. With the growing number of people utilizing these forms of technology, however, the number of ethical questions grow as well, and often developments take place at a faster pace than ethical reflections can take place. Various ethical questions are raised by assisted reproductive technologies (ART), also regarding human sexuality and procreation.

The scholastic movement of the 12th century and in particular, the theology of Thomas Aquinas, has had a lasting influence on both the theology and practices of the Christian Church. Comprising a variety of strands of Thomism, Neo-Scholasticism argued for the sustainability of unbiased moral norms by which to value human deeds and discern whether it is right or wrong. Together with the importance given to the authority of nature, the ends of human nature were identified with "the physical structures of the body."[1] This had the practical implication that the moral good in terms of human sexuality was made to be equal with the determination of the reproductive organs; following this argument, the purpose of reproductive organs is procreation.[2] Others also build on this argument to contend that not only is procreation the purpose of the reproductive organs, and by implication sexual intercourse, but that procreation is also the purpose of marriage. Evan Lenow makes this argument, noting that biblically, this purpose appears earliest in Scripture, making procreation a primary purpose of marriage. Genesis 1:27–28 reads, "God created man in His own image, in the image of God He created him; male and female He created them. God blessed them; and God said to them, 'Be fruitful and multiply, and fill the earth, and subdue it; and rule over the fish of the sea and over the birds of the sky and over every living thing that moves on the earth.'"[3]

Procreation as at least one of the purposes of marriage is a notion that is widely held in Christian thought. If such an argument is made, should not any means to this end be embraced, including utilizing technological advances which make it possible for infertile married couples to conceive biological children? This does not appear to be the case, with much criticism against some or all forms of ART. In the first section of this essay, I provide an overview of the ethical qualms that opponents have, especially from a Christian perspective. As part of this volume, the separation of human sexuality and procreation is focused on in particular, both as conceiving children through technology instead of sexual intercourse, and by making use of donor material. In the second part, I respond to the reservations that critics hold regarding reproductive technology by utilizing theological insights from the notions of embodiment, relationality, creation and birth, in particular a relational theology of the Trinity. In doing so, certain concerns should indeed be held in mind when reflecting on reproductive technology from a Christian theological and ethical perspective, while others could be contested.

---

1. Petri, *Aquinas and the Theology of the Body*, 2–3.
2. Petri, *Aquinas and the Theology of the Body*, 3.
3. Lenow, "Is It Adultery?," 46.

ETHICAL ISSUES RAISED BY ASSISTED REPRODUCTIVE TECHNOLOGY

There is a myriad of ethical aspects that come to the fore in the discussion of ART. ART can be defined as any procedure in which reproduction is assisted through medical intervention. This can include non-invasive treatments such as medicine, or more invasive surgical procedures. Various drugs can be prescribed to assist with ovulation or sperm production, a form of intervention that some would not even classify as ART, or more mechanical forms can be employed, such as artificial insemination, intra-cytoplasmic sperm injection, or *in vitro* fertilization.[4] For the purposes of this contribution and within the broader scope of this volume with its focus on human sexuality, the main aspect that will be emphasized is the ethical aspects regarding sexuality.

SEPARATING CONCEPTION FROM SEXUAL INTERCOURSE

For many theologians, it is the separation of procreation and sexual intercourse that is problematic when it comes to ART. Dennis Hollinger indicates that "God's design is that humans enter the world through the most intimate, loving relationship on earth—the one-flesh covenant relationship of marriage. . . God's intention from creation is that children be born out of a sexual union that is covenantal, permanent, loving, enjoyable, and responsible."[5] This is also echoed by Ishak Mohd and Sayed Haneef, who note that in a biblical view, "human procreation via sexual relations is a God-designed human phenomenon, a natural continuity between sex in marriage and parenthood."[6] Having biological children through ways which does not include sexual union is then, according to this perspective, breaking this continuity in a manner which is ethically improper and the focus in Christian ethical and theological reflection on ART should take its departure from this wrongful act.

Within this line of thought, ethical questions also arise not only in terms of having children separate from sexual intercourse, but also *not* having children through sexual intercourse. Various views have been offered on contraception,[7] but due to the focus of this essay, contraception as such will

4. Lysaught et al., "Assisted Reproductive Technologies," 846–47.

5. Hollinger, *Meaning of Sex*, 102.

6. Mohd and Sayed, "Reproductive Technology," 398.

7. See, for example, Gordon, *The Moral Property of Women*.

not be examined. Choosing to engage in sexual intercourse with no desire or ability to bring forth children, however, is a related matter to the separation of procreation and sexual intercourse.

Karl Barth discussed the reality that there are human beings who do not become parents together with the divine command and while he noted that there is a degree to which such people will experience a lack through their childlessness, he also emphasized that this is mostly from the perspective of those individuals who have become parents and as a result, intimately feel this lack: "Parenthood is one of the most palpable illuminations and joys of life, and those to whom it is denied for different reasons have undoubtedly to bear the pain of loss. But we must not say more. If we can use the rather doubtful expression 'happy parents,' we must not infer that childlessness is a misfortune."[8] Barth emphasizes especially that in such cases we should not speak of an "unfruitful marriage," and that whether a marriage (or partnership) is fruitful or not should not be measured by its physical fruits.

Another interesting question that comes to the fore in terms of separating procreation and sexual intercourse, is whether that would not be a desirable outcome in the view of the well-known Augustinian notion of the transmission of original sin through sexual intercourse? Cristina Richie notes the "startling implication of the Augustinian perspective on the transmission of original sin is that if original sin were passed through concupiscent intercourse, then children created from ARTs would not have original sin."[9] Richie uses this implication to argue against Augustine's conjecture in terms of how original sin is transmitted. Due to the constraints of this essay, this is also not a matter that will be examined in more depth, but it remains a fascinating notion. If this argument would to be followed, then the utilization of ARTs in order to separate sexual intercourse from procreation would not be an ethical conundrum, but rather something that should be embraced and encouraged, a highly desirable application of biotechnology. Richie notes, however, that not only the doctrine of sin and the Augustinian view of the transmission of original sin, is in need of reworking with the advent of ART, but also Christology, soteriology and missiology.[10]

A further issue raised by ART is not only the separation of procreation and sexual intercourse, but also the separation of the genetic material of parents and children. This is particularly in the case when donor material is utilized and a woman may carry and give birth to a child that she will raise,

8. Barth, *Church Dogmatics* III/4, 265.

9. Richie, "Augustinian Perspective," 80.

10. Richie, "Augustinian Perspective," 89.

although that child does not share her or her partner's DNA and, biologically speaking, is not their own. For some, this raises a host of different concerns.

SEPARATING CHILDREN AND PARENTS' GENETIC MATERIAL

Evan Lenow argues that although some view the increasing utilization of ART as a blessing, making use of gametes from third party donors "violates[s] the sanctity of marriage."[11] He mentions that historically, one of the purposes of marriage has been procreation, with the "expectation... that offspring would come from the one-flesh union of the husband and wife."[12] Utilizing donor material, he argues, introduces other parties into the process of procreation, with the consequence that procreation is no longer the result of a union between a husband and wife. While technically, this would not fit the dictionary description of adultery, Lenow argues that utilizing donor gametes "violates the biblical expectations for procreation within the context of marriage and simply adds a scientific step to an action that could only be accomplished before through illicit sexual contact."[13] Accordingly, in his view, ART that uses donor material is equivalent to adultery, although he does allow a distinction between reproductive adultery and illicit sexual intercourse.[14]

While talking about artificial insemination (also called intrauterine insemination) with donor sperm, Dennis Hollinger notes: "With artificial insemination by a donor, however, there are significant ethical issues from a Christian perspective on sex, family, and parenting. Certainly, AID should not be labeled adultery, for there is no physical union between the sperm donor and the wife of the couple desiring a child. There is, nonetheless, an intrusion of a third party into the marital unity, which has been consummated and set apart by the one-flesh union through sexual intercourse."[15]

Thomas Shannon disagrees, however, and makes the argument that there is too much stress placed on particular sexual acts and too little on the entire relationship of marriage partners. He indicates that married couples suffering from infertility and seeking to utilize ART in order to fulfil their desire to have a family are, in doing so, representing their openness to procreation within the setting of marital fidelity. "Why the physical integrity of the sexual act should take moral priority over the intention of the husband

11. Lenow, "Is It Adultery?," 42.
12. Lenow, "Is It Adultery?," 42.
13. Lenow, "Is It Adultery?," 43.
14. Lenow, "Is It Adultery?," 57.
15. Hollinger, *Meaning of Sex*, 204.

and wife to become mother and father through the use of their own genetic is both unexplained and unclear."[16] For Shannon, the question is why a particular sexual act has to be included in human procreation?

These different views highlight different aspects that are deemed problematic when it comes to ART. One of the aspects they share, however, is the stress on the physical reality of embodied existence.

EMBODIMENT AND RELATIONALITY

James Rusthoven remarks that much of biomedical ethics has developed into a discipline that is driven by process; in other words, "much of bio-ethical reflection involved choosing among the various methods available to approach biomedical ethical problems, while little time was devoted to exploring the basic beliefs behind moral positions."[17] He argues in favor of an ethical framework based on the concept of covenant, which is, in his view, both particular in its most complete denotation, as well as able to be generalized to the extent that it can be meaningful also for those outside of the Christian tradition. At its core, such a covenantal ethical framework is based on a relational model that takes as its point of departure human relationships.

Human personhood, Rusthoven indicates, is relational and "distortions of persons will distort relationships and vice versa."[18]

"Defining the image of God in terms of being related to God," remarks Veli-Matti Kärkkäinen, "saves theology from anchoring human dignity in the possession of a quality or commodity."[19] Human dignity is a further concept that is very closely related to the broader discussion of ARTs, but one that this essay will not investigate in much more depth. More important, is the notion of the image of God, which has in recent years been defined with a much stronger emphasis of relationality.

David Kelsey defines the crucial context of God relating to humanity as "living on borrowed breath," a notion in which he describes being created as "having been born," "a theology of birth."[20] For Kelsey, how God relates to not only humanity, but all of creation, is understood in a Trinitarian manner; in the first instance, "God relates to all else creatively," a theological claim that he discusses as "living on borrowed breath." Secondly, "God relates to all else to draw it to eschatological consummation," a theological

---

16. Shannon, *Reproductive Technologies*, 42

17. Rusthoven, *Covenantal Biomedical Ethics*, 3.

18. Rusthoven, *Covenantal Biomedical Ethics*, 212.

19. Kärkkäinen, *Creation and Humanity*, 427.

20. Kelsey, *Eccentric Existence*, 159.

claim that he expresses as "living on borrowed time." Thirdly, "God relates to all else when it is estranged to reconcile it to God," a theological claim that is formulated as "living by Another's breath."[21] It is not only the theme of breath that is utilized in Kelsey's anthropology and specifically, in his discussions of God relating to humanity. The metaphor of birth also plays an important role and is of particular importance for this contribution dealing with questions around having children and bringing them into the world through the assistance of ARTs.

CREATION AND BIRTH

Janice Thompson mentions that a theological interpretation of giving birth is often described as "an image of God's life-giving work of Creator."[22] Sallie McFague serves as a well-known example of this. McFague makes use of images such as Mother, Lover, Friend and Spirit when speaking about the agency of God in the universe. She stresses God's mode of agency in creation as birthing and sustaining when utilizing the metaphor of God as Mother.[23]

Kelsey advises to explain the notion of human creatureliness by making use of the lens of "a theology of birth."[24] Reflecting on Job 10, Job's "lament that he had ever been born," Kelsey indicates that the two different ways in which Job narrates having been born is also "the story of the birth of every human person."[25] After the introduction of Job's tale, Job tells the story of having been born and Kelsey notes these two distinct ways "are wound together in such a fashion that no inconsistency exists between them."[26] The first is the account of having been born of a human mother and coming "to be as a living body"; this narrates a completely natural process. The second is about "being given a living body by God," emphasizing the supernatural act of God in the process of being born.[27] God creates a human, living body, one that already at birth exists in relationships, to the mother who gives birth to the person, to the God who created this living body. The birth process is "at once utterly ordinary and a mysterious gift."[28] Kelsey also stresses that the birthing that is referred to should not only be viewed in a literal

21. Kelsey, *Eccentric Existence*, 10.

22. Thompson, "Making Room for the Other," 395.

23. McFague, *Models of God*, 83–84.

24. Kelsey, *Eccentric Existence*, 242.

25. Kelsey, *Eccentric Existence*, 242.

26. Kelsey, *Eccentric Existence*, 243.

27. Kelsey, *Eccentric Existence*, 245–46.

28. Kelsey, *Eccentric Existence*, 246.

manner, but "must be allowed to stand, not only for natural childbirth, but for any and all medical procedures by which a pregnant woman is helped to give birth to a live newborn."[29] While Kelsey does not follow this argument further, in the context of this essay, the question can then be added whether "any and all medical procedure" of not only the process of birthing, but also of conceiving and carrying a child could be included in this broadening of the metaphor of birth? Could having a child through ARTs also be part of this process, perhaps in doing so highlighting less the "utterly ordinary" and more the "mysterious gift"?

The metaphor of creation and birth emphasizes also relationality, and Kelsey states that "the life of a living body cannot be understood except in terms of that body's dynamic relationship with its environment. . . biology. . . ecology."[30] Relationality is then also another theme that can assist us in reflecting on the ethical challenges that ARTs pose; are the relationships between parents and children harmed when the act of procreation is separated from sexual intercourse? Is the relationship between parents and children harmed when the children do not share their parent/s' genetic material? From the previous statement of Kelsey, relationships appear to be more complex than such a simplistic claim could suggest. A theological reflection of relationality within the context of embodiment also calls to mind the Trinitarian relationality, which is examined in the following section.

EMBODIMENT, RELATIONALITY AND THE TRINITY

One of the aspects stressed in this contribution, is the issue of embodiment. Nicola Hoggard Creegan notes that as human beings we rarely value our bodies or give much thought to whence they came:

> Humans live uneasily, hovering between the world of animals and a world transcending this, determined in some cases to live as though we belong to neither realm—gods of ourselves, and superior and dominating of the animals who have at times been seen as mere machines. Humans are restless creatures, constantly bewailing our bodies, frustrated by the limit of bodies, inspired by nonphysical and complex abstract and spiritual realities that transcend the body.[31]

---

29. Kelsey, *Eccentric Existence*, 247.
30. Kelsey, *Eccentric Existence*, 248.
31. Creegan, "Torn between Body and Soul," 55.

One way in which mediation between the seen and the unseen is possible, is through human embodiment.[32] Creegan also stresses the social dimension of embodiment as part of our evolutionary makeup; caring from others, being aware of others' needs, and observing a social order through stratification are all ways in which our human moral capacities developed from the bedrock of basic animal behavior. Our relationality is part of our biological inheritance and the social accompanies for almost all animals, embodiment. From a theological perspective, the embodied social capacity also serves to make the concept of God as Trinity "less arbitrary and abstract."[33] Karl Rahner asserted that there must be a connection between Trinity and humanity.[34] Denis Edwards argues that the theological discernment of God as relational can serve as the foundation for the "fundamental reality of the universe as relational. . . theology grounds this in the Trinitarian relationships of mutual love. Trinitarian theologians argue that if the Creator's being is radically relational, then this suggests something about the nature of created reality itself."[35] In other words, this is an ontological claim. As stated by John Zizioulas: "It is communion that makes things 'be': nothing exists without it, not even God."[36]

Reflecting on ethical and theological issues that are raised by the utilization of biotechnology such as ART are not only abstract questions for theologians and Christian ethicists. In the first place, these are questions posed by people struggling to make the decision on whether to resort to technology to fulfil their desperate desire to have their own child, and/or whether they should consider one form of ART and not another. It is also at its very core then a pastoral issue. Pembroke notes that "since the relational element is at the very center of pastoral work, it seemed to me that the doctrine of the Trinity must have the potential to make a major contribution to pastoral theory and practice."[37] Relationality is also the primary term in newer approaches to Trinitarian doctrine. "The older metaphysic of substance, despite its usefulness in the task of asserting the equality of the Three, is spoilt by the image of God that is associated with it. God as substance speaks of an isolated, passionless monad. The modern European metaphysic of subjectivity allows for the idea of a person-to-person communication, but ultimately it leads away from the interpersonal relations of

---

32. Creegan, "Torn between Body and Soul," 57.

33. Creegan, "Torn between Body and Soul," 60.

34. Rahner, *The Trinity*, 22.

35. Edwards, *Ecology*, 80.

36. Zizioulas, *Being as Communion*, 17.

37. Pembroke, *Renewing Pastoral Practice*, 7.

the triune God. It is the notion of fellowship or communion that is primary in the renewal of trinitarian thinking."[38]

Catherine LaCugna's main proposition is that "the life of God—precisely because God is triune does not belong to God alone. God who dwells in inaccessible light and eternal glory comes to us in the face of Christ and the activity of the Holy Spirit. Because of God's outreach to the creature, God is said to be essentially relational, ecstatic, fecund, alive as passionate love. Divine life is therefore also our life. The heart of the Christian life is to be united with the God of Jesus Christ by means of communion with one another."[39] With this perspective on the Triune God, her Trinitarian theology could be considered "as par excellence a theology of relationship, which explores the mysteries of love, relationship, personhood, and communion within the framework of God's self-revelation in the person of Christ and the activity of the Holy Spirit."[40] In this way, LaCugna laid the foundation for focusing on the practical implications of a relational understanding of the doctrine of the Trinity for Christian spirituality and faith praxis, also when responding to new ethical issues such as those brought about by ART.

BIBLIOGRAPHY

Barth, Karl. *Church Dogmatics* III/4. Translated by A. T. Mackay et al. Edinburgh: T. & T. Clark, 1961.

Creegan, Nicola Hoggard, "Torn between Body and Soul: The Evolved Body in Theological Perspective." In *Theology and the Body: Reflections on Being Flesh and Blood*, edited by S. Garner, 55–72. Adelaide: ATF, 2011.

Edwards, D. *Ecology at the Heart of Faith: The Change of Heart that Leads to a New Way of Living on Earth*. Maryknoll: Orbis, 2006.

Gordon, Linda. *The Moral Property of Women: A History of Birth Control Politics in America*. Chicago: University of Illinois Press, 2007.

Hollinger, Dennis R. *The Meaning of Sex: Ethics and the Moral Life*. Grand Rapids: Baker, 2009.

Kärkkäinen, V. *Creation and Humanity*. Vol. 3, *A Constructive Theology for the Pluralistic World*. Grand Rapids: Eerdmans, 2015.

Kelsey, David H. *Eccentric Existence: A Theological Anthropology*. Louisville: Westminster John Knox, 2009.

LaCugna, Catherine M. *God for Us: The Trinity and Christian Life*. San Francisco: Harper Collins, 1991.

Lenow, Evan. "Is it Adultery?: The Use of Third-Party Gametes in Assisted Reproductive Technology." *Southwestern Journal of Theology* 59.1 (2016) 41–57.

38. Pembroke, *Renewing Pastoral Practice*, 10.

39. LaCugna, *God for Us*, 1.

40. LaCugna, *God for Us*, 1.

Lysaught, M. Therese, et al. "Assisted Reproductive Technologies." In *On Moral Medicine: Theological Perspectives in Medical Ethics*, edited by M. Therese Lysaught et al., 846–850. 3rd ed. Grand Rapids: Eerdmans, 2012.

McFague, Sally. *Models of God*. Philadelphia: Fortress, 1987.

Mohd, S. Ishak, and Sayed Sikandar Shah Haneef. "Reproductive Technology: A Critical Analysis of Theological Responses in Christianity and Islam." *Zygon* 49.2 (2014) 396–413.

Pembroke, Neil. *Renewing Pastoral Practice: Trinitarian Perspectives on Pastoral Care and Counseling*. Aldershot: Ashgate, 2006.

Petri, Thomas. *Aquinas and the Theology of the Body: The Thomastic Foundations of John Paul II's Anthropology*. Washington, DC: Catholic University of America Press, 2016.

Rahner, Karl. *The Trinity*. Translated by Joseph Donceel. New York: Herder and Herder, 1970.

Richie, Cristina. "The Augustinian Perspective on the Transmission of Original Sin and Assisted Reproductive Technologies." *Religious Studies and Theology* 37.1 (2018) 79–91.

Rusthoven, James J. *Covenantal Biomedical Ethics for Contemporary Medicine: An Alternative to Principles-Based Ethics*. Eugene, OR: Pickwick, 2014.

Shannon, Thomas A. "Reproductive Technologies: Ethical and Religious Issues." In *Reproductive Technologies: A Reader*, edited by Thomas A. Shannon, 39–56. New York: Rowman and Littlefield, 2004.

Thompson, J. A. "Making Room for the Other: Maternal Mourning and Eschatological Hope." *Modern Theology* 27.3 (2011) 395–413.

Zizioulas, J. D. *Being as Communion: Studies in Personhood and the Church*. Crestwood: St. Vladimir's Seminary Press, 1993.

SECTION 2

Biblical Reflections

6

Voicing Reproductive Loss

Rachel's Cry in Conversation with The Light Between Oceans[1]

L. JULIANA CLAASSENS

A voice was heard in Ramah,
wailing and loud lamentation,
Rachel weeping for her children;
she refused to be consoled, because they are no more. (Matt 2:18)

INTRODUCTION

The topic of reproductive loss for the longest time has been met with an overwhelming silence. Both in contemporary faith communities, but also in the biblical text, the profound grief regarding miscarriage is rarely mentioned—this despite the fact that it is estimated that as many as 1 in 4

1. This essay, which was initially presented at the Reconceiving Reproductive Health Gender Unit conference at the Faculty of Theology, Stellenbosch University, May 30–31, 2018, was reworked and expanded to form part of ch.2, "Narrating Reproductive Loss: The Story of Rachel and *The Light Between the Oceans* (M. L. Stedman)," of my monograph, *Writing and Reading to Survive: Biblical and Contemporary Trauma Narratives in Conversation* (Sheffield Phoenix Press, 2020). This current essay is published with the permission of the Publisher.

pregnancies is said to end in miscarriage.[2] Moreover, the very few references to miscarriage in the Hebrew Bible are always presented from a male point of view. For instance, in Exodus 21:22–23, one finds some laws that speak to what would happen when a pregnant woman is injured to the extent that she loses the child. Not at all interested in the woman's experience of this miscarriage, rather, these laws focus on monetary matters with the husband said to determine the amount of the fine that ought to be paid to him.[3]

It is no wonder then that, when journeying with her friend Wendy as she sought to come to terms with yet another miscarriage (her fourth!), Serene Jones was struck by the absence of any sort of meaningful reflection on the devastating nature and effects of reproductive loss within the Protestant Church tradition that constitutes her faith community.[4] Aside from the paucity of biblical and theological images and narratives that could assist women and men in dealing with the trauma of reproductive loss, Jones moreover writes how the best tools in her feminist theological toolbox fell short as well in dealing with her friend's grief. To pray to God Our Mother almost seemed cruel to Jones given her friend's inability to become a mother herself.[5] And popular feminist discourses such a woman's right to choose, or a feminist ethic of care were unable to console her friend who, like so many other women like her, was paralyzed by her profound inability to exercise any measure of agency or choice in terms of having and nurturing a child. Jones writes that what she and her friend wanted were "images, a drama, a story, a vivid language that could draw together" their so very painful experience of reproductive loss and "the faith and feminism, which have so profoundly formed [them]."[6]

As more and more women (and men) across the globe are struggling with infertility, it is important to find imaginative ways of voicing reproductive loss, which according to Jones includes infertility, miscarriage, and stillbirth.[7] As part of a larger project on reading trauma narratives, this essay

2. Serene Jones cites statistics pertaining to her US context that 10 percent of American women experience infertility, 25 percent of all childbearing women will experience a miscarriage in their lifetime, and one in eighty pregnancies will end in stillbirth (Jones, "Hope Deferred," 128).

3. Setel, "Exodus," 34; Scholz, "Exodus," 44–45. See also Cheryl Anderson who argues that "[t]he perspective on women offered by these examples is one in which they are understood solely as the property of fathers or husbands." In particular, the view that "a rapist must marry his victim (22:6) underscores the extent to which the text is devoid of female perspective" (Anderson, *Ancient Laws*, 33).

4. Jones, "Hope Deferred," 128.

5. Jones, "Hope Deferred," 127.

6. Jones, "Hope Deferred," 128–29.

7. Jones, "Hope Deferred," 130. Jones defines infertility as a "biological condition in

seeks to explore the often hidden trauma of reproductive loss by employing the courageous representation of this topic in the 2012 novel *The Light Between Oceans* by M. L. Stedman (cf. the film adaptation in 2016 with director Michael Fassbender)[8] as a way to help us reconsider the way reproductive loss is voiced in the biblical traditions. So, Rachel, one of the four wives of Jacob whose struggle with infertility is narrated in Genesis 30, serves as one of the few exceptions to the androcentric portrayal of reproductive loss in the Hebrew Bible. In Genesis 30:1, we ever so briefly catch a glimpse of the woman's voice as Rachel exclaims as following with reference to her struggles to conceive: "Give me children or I'll die!" Rachel's grief regarding reproductive loss moreover has come to represent on a metaphorical level the grief of a nation mourning the loss of its children (Jer 31:15; Matt 2:18). In conversation with a contemporary trauma narrative such as *The Light Between Oceans*, I propose that the figure of Rachel might be reclaimed as a biblical symbol of reproductive loss that may serve as a much-needed resource as we initiate conversations pertaining to this neglected issue. Trauma narratives that voice the pain of reproductive loss, and do not shy away from exploring the complexities associated with dealing with the profound grief associated with infertility, miscarriage and stillbirth are important as they create space for women and men to begin to share their own experiences regarding the reality and effects of reproductive loss. In this regard, a contemporary trauma narrative such as *The Light Between Oceans* may help us to imagine that which is not voiced in the biblical text itself.

FACING THE EFFECTS OF REPRODUCTIVE LOSS IN THE LIGHT BETWEEN OCEANS

In her profound essay on reproductive loss in *Trauma and Grace,* Serene Jones offers some helpful insights into the effects of reproductive loss on women like her friend Wendy. Jones argues that reproductive loss has a distinct effect on a woman's sense of agency. She writes how powerless her

---

which conception cannot take place . . . ; a miscarriage [as] the loss of pregnancy but before twenty-four weeks [and] stillbirth [as] the loss of a pregnancy any time from twenty-four weeks to term in which the fetus dies in utero or immediately following delivery." Important to note, Jones does not focus in her essay on abortion, but rather on the experience of women "who try but cannot biologically reproduce." The reason for this is that "even though many women go through a period of grief after an abortion, their grief does not usually include mourning the failure of the body to either conceive or carry a pregnancy" (Jones, "Hope Deferred," 131).

8. This article will be focused on the novel by M. L. Stedman, *The Light Between Oceans* (2012). Engagement with the film version would constitute another essay altogether.

friend felt, unable to stop the blood from pouring out, washing away—hence signaling the inevitable, i.e. that she is losing her child.[9] At the same time, accompanied with these feelings of being profoundly powerless also was the idea that somehow she was responsible for this loss; that she had done something to cause this pregnancy from spontaneously terminating.[10]

According to Jones, a second feature of reproductive grief is the overwhelming loss of a future that is closely linked to what it means to be expecting a child. Important to note that when a woman loses a child due to miscarriage, stillbirth or a failed in vitro fertilization, she may very much be experiencing this loss in terms of the death of her unborn child, and with it, all hope for the future. As Jones writes: "Because the child that dies exists so completely in the space of hope and imagination, its death produces in the self its negative mirror image: the death of hope of the capacity to relate to time as the space of expectancy, a welcoming space into which the self is invited to walk."[11]

Third, Jones's speaks of "the loss of bodily integrity," what she calls "the rupturing of self" that forms a central aspect of reproductive loss. In terms of her thoughts and her emotions, the woman facing reproductive loss may become confused about who she is, which is mirrored in the further "dissolution" that "happens to her each time she sees the unwanted blood of her cycle, a blood whose cramping flow once again announces the advent of a dying, not a living."[12] And finally, related to this inability of the woman's body to sustain life is the particularly harrowing thought that the very womb that was supposed to be the site of new life, in a macabre way actually has become the unborn child's tomb.[13]

These theoretical insights come to life in a striking fashion in the beautifully written novel by ML Stedmen, *The Light Between Oceans*. This novel, which very much can be said to be a multi-layered story of trauma, with multiple characters experiencing a variety of greatly traumatizing events of which the ongoing effects intersect for better or for worse. The novel is set against the backdrop of the Great War, with the main character Tom, who recently returned from the battlefield in Europe, taking up a position as lighthouse keeper on the island of Janus, as far away removed from the mainland as he possibly could be. The novel is framed very much as a trauma narrative as Tom is seeking to come to terms with the terrible things he

9. Jones, "Hope Deferred," 135.

10. Jones, "Hope Deferred," 135–36.

11. Jones, "Hope Deferred," 137.

12. Jones, "Hope Deferred,"138.

13. Jones, "Hope Deferred," 138–39.

had seen. As he reflects on this traumatic past that ever so often interrupts attempts to live and love again: "Yet the sensation leads him back into the darkness, back into the galleries of wounded flesh and twisted limbs. To make sense of it—that's the challenge. To bear witness to the death, without being broken by the weight of it."[14]

Tom falls in love with a local girl, Isabel, who herself grew up in a house with a mother mourning the tragic demise of three sons in that terrible war. The profound effect of this loss is evident in Isabel's reminiscing about her upbringing: "Coming back last time to the house she grew up in, Isabel had been reminded of the darkness that had descended with her brothers' deaths, how loss had leaked all over her mother's life like a stain."[15]

Isabel and Tom marry and move to their isolated island outpost called Janus, only to return every couple of years to the mainland. Their blissful existence on this island paradise is ruptured though by Isabel's inability to have a much-desired child, with two devastating miscarriages as well as a stillbirth. The following scene hauntingly captures the experience of a bereaved mother mourning the loss of her stillborn son:

> The old clock on the kitchen wall still clicked its minutes with fussy punctuality. A life had come and gone, and nature had not paused a second for it. The machine of time and space grinds on, and people are fed through it like grist through the mill. Isabel had managed to sit up a little against the wall, and she sobbed at the sight of the diminutive form, which she had dared to imagine as bigger, as stronger—as a child of this world. 'My baby my baby my baby my baby,' she whispered like a magic incantation that might resuscitate him. The face of the creature was solemn, a monk in deep prayer, eyes closed, mouth sealed shut: already back in that world from which he had apparently been reluctant to stray.[16]

And a couple of weeks later, we are shown a glimpse of the heart-rending effects of this experience of reproductive loss upon loss upon Isabel:

---

14. Stedman, *The Light Between Oceans*, 61. Tom continues: "There's no reason he should still be alive, un-maimed. Suddenly Tom realizes he is crying. He weeps for the men snatched away to his left and right, when death had no appetite for him. He weeps for the men he killed."

15. Stedman, *The Light Between Oceans*, 133. Isabel reflects furthermore: "As a fourteen-year-old, Isabel had searched the dictionary. She knew that if a wife lost a husband, there was a whole new word to describe who she was: she was now a *widow*. A husband became a *widower*. But if a parent lost a child, there was no special label for their grief. They were still just a mother or a father, even if they no longer had a son or daughter."

16. Stedman, *The Light Between Oceans*, 100–101.

Isabel's lips were pale and her eyes downcast. She still placed her hand fondly on her stomach sometimes, before its flatness reminded her it was empty. And still, her blouses bore occasional patches from the last of the breast milk that had come in so abundantly in the first days, a feast for an absent guest. Then she would cry again, as though the news were fresh.[17]

Just how hopeless Isabel feels is evident in the description of her emotional state: "Only weeks ago she had been so full of expectation and vigor. Now the room felt like a coffin, and her life stopped at its edges."

This devastating reproductive loss felt so intensively by Isabel also has an effect on Tom, who as the doting husband, is torn apart by his beloved wife's disintegration. As Tom expresses his own pain after the stillbirth of his son:

As darkness fell, he sat at the table and lit the lamp. He said a prayer over the little body. The vastness, the tiny body, eternity and the clock that accused the time of passing: it all made even less sense here than it had in Egypt or France. He had seen so many deaths. But there was something about the quietness of this one: as though, in the absence of the gunfire and the shouting, he was observing it unobscured for the first time. The men he had accompanied to the border of life would be mourned by a mother, but on the battlefield, the loved ones were far away and beyond imagining. To see a child torn away from his mother at the very moment of birth—torn away from the only woman in the world Tom cared about—was a more dreadful kind of pain.[18]

We continue to follow Isabel as she is going through the motions, keeping busy with chores, but then also heading up to the cliff to go engage in an act of mourning amongst the makeshift graveyard, with a new cross joining the "the two older crosses, now finely crystalled with years of salt, the rosemary growing doggedly despite the gales."[19]

Isabel's act of making crosses from driftwood to commemorate the babies she had lost, by planting rosemary as a sign of life amidst death signals an important sign of agency. With reference to their own ritual of digging a makeshift grave in the backyard in the aftermath of yet another miscarriage, Serene Jones remarks that this seemingly futile act allowed her friend Wendy to feel that she was doing something she could control: "She felt like

17. Stedman, *The Light Between Oceans*, 95.

18. Stedman, *The Light Between Oceans*, 103.

19. Stedman, *The Light Between Oceans*, 95.

an agent whose intentional actions, even the simple action of turning over mud were controlled and had measurable consequences."[20]

However, beyond its candid portrayal of reproductive loss and the tentative attempts by both Tom and Isabel to mitigate its effects, what makes *The Light Between Oceans* such a memorable story is a dramatic turn of events that quite ironically is responsible for the return of agency on behalf of Isabel, which restores her ability to imagine a future, in addition to re-assemble her shattered self. As Isabel is busy tending the graves of her unborn children, a small boat arrives with a dead father and a tiny crying baby. Isabel immediately takes to the child and starts to care for the little girl. Isabel convinces Tom to keep the baby, and not to report the foundling nor her deceased father to the authorities. It is significant how this account is told twice. In the prologue to the novel, one finds the account told from Tom's point of view, which already reflects some of the moral ambiguity concerning their actions of taking this child as their own. However, later in the novel in the context of the devastating effects of the third miscarriage that ended in the stillbirth of a baby son, the same account is told once more, however this time from Isabel's point of view. This second account focuses very much on how Isabel seamlessly falls into caring for this child, expounding on the need to care for this starving baby whom she feeds, bathes, clothes, and comforts:

> Back in the cottage, Isabel's belly quickened at the very sight of the baby—her arms knew instinctively how to hold the child and calm her, soothe her. As she scooped warm water over the infant, she registered the freshness of her skin, taut and soft and without a wrinkle. She kissed each of the tiny fingertips in turn, gently nibbling down the nails a fraction so the child would not scratch herself. She cupped the baby's head in the palm of her hand, and with the silk handkerchief she kept for best, dabbed away a fine crust of mucus from under her nostrils, and wiped the dried salt of tears from around her eyes. The moment seemed to merge into one with another bathing, another face—a single act that had merely been interrupted.[21]

They call the little girl Lucy, meaning light, who breaks into their darkness, and can be said to save Isabel as she fully embraces her role as Lucy's adoptive mother, having been given the opportunity to finally fulfill her deep desire of caring for a child. When she nurses the child, Tom

20. Jones, "Hope Deferred," 134–35.
21. Stedman, *The Light Between Oceans*, 96.

observes that, "That afternoon, Isabel's eyes were alive with a light Tom had not seen for years."[22]

The Light Between Oceans is a powerful novel that in some very concrete ways show the effects of reproductive loss on both women and men. Through its intriguing plot line, with a baby drifting in with the tide, this novel offers a novel twist on the question of not only the trauma of reproductive loss but also recovery as Isabel's act to take the presumed motherless child into her home as well as into her heart.

However, the novel also does not shy away from the complexity associated with these acts that are so deeply rooted in self-preservation. Particularly the character of Tom is plagued with doubts as he contemplates the unavoidable reality that Lucy is another grieving mother's child, who is also mourning the loss of child whom she believes to be dead. Later in the novel, it will be revealed that this birth mother's story is profoundly shaped by trauma as well, that includes being an outsider to the community, which in the end is responsible for the fact that the baby and her father ended up in a boat in the first place. And not to give away the ending, *The Light Between Oceans* definitely does not have a classic happy ending with mothers on both sides of the ocean suffering loss in different ways in terms of their relationship with Lucy, or Grace as she originally was called.

The Light Between Oceans thus offers a honest portrayal of the moral ambiguity associated with the various ways in which its characters act in the face of reproductive loss. The novel draws the reader in and asks him/her to read with compassion. But it very much reminds us as well that, when traumatized individuals act out of their trauma, actions may have consequences that lead to further trauma for the self as well as others along the way, which is the topic of the second half of the novel, that falls though outside the scope of this current inquiry on the representation of reproductive loss in trauma narratives.

RACHEL'S VERSION OF REPRODUCTIVE LOSS

This compassionate, though complicated look at a contemporary story of reproductive loss in *The Light Between Oceans* offers a framework for helping us to take a second look at the story of Rachel's lament that reverberates across the canon. In conversation with this contemporary novel on reproductive loss, we might be less inclined to skip over Rachel's desperate attempts to conceive.

Rachel's story starts with the very personal account of a woman who desperately wants a child of her own. Her anguish is evident in her exclamation

22. Stedman, *The Light Between Oceans*, 106.

to her husband: "Give me children or I'll die" (Gen 30:1). Caught in the so-called "baby wars," Rachel competes with her sister Leah for her husband Jacob's affection, in the process utilizing her servant Bilhah in order to comply with the societal expectations of bringing sons into the world.[23] However, more seems to be at stake as evident in the intensity of her desire to have children that is not satisfied by a surrogate fulfilling her reproductive role.[24]

In her essay that seeks to delineate the narratological pattern of the barren hero, Rachel Havrelock argues that one can discern a clear pattern in the way the barren hero motif is presented in the Hebrew Bible. For instance, pertaining to Rachel, one finds how she clearly articulates her discontent about her inability to give birth, so imploring her husband Jacob to intercede on her behalf as his father Isaac had done for his wife Rebecca. When Jacob is dismissive of her request, Rachel turns to surrogacy as a way in which "the matriarchs employ a foreign body as an extension of their own" (cf. the reference in Gen 30:3 regarding Bilhah, "she will give birth on my knees so that *I* also will be built up through *her*), but which as evident in the example of Rachel, "remain[s] unsettled until they themselves give birth."[25] When these attempts fail to fill the void, this most desperate woman turns to what Susan Ackerman describes as "magical practices that can be exercised outside the cultic sphere" as evident in the mandrakes that Leah's son, Reuben, procured for his mother.[26]

Rachel's attempts to address her failure to conceive shows on the one hand the effects of reproductive loss on an individual, but also demonstrates a measure of agency on the part of Rachel, underscoring just how far she would go in order to overcome her state of infertility. However, even though we can deduct from Rachel's desperate actions the depths of her longing to have a child, what is missing from the biblical account is Rachel's experience of what must have been many years filled with one reproductive loss upon another. This brings us to the first instance in which the conversation between *The Light Between Oceans* and the biblical traditions associated with

23. For a compelling exposition on the effect of Rachel's actions on her "womb-slave," see Gafney, *Midrash*, 67–70; Scholz, *Sacred Witness*, 56–7. See also the forthcoming article of Claassens, "Reading Trauma Narratives," for a more in-depth treatment of the importance of reading Rachel's suffering also in the context of her relationship with her sister, Leah, as well as their handmaids, Bilhah and Zilpah.

24. Baden, "The Nature of Barrenness," 16. See also Jacobs, *Gender, Power, and Persuasion*, 167.

25. Havrelock, "The Myth of Birthing the Hero," 168–69.

26. Ackerman, "The Blind, the Lame, and the Barren," 38. See also Havrelock's description of the movement from "imitative to contagious magic" in the utilization of what Gafney calls "love fruit" (Havrelock, "The Myth of Birthing the Hero," 169; Gafney, *Womanist Midrash*, 58).

Rachel's struggle with infertility offers interesting insights. In particular, Isabel's point of view as reflected in *The Light Between Oceans* may help us to fill in the narrative gaps in the biblical account, imagining the depths of the unspoken grief suffered by Rachel that is glossed over in the Genesis account. Month after month, and year after year, Rachel saw her sister and servants conceive, with her own body unable to sustain and nurture new life. Or perhaps also the experience of a fragmented self conceivably experienced by Rachel, which is all the more pronounced in a society that is profoundly shaped by a women's reproductive role. Considering the fact that both Isabel and Serene Jones' friend Wendy are shown to engage in acts of burial in response to reproductive loss, what rituals Rachel and her closest confidants may have enacted in order to make sense of her grief and despair?

Second, it is significant that in the case of Rachel and the other barren matriarchs, the woman's act of naming her newborn child plays an important role in in allowing the mothers to tell their story from barrenness to fertility, which on some level also serves as a testimony of the effect of reproductive loss.[27] For instance, Rachel calls the son that Bilhah gives birth to "Naphtali"—a name that reflects her struggle with reproductive loss that she describes as wrestling with and prevailing over her sister Leah.[28] And her own struggle with reproductive loss is evident in the dual explanation she offers for the name she gives to her first biological son: First saying, "God has removed my disgrace," which would have made her son's name, "Asaph," she then proceeds to call her newborn son "Yosef," which means "may God add another son for me" (Gen 30:24). According to Havrelock, in this act of name-giving, Rachel at the very moment of fulfilling her lifelong desire already is strategizing to have another child.[29] Also the son whom she names shortly before dying in childbirth, "Ben-amoni," "Son of my Suffering" (Gen 35:16) documents the long and painful journey with reproductive loss that ends in tragedy.[30]

Third, one finds how both trauma narratives seek to make sense of reproductive loss in terms of some sort of theological construction. In the story of the matriarch, the ability to conceive is typically connected to divine intervention as evident in the reference in Genesis 30:22 of God responding with three actions to Rachel's threefold attempts to overcome her barrenness: God remembered Rachel; God listened to her, and as a result, God

27. Havrelock cites the work of Meir Sternberg, who proposes that the naming of a child reveals "more about the character of the name-giver than the recipient" (Havrelock, "The Myth of Birthing the Hero," 175–76).

28. Havrelock, "The Myth of Birthing the Hero," 167–68.

29. Havrelock, "The Myth of Birthing the Hero," 177.

30. Kalmanofsky, *Dangerous Sisters*, 33; Gafney, *Womanist Midrash*, 61.

opened her womb. As Havrelock says it well: "Her struggle results in an encounter with God in which her memory is assured, her voice heeded, and the barrier to conception lifted."[31]

Also, in *The Light Between Oceans,* from Isabel's point of view, there is no doubt; this baby is a gift of God who fills the huge void left by the series of reproductive losses that have devastated her:

> Looking into those eyes was like looking at the face of God. No mask or pretense: the baby's defenselessness was overwhelming. That this intricate creature, this exquisite crafting of blood and bones and skin, could have found its way to her, was humbling. That she could have arrived now, barely two weeks after. . . It was impossible to see it as mere chance. Frail as a falling snowflake, the baby could so easily have melted into oblivion had the currents not borne her, arrow-true and safe, to Shipwreck Beach.[32]

Even though such theological constructions have its place in helping individuals make sense of the ongoing trauma of reproductive loss, one should be vigilant about the potentially harmful effects of such explanations on the lives of oneself as well as others. The unintended consequences of Isabel's attempts to overcome reproductive loss in the second part of *The Light Between Oceans* serves as a clear case in point.

Finally, the moral ambiguity at the heart of *The Light Between Oceans* associated with the effects of attempts to overcome reproductive loss on the lives of so many people (cf. e.g., the birthmother of Lucy, who is actually called Grace, as well as her husband Tom, who will land in jail in an effort to exonerate his wife), helps one to also be more cognizant of the effects Rachel's actions may have had on her servant Bilhah as Rachel utilizes her as a surrogate mother. Both Rachel's and Isabel's intense desire to overcome infertility in different ways conceivably also draws our attention to the grave potential for abuse in terms of today's Zilpah's and Bilhah's as e.g., represented by the growing trend of the surrogate mother industry in India, which raises important questions regarding the role of race and class.[33]

---

31. Havrelock, "The Myth of Birthing the Hero," 173.

32. Stedman, *The Light Between Oceans*, 96.

33 Bailey, "Reconceiving Surrogacy," 715–41. See also Smith, "Fashioning Our Own Souls," 169. Delores Williams's work on surrogate motherhood and the African-American women's experience is further worth noting; see Williams, *Sisters in the Wilderness* (1993).

REPRODUCTIVE LOSS AND TRAGEDY

In the previous section, we have seen a number of instances in which the contemporary trauma narrative *The Light Between Oceans* offered some intriguing perspectives on the biblical account of Rachel's reproductive loss. However, by reading these two trauma narratives together, one finds how Rachel's story also talks back at that of Isabel in *The Light Between Oceans* that may help in this process of finding ways to voice reproductive loss, which may contribute to our goal of finding ways to meaningfully speak about reproductive loss in our respective communities of faith.

So, it is quite interesting to see the way in which Rachel's story reverberates far beyond the book of Genesis where we first encounter her narrative. Rachel re-emerges in Jeremiah 31 as the paradigmatic mother who has experienced reproductive loss in order to represent the countless suffering experienced by the mothers of the people of Judah who all are mourning the loss of their children. In a book filled with images of women in labor (Jer 4:31, 6:24, 13:21, 22:23; 30:6), some stuck in an anguished filled labor without end, the theme of Rachel weeping for her lost children, and refusing to be comforted seems more than fitting.[34]

In this regard, Ekaterina Kozlova portrays Rachel as the "bereaved mother engaged in a series of mourning rites in Jer 31:15–22."[35] Apart from Rachel's haunting lament, Kozlova in an interesting interpretation views the enigmatic reference to "a woman shall surround a man" in Jer 31:22 as a profound expression of maternal grief. In light of Ancient Near East evidence of funerary dances and the kinetic nature of grief often associated with women, Kozlova suggests that Rachel in this text is engaging in a funerary dance over the lost children of Israel who poetically is portrayed as encircling (*sbb*) the body of her deceased son in "a solemn dance of the matriarch par excellence."[36] Moreover, in yet another profound act of mourning, reminiscent of the act of Isabel and Wendy cited earlier of constructing crosses to mark their profound loss, Kozlova interprets the reference to signposts in Jer 31:21 in terms of a ritual act of grave marking.[37] Together with the circularly funerary dance, this "corrective mortuary duty" has the purpose of honoring the dead, particularly in the absence of burial practices that is pervasive throughout the book of Jeremiah.[38] This compelling inter-

---

34. Claassens, "The Rhetorical Function," 68, 70.

35. Kozlova, *Maternal Grief,* 157.

36. Kozlova, *Maternal Grief,* 177.

37. Kozlova, *Maternal Grief,* 188–92.

38. Kozlova, *Maternal Grief,* 195.

pretation of Rachel mourning for her lost children points to the very human need for rituals to accompany the process of facing reproductive loss.

Within this profound expression of maternal grief, it is furthermore significant to see how the image of Rachel weeping for her lost children, which is rooted in her own painful struggle to come to terms with reproductive loss as narrated in the Genesis traditions is not confined to her own desperate struggle to become a mother. In Jer 31:15 as well as in Matt 2:18, Rachel represents the depths of despair of mothers past, present and future who are faced with the loss of the infant children who brutally have been murdered by means of the horrors of imperial violence, and hence represent the loss of children on a national level.[39]

In the story of Rachel's cry, a woman's very personal account of reproductive loss thus is set against the backdrop of a much greater story of national trauma and loss. This is also true in the case of *The Light Between Oceans* in which Isabel's and Tom's story of reproductive loss is told within a broader context of trauma according to which so many mothers were forced to deal with the loss of their sons during the time of the Great War:

> Nineteen fourteen was just flags and new-smelling leather on uniforms. It wasn't until a year later that life started to feel different—started to feel as if maybe this wasn't a sideshow after all—when, instead of getting back their precious, strapping husbands and sons, the women began to get telegrams. These bits of paper which could fall from stunned hands and blow about in the knife-sharp wind, which told you that the boy you'd suckled, bathed, scolded and cried over, was—well—wasn't. Partageuse joined the world late and in a painful labor."[40]

To reclaim the tragic nature of reproductive loss may yield an important insight for Rachel and Isabel, but also other women struggling with reproductive loss. By expanding the definition of reproductive loss so as to include also other mothers and fathers losing their children, we are able to reconceive miscarriage and infertility for what it is. Reproductive loss signifies not only the loss of a child but also of the vision of oneself as the mother of this child and the death of the hopes and dreams mothers and fathers have for their children, born and unborn. The tragic nature associated with reproductive loss on a broader scale is encapsulated in the following quote from *The Light Between Oceans:*

---

39. Jones, "Hope Deferred," 109.
40. Stedman, *The Light Between Oceans*, 23.

Of course the losing of children had always been a thing that had to be gone through. There had never been guarantee that conception would lead to a live birth, or that birth would lead to a life of any great length. Nature allowed only the fit and the lucky to share this paradise-in-the-making. Look inside the cover of any family Bible and you'd see the facts. The graveyards, too, told the story of the babies whose voices, because of a snakebite or a fever or a fall from a wagon, had finally succumbed to their mothers' beseeching to "hush, hush, little one."[41]

Such an understanding of the tragic nature of reproductive loss serves as an important counter narrative that serves as an essential part of the process of sense-making that is so crucial for coming to terms with trauma. Viewing reproductive loss for the tragedy that it is resists the widespread belief that in some way miscarriage or infertility or stillbirth can be ascribed to something the mother did wrong. In this regard, it is significant that in none of the stories of the five biblical women that are said to be barren (Sarah, Rebekah, Rachel, Hannah, and Samson's mother), there seems to be a link between sin and barrenness.[42] Reproductive loss just is what it is: unfortunate, tragic, heartbreaking.[43]

IMAGINING THE RETURN OF A FUTURE AND THE POSSIBILITY OF GRACE

In the previous section, it was shown how reclaiming tragedy is a productive means of making sense of reproductive loss that is vital for the process of recovery to occur. Women like Serene Jones' friend Wendy, but also the Isabels, Rachels and the countless women we know, or do not know, are struggling to overcome reproductive loss are though in desperate need of something more—something that Jones describes as "new narratives that enable the return of a future and the possibility of grace to take hold of those traumatized by loss."[44]

In this regard, it is significant that the image of Rachel's cry is actually situated in a section in the book of Jeremiah that is called the Little Book of Comfort that offers us a brief glimpse of the arduous journey of recovering

41. Stedman, *The Light Between Oceans*, 23–24.

42. Baden, "The Nature of Barrenness," 21.

43. Baden, "The Nature of Barrenness," 18. As Baden rightly points out, we are introduced to these women as barren in a matter-of-fact way before anything else about them is known.

44. Jones, "Hope Deferred," 150.

from the trauma of the Babylonian invasion. In Jer 31:16–17 it is Godself who is comforting Rachel, who proclaims:

> Keep your voice from weeping, and your eyes from tears; for there is a reward for your work, says the LORD, they shall come back from the land of the enemy, there is hope for your future, says the LORD: your children shall come back to their own country.

The figure of a bereaved mother serves here as an image that spans past, present, and future—her act of voicing the profound pain regarding her and her nation's reproductive loss being taken up into a vision of restoration that promises the return of a future that was thought to be lost.[45] But how is this image helpful?

In contemplating how Rachel's cry may be reconfigured to serve as a way to imagine the return of a future and the possibility of grace, Jones actually offers an imaginative dialogue between Rachel who is perpetually weeping for her lost children and Mary who is singing in the Magnificat in Luke 1:46–55 of being blessed; of the Lord doing great things for her; lifting up the lowly and filling the hungry with good things. In this imaginary encounter, Jones proposes that in her engagement with Mary, "Rachel is able to catch a glimpse of grace, a fleeting hint of redemption, a sense of hope that long ago faded."[46] It is this grace that "enlarg[es] our imaginations and expan[ds] the borders of our usual actions."[47] Jones describes this grace a powerful force "that moves deep within our being, sharing our plight, conforming to our reality, and in that identification, opening up new avenues of experience and hope."[48]

But at the same time, one should not forget that Rachel also is there to remind Mary "that not all the hungry have yet been filled with good things. . . that the greedy powers are all too present," as evident in all those lost children Rachel has mourned and continues in many instances to mourn.[49] Something which Mary herself ultimately will learn at Golgotha when she herself is weeping for a lost son.

---

45. This briefest glimpse of hope occurs though within a book filled with a seemingly unending supply of violence and devastation. Following Rachel's appearance in Jeremiah 31, there will be many more chapters where the future promised seems nowhere on the horizon. See also O'Connor, *Jeremiah*, 103–04.

46. Jones, "Hope Deferred," 122.

47. Jones, "Hope Deferred," 123.

48. Jones, "Hope Deferred," 123.

49. Jones, "Hope Deferred," 120–121.

CONCLUSION

Every woman who has ever suffered miscarriage or a failed in-vitro procedure knows that one has to go on. As one goes on, whether one ultimately
succeeds in one's effort to become a mother, or finds ways to mother in some
other way, voicing reproductive loss is vital for all women and men as they
are seeking to recover from reproductive loss.

The examples of reproductive loss cited in this essay points to the fact
that there is no single ending possible for an essay on reproductive loss.
Rachel gave birth to two sons before dying in childbirth—her anguish being
taken up in mothers everywhere who are mourning reproductive loss, also
those who lost children in acts of violence as evident in the laments going
up in Jerusalem and Ramah. Isabel, after a series of miscarriages, culmi-
nating in a stillbirth, raises a daughter brought by the waves of the ocean
before having to give her up which can only be described as yet another
devastating reproductive loss. I myself after many years of going through
one failed in-vitro procedure after another as well as a miscarriage feel very
lucky indeed to have a beautiful daughter who now almost is 9!

Regardless thus if one has a child after facing reproductive loss, has a
child and loses a child, or never has a child at all, one has to keep on living
before, during, and also after having voiced reproductive loss. Towards the
end of *The Light Between Oceans* there is a touching dialogue between husband and wife about how to go on, how to live again after their harrowing
journey with reproductive loss. Isabel admits that "[l]osing Lucy—it's as if
something has been amputated." The effect of this loss is evident also in her
lament: "Everything's ruined. Nothing can ever be put right." To which Tom
responds. "We've put things right as well as we can. That's all we can do. We
have to live with things the way they are now."

And live they do. They live with the memory of Lucy who according
to Isabel "got under [their] skin" and "opened up [their] heart[s] somehow."
Brief as this experience may have been, they both agree, it was worth it—a
perspective poignantly captured in the accompanying image of the couple
eating honeysuckle from its vine:

> She was holding the strand of honeysuckle, stroking the leaves
> absently. Tom plucked one of the creamy blooms from it. "We
> used to eat these, when we were kids. Did you?"
> "Eat them?"
> He bit the narrow end of the flower and sucked the droplet
> of nectar from its base. "You only taste it for a second. But it's
> worth it." He picked another, and put it to her lips to bite.[50]

50. Stedman, *The Light Between Oceans*, 352.

BIBLIOGRAPHY

Ackerman, Susan. "The Blind, the Lame, and the Barren Shall Not Come into the House." In *Disability Studies and Biblical Literature,* edited by Candida R. Moss, and Jeremy Schipper, 29–45. New York: Palgrave MacMillan, 2011.

Anderson, Cheryl. *Ancient Laws and Contemporary Controversies: The Need for Inclusive Biblical Interpretation.* Oxford: Oxford University Press, 2009.

Baden, Joel S. "The Nature of Barrenness in the Hebrew Bible." In *Disability Studies and Biblical Literature*, edited by Candida R. Moss and Jeremy Schipper, 13–27. New York: Palgrave MacMillan, 2011.

Bailey, Alison. "Reconceiving Surrogacy: Toward a Reproductive Justice Account of Indian Surrogacy." *Hypatia* 26.4 (2011) 715–41.

Claassens, L Juliana. "Reading Trauma Narratives: Insidious Trauma in the Story of Rachel, Leah, Bilhah and Zilpah (Genesis 29–30) and Margaret Atwood's *The Handmaid's Tale*," OTE 33/1 (2020) 10–31.

———. "The Rhetorical Function of the Woman in Labor Metaphor in Jeremiah 30–31: Trauma, Gender and Postcolonial Perspectives." *Journal of Theology for Southern Africa* 150 (2014) 67–84.

———. *Writing and Reading to Survive: Biblical and Contemporary Trauma Narratives in Conversation.* Sheffield: Sheffield Phoenix Press, 2020.

Gafney, Wilda C. *Womanist Midrash: A Reintroduction to the Women of the Torah and the Throne.* Louisville: Westminster John Knox, 2017.

Havrelock, Rachel. "The Myth of Birthing the Hero: Heroic Barrenness in the Hebrew Bible." *Biblical Interpretation* 16 (2008) 154–78.

Jacobs, Mignon R. *Gender, Power, and Persuasion: The Genesis Narratives and Contemporary Portraits.* Grand Rapids: Baker Academic, 2007.

Jones, Serene. "Hope Deferred: Theological Reflections on Reproductive Loss." In *Trauma and Grace: Theology in a Ruptured World,* 113–28. Louisville: Westminster John Knox, 2009.

Kalmanofsky, Amy. *Dangerous Sisters of the Hebrew Bible.* Minneapolis: Fortress, 2014.

Kozlova, Ekaterina E. *Maternal Grief in the Hebrew Bible.* Oxford: Oxford University Press, 2017.

O'Connor, Kathleen M. *Jeremiah: Pain and Promise.* Minneapolis: Fortress, 2011.

Scholz, Susanne. "Exodus: The Meaning of Liberation from 'His' Perspective." In *Feminist Biblical Interpretation: A Compendium of Critical Commentary on the Books of the Bible and Related Literature,* edited by Luise Schottroff et al., 33–50. Grand Rapids, Eerdmans, 2012.

———. *Sacred Witness: Rape in the Hebrew Bible.* Minneapolis: Fortress, 2010.

Setel, Drorah O'Donnell. "Exodus." In *The Women's Bible Commentary,* edited by Carol A. Newsom and Sharon H. Ringe, 26–35. Louisville: Westminster John Knox, 1992.

Smith, Mitzi. "Fashioning Our Own Souls: A Womanist Reading of the Virgin–Whore Binary in Matthew and Revelation," in *I Found God in Me: A Womanist Biblical Hermeneutics Reader*, edited by Mitzi J. Smith, 158–82. Eugene: Cascade, 2015.

Stedmen, M. L. *The Light Between Oceans.* New York: Scribner, 2012.

Williams, Delores S. *Sisters in the Wilderness: The Challenge of Womanist God-Talk.* Maryknoll: Orbis, 1993.

7

"The Bra Is Wearing a Skirt!"

*Queering Joseph in the Quest to
Enhance Contextual Ethical Gender
and Sexuality Engagements*

CHARLENE VAN DER WALT

RESISTING THE SOLIDITY OF CONSTRUCTION

NOMZAMO'S RIVER

Can we not do statues?
Can we not ERECT Her?
All of Her.

Can we call rivers and streams in Her name?
The name she answers to.
So we find her in distant lands.

If the water dries up, we'll sink deep in our bellies and weep for her.
Fill up the streams with grief and memory.

We saw what humans can do to statues;
We saw what statutes make of us.
This time when history reveals more bewitched and opaque stories of
who she really is;
This Mamlambo,

We'll boil her water; toss her outside; block her
flow so that her stream shifts in other directions.

To grow and nurture other lands.
Those rivers and streams will have other names.
New waters flowing on umhlaba wethu.

The initial conceptual inspiration for this contribution that aims at a critical
reflection on the intersection of sexuality, gender and religion was sparked
by the challenging poetry of the inspiring young South African theatre-
maker, Pumelela 'Push' Nqelenga.[1] The poem poignantly articulates one of
the central overarching imperatives of the contribution when it succeeds in
giving pertinent expression to the impulse of resistance when engaging with
the apparent stability and unquestionability of hard and fast constructions,
definitions, and systems.

Nqelenga's reflection is aimed at the landscape of remembrance and
honoring. She asks critical questions engaging how we remember and honor
those who have courageously gone before us. She appeals to us as listeners
and viewers of the poem to resist the stable, permanent, one-dimensional
memory mode that finds expression in statues. "We saw what humans can
do to statues" she remarks and, in the process, vividly reminds us of the
complicated and traumatic events that transpired in the unfolding of the
#Rhodesmustfall movement at the University of Cape Town and the linked
yet unique #Feesmustfall movement that swept across the higher education
sector in 2016/17 in the South African landscape.

She continues chillingly when stating, "We saw what statutes make of us"
and in the process, captures something of the simplifying and profoundly dehumanizing effects of remembering selectively or partially and then proceeding to consider the partial or selective to speak to all experiences, constituting
the realities and histories of everyone. Beyond the reality of not including all
experiences in this mode of remembrance or honoring, this mode of remembrance's solidity and temporality also binds the one remembered or honored
to one expression, a solid manifestation as a single representation.

1. The poem was installed as a visual installation in 2019 at the Durban Art gallery
as part of an exhibit reflecting on the status of women in contemporary South African
society. I appropriate it here with written consent obtained from the poet.

She challenges us, as the interpreters of the poem, to remember and honor with greater fluidity, to resist singular or one-dimensional representations, and in the process to allow for greater flow, movement, and acknowledgment of complexity.

This rigidness of stable constructions and the instance on categorization finds remarkable resonance in the field of gender and sexuality studies, and it is to the intersectional landscape that I now turn my attention. When reflecting on the development of thought regarding dominant constructions of gender and sexuality, Mary-Ann Tolbert remarks: "Gender from a modernist perspective is generally understood as a set of innate social traits that naturally accompany biological sex. Thus, in modernist though, gender becomes the universal and essential social correlative of binary biological differentiation."[2]

Although post-modernist developments have gone a long way to destabilize the solidity of the pervasive binary understanding of gender through social-constructivism, men and women, understood in the cisgender and essentialist manner, are still often assumed to be polar opposites. As a result of the process of "othering" within the binary construction of gender, men are pitted over against women, as women are not only understood as being other to men but also somehow of lesser value and importance. The rigid binary construction of gender further erases the possibility or visibility of gender diversity expression on a spectrum or continuum. The ideal or normative state of being a human being, within a robust binary construction of sex and gender is to be a man. Apart from men being defined over and against women, men are also ideally framed relationally in liaison with women. Within a binary construction of gender, a real man is thus one who is heterosexual, preferably married to a woman, and successful as the protector, penetrator, and provider.

The foundational underpinning upon which the notion of a normal or ideal state is based is heteropatriarchy. Heteropatriarchy derives from the conceptual combination of two foundational ideological frames, namely heterosexuality or heteronormativity and patriarchy. Feminist theorists[3]

---

2. Tolbert, "Gender," 99.

3. Ruether describes feminism as "a critical stance that challenges the patriarchal gender paradigm that associates males with human characteristics defined as superior and dominant and females with those defined as inferior and auxiliary" (Ruether, *Sexism and God-Talk*, 3). Ackermann elaborates by defining the term as: "The commitment to the praxis of liberation for women from all that oppresses us. Feminism does not benefit any specific group, race, or class of women; neither does it promote women's privilege over men. It is about a different consciousness, a radically transformed perspective which questions our social, cultural, political, and religious traditions and calls for structural change in all these spheres" (Ackermann, "Meaning and Power," 24).

termed the system of male dominance patriarchy to conceptually frame how men benefit from their "privilege, power and authority [that] are invested in masculinity and the cultural, economic and/or social positions."[4] Heteronormativity is the result of a systematic normalization of heterosexuality and is often informed by a certain way of reading the Bible and infused by patriarchy and static understandings of culture. Gust Yep describes this process as follows:

> The process of normalizing heterosexuality in our social system actively and methodically subordinates, disempowers, denies, and rejects individuals who do not conform to the heterosexual mandate by criminalizing them, denying them protection against discrimination, and refusing them basic rights and recognition, or all of the above.[5]

Heteronormative discourse describes reality primarily and exclusively from the position of the heterosexual. According to Andrew Martin,

> [T]his is the idea, dominant in most societies, that heterosexuality is the only "normal" sexual orientation, only sexual or marital relations between women and men are acceptable and each sex has certain natural roles in life, so-called gender roles.[6]

Within the heteronormative, there is only space for heterosexual experiences, constructions, and realities, and no other alternatives are tolerated. The stability of heteronormativity is underpinned and bolstered by patriarchal religious and cultural foundational ideologies, teachings, and practices. Heteronormativity and the resulting intolerance of sexual diversity often give rise to homophobic attitudes, hate crimes, and violence.[7]

4. Cranny-Francis et al., *Gender Studies*, 15; Thatcher, *God, Sex, and Gender*, 26.

5. Yep, "Violence of Heteronormativity," 24.

6. Martin, "Hate Crimes," 1.

7. South Africa is also considered to be the birthplace of so-called "corrective rape": an act of violence against women committed by men ostensibly to "cure" lesbians of their non-conforming sexual orientation—or correct it—the belief being that homosexuality is "an imported white disease (from the colonial empire)." It is especially African women and girls thought to be lesbian that become victims of corrective rape, with the claimed purpose of turning them into "real African women." Attackers, often family members, friends, or neighbors of the victims, say they are teaching lesbian women "a lesson" by raping them and "showing them how to be a real woman." Although black lesbians are the main targets of corrective rape, any woman with a non-conforming sexual identity is at risk, seeing that the aim or goal is to "cure" or simply to punish any non-conforming sexual orientations. Thus, any woman thought to be "too different or insufficiently feminine" and who fails to stay invisible is at risk. Accordingly, 86 percent of black lesbians from the Western Cape said they lived in fear of sexual assault (Di Silvio, "Correcting Corrective Rape," 1469).

To maintain and protect the stability of heteropatriarchy, those who are gender non-conforming or who somehow do not fit the bill prescribed within the framework of heteropatriarchy have to be policed, surveilled, or at its most extreme, corrected or annihilated.

DOING AND UNDOING GENDER

As hinted at in the discussion above, and significantly informed by the growth in third-wave feminism and its insistence on intersectionality, a far more complex understanding of sex, gender, and sexuality has developed, consequently pushing back against normative, stable, binary, and heteronormative constructions. Intersectionality, a term coined by Kimberly Crenshaw in 1989, highlights the "interaction between gender, race, and other categories of difference in individual lives, social practices, institutional arrangements, and cultural ideologies."[8] The understanding that gender is socially constructed and is constituted differently in different social locations draws heavily on the notion of "gender performativity," as proposed by Judith Butler.[9] Thatcher eloquently engages Butler's notion of gender performativity when stating:

> We become the women and men we are by the repeating of countless gendered acts every day of our lives in every space that we navigate—also faith communities. We *perform* our genders through our actions. The clothes that we wear, the way in which we walk, the gestures that we make, the perfume or cologne that we wear are all "learned performances" through interacting with our peers, with family, and friends. Through repeating actions, we confirm in ourselves, we modify and accept or renounce them. There is thus, freedom in this and gender can be done or undone with this affirmation of acceptance or rejection of what peers, family, and friends offer.[10]

The title of this contribution, *The Bra is wearing a skirt!,* links to this notion of doing and undoing of gender as explained above. The setting for the tale informing the exclamation is a late-night/early-morning back-alley on the fringe of the city of Cape Town. After an unfortunate clothing malfunction due to the nighttime activities engaged in, the best solution at the time, it being 2 o'clock in the morning, seemed to be that two friends, one

8. Davis, "Intersectionality," 68.

9. For more in this regard, see Butler, *Gender Trouble*, 2011.

10. Thatcher, *God, Sex, and Gender*, 19–20.

a man and one a woman, change the bottoms of their respective attire. On witnessing the result of the transition, a local casual passerby exclaimed to his friend: "Look, that Bra is wearing a skirt!" This little, and often commented and reflected on incident, highlights something of the constructed and co-constructed ways of doing gender. The Bra, a local slang word for a man, was clearly not performing gender in the expected way, by wearing a skirt, and this provoked a corrective normalizing reaction. From this anecdote, it follows that the stabilizing patterns that often find expression in what we wear, create a grid or a frame for what is considered normal or acceptable. This in turn, leads to stable constructions of what it means to be a man or woman and how one must look as a member of a particular gender sub-group. Secondly, in our collective participation in the production and re-production of gender we also hold each other accountable. Although in the case of this anecdote the gender-policing was done though a humoristic exclamation, more often than not corrective gender and sexual policing takes on more violent forms that varies from name calling, denial to gender affirming healthcare and misgendering to violent annihilation. Besides highlighting the pervasive stability of dominant co-created gender construction and how it is kept in place through policing and surveillance, the anecdote also illustrates something of the possibility of undoing gender though pushing–back or destabilizing that which is considered un–questionable, stable, and normal. If we indeed co-construct gender though the myriad of our gendered actions, expectations and assumptions, it follows that we have the potential also to destabilize, trouble, and un-do gender.

Before turning my attention to a biblical Bra that wears a skirt of many colors, I focus on queer theory in the next part of this contribution in order to posit the theoretical landscape that offers tools for disrupting, destabilizing, and troubling stable and pervasive binary gender constructions.

I intentionally choose to use the term *queer*, and the methodological insights developed from this approach, rather than one of the more stable identity markers associated with identity politics, firstly because of the overt ideological and political intentionality and positionality of this approach as it articulates its focus as push-back or disruption of the normative in service of liberation and justice. Secondly, I believe that this approach creates space for a diversity of non-binary and non-conforming identities and positionalities. Precisely because the aim is not to create a new master narrative, but rather to destabilize and disrupt, it does not insist on a singular positionality but instead articulates the possibility of a multiplicity and even contradiction of experience. While at the same time taking stock of the myriad of ways in which heteropatriarchy police, silence, and perpetuate violence against those who do not fit the heteronormative ideal, the approach also accounts for creative and dynamic forms of agency that allows for sense-making, meaning-making and counter-community formation. Thirdly, I believe that this approach creates space for more bodies to matter and for allies with political empathy with the plight of those outside the norm to become part of aggravating for justice. Queer creates space for all those who want to query or trouble or make trouble despite the heteronormative norm's confines. Finally, queer is not singularly confined to gender and sexuality issues, but rather represents an intersectional ideological commitment to the interrogation and destabilization of any social construct and the privilege that insider states hold to any dominant construction, be it race, class, age, gender, sexuality, and ability.[11]

When Patrick Cheng engages queer theory, he identifies three strands, namely queer as an umbrella term that collectively refers to lesbian, gay, bisexual, transgender, intersex, questioning and other individuals who identify with non-normative sexualities/gender identities. Secondly and linking to the reflection above, Cheng refers to queer as a verb that insists on transgressive action aimed at disrupting the normative. Thirdly, he draws on the insight offered by Foucault in an attempt to "erase boundaries" in the process of disrupting or challenging stable or normative notions of gender and sexuality.[12] When translating these main strands of queer theory for the theological landscape, Cheng maintains the three stands when stating that queer theology is LGBTIQA+ people talking about God and developing theology by LGBTIQA+ people for LGBTIQA+ people. Secondly, queer theology seeks to destabilize power by illuminating the hidden perspective and disrupting normative understandings. Finally, queer theology is a way of doing theology that is rooted in queer theory and that aims at erasing the boundaries of essentialist categories.[13]

Fundamental, however, to this contribution is the appropriation of queer theoretical insights for the landscape of biblical hermeneutics. Teresa Hornsby and Ken Stone explain that the aim of queer biblical hermeneutics is to "trouble the text" for the purposes of gaining new insight over-against normative interpretations.[14] Generally, queer biblical hermeneutics is an ex-

---

11. Schneider describes the task of queer theory: "In general, queer theory seeks to disrupt modernist notions of fixed sexuality and gender by appropriating post structuralism critiques of 'natural' identities . . . Queer theory 'queers' taken-for-granted cultural associations concerning all sexual identities (and the social placements that adhere to those identities) by revealing the vulnerability of history and politics and therefore to change" (Schneider, "Homosexuality," 6).

12. Cheng, *Radical Love*, 2–25.

13. Cheng, *Radical Love*, 2–25.

14. Hornsby and Stone, "Introduction," ix.

tremely diverse and non-conformist way of looking at the Bible which goes beyond the familiar heteronormative ways in which the Bible is read.[15] Punt offers a summary of queer biblical hermeneutics when stating that firstly queer theory is employed in biblical interpretation to challenge fixed notions of gender and sexuality which are enforced through common forms of biblical interpretation, and secondly by reinterpreting commonly used texts and employing other texts to legitimate other forms of sexuality.[16]

When surveying the landscape of queer biblical hermeneutics, Koch offers a poignant critique of three commonly appropriated strategies when it comes to engaging the issue of sexual diversity and the Bible. Firstly, *The pissing contest*, a Christian apologetic engaging the so-called six-shooter texts where scholars often weigh in with for—and against—arguments when appropriating these texts. Secondly, an approach described as *Jesus is my trump card*, where all Christians are called to love as Christ expressed love and, in the process, include all who are diverse or "other." Finally, in an approach entitled, *I can fit the glass slipper, too!*, Koch points to scholarly trends where sexually diverse characters are excavated and documented within the text. Beyond offering this critique, Koch appropriates queer lingo to explain his own engagement with the text when discussing the notion of *cruising texts*. In this mode of interpretation, he reads different texts for the various ways in which queer individuals experience the world and encounter hostility, friendship, criticism, or celebration, without an expectation that the Bible actually validates and celebrates queerness.[17] Yip also offers a systematic description that offers a critique of "defense apologetics" and reflects on the strategy of "cruising texts" to uncover the queer nature of biblical texts in order to celebrate sexual diversity. He highlights how these strategies are appropriated in the queer process of "turning Theology upside down."[18]

I started this contribution with a reflection on the systemic realities underpinned by the pervasive ideology of heteropatriarchy. The foundational ideology combines stands from heteronormativity and patriarchy and informs dominant normative constructions of gender, sexuality, and relationality. Those who find themselves embodied outside the heteronormative script's confines often experience attempts at correction that varies from name-calling and being made fun of, to violent annihilation. African queer people who express gender and sexuality outside the heteropatriarchal norm is particularly vulnerable to exclusion, victimization, and violence. Rather

15. Punt, "Intersections," 321.
16. Punt, "Sex and Gender," 385–86.
17. Koch, "Homoerotic Approach," 12–16.
18. Yip, "Coming Home," 35–50.

than being spaces of safety, care, and hospitality, faith institutions often contribute to the stigmatization and violence committed to LGBTIQA+ people in the African context. The Bible is frequently and pervasively used as a tool to exclude queer believers from the church as a community of care, celebration, and support. Even further, it is often cited as a source document that incites hate and violence again LGBTIQA+ people in the African context.

Considering the above-mentioned life-denying complexities and after reflecting on the theoretical underpinnings of queer biblical hermeneutics, in the last part of this contribution I aim to offer an example of a queer reading of selected episodes of the Joseph narrative cycle. I propose that queer biblical hermeneutics is a helpful theoretical tool because it questions dominant ideas rooted in heteronormativity by critiquing hegemonies that exist in the use of biblical texts or even within biblical text themselves, and it also enables the opening of space for more experiences to matter in the interpretation process. I fundamentally offer these reflections in order to illustrate how the Joseph narrative could function as a reflective surface for contemporary African queer believers. I aim to draw on biblical scholarship insights by using both literary-narrative and socio-historical modes of analysis to identify and read with marginalized "voices" in, under, above, and behind biblical texts. In the process, I propose that the ancient figure of Joseph become a dialogue partner for the contemporary marginalized communities, as the text functions as a dynamic reflective surface.[19] Considering that the Bible is often understood by LGBTIQA+ people as the property of either the church or the academy to be overseen by faith leaders and scholars, queer Bible readings opens up the possibility for LGBTIQA+ people to "take back the Word" and to reclaim and strengthen positions of agency.[20]

THE BRA IS WEARING A MULTI-COLORED SKIRT!

When considering the role of religion in as it pertains to contextual embodied issues within the landscape of sexual reproductive health and rights, the common perception is often that faith speaks with a singular, predominantly negative voice and that God's will is clearly deducible from the sacred scriptures. In the pursuit of sexual and reproductive justice, as proposed by

19. For more on how the Bible functions as a reflective surface in the process of contextual Bible study, see Van der Walt, "'It's the Price,'" 57; Van der Walt and Terblanche, "Reimagining," 176–94; and Van der Walt, "To the Wonder," 170.

20. I borrow this term from a publication by the same name aimed at highlighting the life-affirming contours of queer biblical hermeneutics. For more in this regard, see Goss and West, *Take Back the Word,* 2000.

Catriona Macleod and others, faith actors are often deemed obstructionist or counter the ideals of a reproductive justice approach, that draws on a social justice framework and emphasizes systemic or holistic analyses, seeking to illuminate the complex array of social, economic, cultural and healthcare possibilities and challenges that serve to either enhance or hinder women's reproductive freedoms and the rights of those identifying within the spectrum of sexual fluidly.[21]

At the heart of this contribution is a concern for the integrity and soul of the process of biblical hermeneutics in the pursuit of ethical decision making as much of the debate around SRHR issues in general and sexual diversity, in particular, boils down to divergent understandings of the role and nature of Scripture and a violent clash in the epistemological underpinnings foundational to conflicting methods of interpretation.

When considering the role of the Bible in the process of ethical decision making, especially when it comes to sex and gender, the dominant trend is often to make icons of certain central characters. Beyond the textual representation of these characters, the ideas or caricatures that develop often become fixed or stable and quickly lead to an uncritical and decontextualized emulation of certain characters. In the process of engaging this notion of biblical characters taking on a life of their own and as such becoming hero figures informing ethical reflection, Jacqueline Lapsley argues:

> For the most part, I want to move away from asking which characters are worth emulating or not, and which text is "good" or "bad". As a rule, the kind of ethical reflection I propose here asks the reader to allow herself to be drawn into a complex moral world evoked by the narrative. In the narrative worlds of the Old Testament, easy moral judgments are elusive and most often miss the mark. The kind of ethics I envision has more to do with how the reader enters into the story—it is narrative ethics—and less to do with the reading standing outside the story making ethical judgments about character.[22]

In an attempt to make trouble and play around with some of the theoretical insights highlighted above in the process of engaging Bible stories and central biblical characters in the process of ethical decision making when it comes to issues within the intersection of sexuality and gender, I

---

21. For more regarding the reproductive justice framework, see Chiweshe et al., "Reproductive Justice in Context," 203–24; Macleod et al., "Articulating Reproductive Justice through Reparative Justice," 601–15; and Macleod, "Expanding Reproductive Justice," 46–62.

22. Lapsley, *Whispering the Word*, 11.

now turn my attention to the character of Joseph as embedded in the narrative cycle at the tail end of the book of Genesis.

As stated above, Joseph could indeed be considered a poster-boy biblical patriarch and one worth emulating. Kim remarks regarding Joseph's emulatability that "Joseph's dramatic progress from humble origins to imperial governor certainly makes him an extraordinary figure."[23] Joseph's success is further remarkable, especially when it is read against the likely socio-historical setting of the rebuking and survival periods under the Persian Empire.

However, this notion of Joseph as a superhero has recently been troubled by contextually informed interpretations and receptions. Scholars employing contextual ideological critical approaches have raised poignant concerns regarding the simple positive appropriation of the Joseph character. Kim, therefore, continues from his positive remarks above regarding Joseph's successes in Egypt by addressing the complexity of Joseph's hybrid identity construction and simultaneous insider/outsider status in Egypt when stating, "Joseph, though once an outsider, has become not only an insider but also a typically authoritative overlord."[24] Fontaine also picks up on this dimension when stating that "Our hero is a survivor of human trafficking who becomes a successful state food aid distributor. He then colludes to enslave people in their own lands in return for the bread he has stored up with God's help."[25] Parris continues:

> We need to be fairly clear about what Joseph represents. Joseph used the extreme needs of the people to compel them to sell all their land, their possessions and even themselves to their new ruler. He used his extraordinary abilities to create and install an inhuman economic system in which ownership of all land and farm animals, with all property and wealth, belonged to Pharaoh.[26]

It is clear that a great deal of hero disruption has taken place in the process of socio-economic ideological critical engagements with the Joseph narrative. There has also been a resurgence of queer readings of the Joseph narrative, and it is to this discourse that I aim to contribute. However, the aim in queering Joseph is not to discredit or devalue Joseph as a character, but rather to undermine or trouble stable heteropatriarchal readings of

---

23. Kim, "Reading the Joseph Story," 22.
24. Kim, "Reading the Joseph Story," 22.
25. Fontaine, "Here Comes This Dreamer," 140.
26. Parris, "Iconic Joseph," 96.

Joseph as patriarch and, in the process, to crack open space for contemporary readers to relate and appropriate Joseph in new and subversive ways.

In the course of queering Joseph's character, I have found the work of the queer drama scholar Peterson Toscano exceptionally helpful in the process of intersecting the religio-cultural and socio-economic with gender and sexuality.[27] Toscano picks up on Joseph's gender non-conforming character in one of his performance lectures, and I initially drew from this creative work in order to reflect on Joseph, the indoorsy and dreamy favorite son, as an example of a character who transgresses gender norms in the Bible and one who does not adhere to prescribed gender constructions or expectations. Although there are numerous sub-sections to the overall narrative that lends itself to queer interrogation, I limit my discussion in the final part of this contribution to three interrelated themes, namely othering, punitive violence and counter-dominant masculinity constructions.

Firstly, we turn our attention to how Joseph is set apart in the narrative. Joseph's less than favorable position amongst his brothers does not seem so surprising because Joseph lords his lofty, some might even say egotistical, dreams over his brothers and snitches on their boys-will-be-boys activities to the patriarch. The text, however, clearly states that Jacob loved Joseph more than any of his other children. This special affection is undoubtedly informed not only by the fact that Joseph is the son of Jacob's favorite wife, Rachel but also because he recognizes his own proneness to dwell amongst the tents in the young dreamer.[28] In a difficult to understand parental strategy, Jacob gifts Joseph with a coat of many colors. The gift is probably remarkable in and of itself, but that this garment, which has the clear function of an identity marker, is described by the same word that is used to describe Tamar's dress, fit for a princess, in 2 Samuel 13 opens up an array of queer interpretative possibilities. Jacob gifts Joseph with a princess dress, and in the process, the outsider is colorfully othered. Joseph who is already set apart due to the uncensored way in which he flaunts his visions in front of his extended family is queerly set apart by his transgressive dress. The Bra is indeed wearing a skirt, and he flaunts it everywhere like a multi-colored butterfly.

Secondly, Joseph's distinctly marked otherness, which is amplified by the princess dress, evokes his brothers' punitive reaction. They see him from afar prancing in the field with his princess dress, where they are doing real men's work, and is affronted by his display of otherness. Their physical disciplinary action to his queerness is reminiscent of similar "corrective/curative" behavior expressed though the rape of lesbian women in the African

---

27. For more on Toscano's work, see https://petersontoscano.com/.

28. For more in this regard, cf. Jennings, *Jacob's Wound*, 2005.

context who do not conform to the heteronormative ideal. The violence is punitive, they want to teach him a lesson for not fitting the dominant and communally constructed and upheld gender norms. Linked to the "corrective/curative" behavior displayed by the brothers are questions about Jacob's positionality and responsibility when it comes to the punitive violence committed by the brothers in an attempt to "correct" Joseph. We read that it is Jacob who sends Joseph to his brothers. He does this directly after reprimanding Joseph for flaunting his dreams not only in front of his brothers, but also including the patriarch in the dream divulgence. Although merely troublemaking speculation it is indeed something to consider. Did Jacob send Joseph to his brothers in the field for a bit of man-making activity to get him to understand his place in the pecking order?

Thirdly, and connected to the previous points, the counter-dominant construction of Joseph's masculinity makes him an ideal character to engage in contemporary discussion on dominant notions of masculinity and related sexuality and gender identity discussions. In Egypt, Joseph is described as beautiful, and he is valued and desired for his gender-fluid expression. His lack of sexual vigor with Potiphar's wife and the apparent speed with which he climbs the influence ladder raises questions regarding his masculinity construction, especially if one considers the high value placed on sexual conquest as an illustration of hegemonic masculinity in the Hebrew Bible.[29] Rather than respond to the violence committed to him by his brothers with violence, we find Joseph often overcome with emotion and swift to forgive when they meet again as vulnerable climate migrants before him in full Egyptian drag. In his forgiveness of his brothers and his willingness to seek for the possibility of reconciliation, we find Joseph moving beyond typical masculine modes of conflict engagement.

SO WHAT?

For those who appropriate the Bible when ethically engaging issues in the intersectional gender and sexuality landscape in an uncritical and decontextual way, the probing outlined in the final section of this contribution will surely be a bridge too far. It will be dismissed as disrespectful by the faithful or unscientific by the scholars. So, why bother? Why make this trouble? Why ask questions and make suggestions that will lead to discomfort, and that will destabilize the neat and clean ways of understanding and interpreting?

29. For more in this regard, please see: Creangă, *Men and Masculinity*; Haddox, "Masculinity Studies"; and Creangă, *Hebrew Masculinities Anew*.

Beyond offering conclusions or how-to guides for engaging the Biblical text the aim of this contribution was to illustrate how it is possible for queer believers to engage the biblical text because of all the interpretive possibilities that exist in the queer twists and turns of biblical narratives. The fact that Joseph is visibly othered in the narrative creates space for those who are often positioned as the "other" in African faith landscapes to discover a kindred spirit. The painful depiction of Joseph's punitive gender correction cracks open space for contemporary conversations about hate-crimes, curative violence and other forms of dehumanization. The fact that Joseph, on more than one occasion, has to leave the room to cry and succeeds in reaching across the divide to forgive his brothers invites us in to have serious conversations about toxic constructions of masculinity and the possibility for redemption. The fact that the Bra is wearing a skirt enables us to critically engage the myriad of ways in which we limit ourselves and others by blindly accepting the stable normalcy prescribed by heteropatriarchy. We have these conversations because as Pumelela 'Push' Nqelenga so chillingly reminds us:

> We saw what humans can do to statues;
> We saw what statutes make of us. . .

BIBLIOGRAPHY

Ackermann, Denise. "Meaning and Power: Some Key Terms in Feminist Liberation Theology." *Scriptura* 44 (1993) 19–33.

Butler, Judith. *Gender Trouble: Feminism and the Subversion of Identity.* New York: Routledge, 2011.

Cheng, Patrick S. *Radical Love: An Introduction to Queer Theology.* New York: Seabury, 2011.

Chiweshe, Malvern T., et al. "Reproductive Justice in Context: South African and Zimbabwean Women's Narratives of their Abortion Decision." *Feminism and Psychology* 27.2 (2017) 203–24.

Cranny-Francis, Anne, et al. *Gender Studies: Terms and Debates.* New York: Palgrave, 2003.

Creangă, Ovidiu. *Hebrew Masculinities Anew.* Sheffield: Sheffield Phoenix, 2019.

———. *Men and Masculinity in the Hebrew Bible and Beyond.* Sheffield: Sheffield Phoenix, 2010.

Davis, Kathy. "Intersectionality as Buzzword: A Sociology of Science Perspective on What Makes a Feminist Theory Successful." *Feminist Theory* 9.1 (2008) 67–85.

Di Silvio, Lorenzo. "Correcting Corrective Rape: Carmichele and Developing South Africa's Affirmative Obligations to Prevent Violence Against Women." *Georgetown Law Journal* 99.5 (2011) 1469.

Fontaine, Carole R. "'Here Comes This Dreamer': Reading Joseph the Slave in Multi-cultural and Interfaith Contexts." In *Genesis*, edited by Athalya Brenner et al., 131–45. Philadelphia: Fortress, 2010.

Goss, Robert E., and Mona West, eds. *Take Back the Word: A Queer Reading of the Bible.* Cleveland: Pilgrim, 2000.

Haddox, S. E. "Masculinity Studies of the Hebrew Bible: The First Two Decades." *Currents in Biblical Research* 14.2 (2016) 176–206.

Hornsby, Teresa J., and Ken Stone. "Introduction." In *Bible Trouble: Queer Reading at the Boundaries of Biblical Scholarship*, edited by Teresa J. Hornsby and Ken Stone, ix–xiv. Atlanta: Society of Biblical Literature, 2011.

Jennings, Thedore W. *Jacob's Wound: Homoerotic Narrative in the Literature of Ancient Israel.* New York: Bloomsbury, 2005.

Kim, Hyun C. P. "Reading the Joseph Story (Genesis 37–50) as a Diaspora Narrative." *Catholic Biblical Quarterly* 75.2 (2013) 219–38.

Koch, Tim R. "A Homoerotic Approach to Scripture." *Theology and Sexuality* 14 (2001) 10–22.

Lapsley, Jacqueline E. *Whispering the Word. Hearing Women's Stories in the Old Testament.* Louisville: Westminster John Knox, 2011.

Macleod, Catriona I. "Expanding Reproductive Justice through a Supportability Reparative Justice Framework: The Case of Abortion in South Africa." *Culture, Health, and Sexuality* 21.1 (2019) 46–62.

Macleod, Catriona I., et al. "Articulating Reproductive Justice through Reparative Justice: Case Studies of Abortion in Great Britain and South Africa." *Culture, Health, and Sexuality* 19.5 (2017) 601–15.

Martin, A., et al. "Hate Crimes: The Rise of Corrective Rape in South Africa." *ActionAid*, March 2009. https://www.actionaid.org.uk/sites/default/files/doc_lib/correctiveraperep_final.pdf.

Parris, G. "The Iconic Joseph: Contesting the African Migrant Churches' View of Joseph." *Black Theology* 9.1 (2011) 77–107.

Punt, Jeremy. "Sex and Gender, and Liminality in Biblical Texts: Venturing into Postcolonial, Queer Biblical Interpretation." *Neotestamentica* 41.2 (2007) 382–98.

———. "Intersections in Queer Theory and Postcolonial Theory, and Hermeneutical Spin-offs." *Bible and Critical Theory* 4.2 (2011).

Ruether, Rosemary Radford. *Sexism and God-Talk: Toward a Feminist Theology.* London: SCM, 2002.

Schneider, L. C. "Homosexuality, Queer Theory, and Christian Theology." *Religious Studies Review* 26.1 (2000) 3–12.

Thatcher, Adrian. *God, Sex, and Gender: An Introduction.* Chichester: Wiley-Blackwell, 2011.

Tolbert, Mary A. "Gender." In *Handbook of Postmodern Biblical Interpretation*, edited by A. K. M. Adam, 99–105. St. Louis: Chalice, 2000.

Van der Walt, Charlene. "'It's the Price I Guess for the Lies I've Told that the Truth it No Longer Thrills Me . . .': Reading Queer Lies to Reveal Straight Truth in Genesis 38." In *Restorative Readings: The Old Testament, Ethics, and Human Dignity*, edited by L. Juliana Claassens and Bruce C. Birch, 57–75. Eugene: Pickwick, 2015.

———. "'To the Wonder': Finding God in the Most Unexpected Places." In *Considering Compassion: Global Ethics, Human Dignity, and the Compassionate God*, edited by L. Juliana Claassens and Frits de Lange, 170–86. Eugene: Pickwick, 2018.

Van der Walt, Charlene, and Judith Terblanche. "Reimagining a Solitary Landscape: Tracing Communities of Care in Exodus 1–2 and the Film Shirley Adams." *Old Testament Essays* 29.1 (2016) 176–94.

Yep, Gust A. "The Violence of Heteronormativity in Communication Studies: Notes on Injury, Healing, and Queer World-Making." In *Queer Theory and Communication: From Disciplining Queers to Queering the Discipline(s)*, edited by Gust A. Yep et al., 11–60. New York: Routledge, 2014.

Yip, Andrew K. T. "Coming Home from the Wilderness: An Overview of Recent Scholarly Research on LGBTQI Religiosity/Spirituality in the West." In *Queer Spiritual Spaces: Sexuality and Sacred Spaces*, edited by Kath Browne et al., 35–50. Farnham: Ashgate, 2010.

8

Theology on Gender Reformation for the (South)[1] African Reconstruction Process

Perceptions from Exodus 21:7 and Deuteronomy 15:12, 17

Ntozakhe Cezula

INTRODUCTION

According to Dominique Dryding,

> (m)ost South Africans say gender equality has been achieved with regard to jobs, land, and education. . . but even amid widespread support for women's rights, popular attitudes point to persistent barriers to full equality. . . A majority of both men and women believe that homemaking and child-rearing should mainly be a

---

1. South is bracketed because this argument is relevant for the whole of Africa as well, but the author focuses on South Africa because it is the part of Africa he is most familiar with.

woman's responsibility. And while most South Africans reject domestic violence, one in five still see wife-beating as justifiable.[2]

Earlier, Bongani Finca observed:

> There are some within the Church who deal with the gender issue as a matter of charity—some kindness which the church must show women. I believe that the Church must deal with the gender issue because it is fundamental to our calling as the Church which liberates and sets free. . .[3]

Dealing with the gender issue as a matter of charity to women is an attestation to politically correct behavior with a worldview background which is biased against women. Biblical texts that are biased against women reinforce such a worldview. This essay argues that any behavioral change that is not backed by an affirming worldview is artificial. In an attempt to challenge the worldview itself, I set out to explore two texts, namely Exodus 21:7 and Deuteronomy 15:12 and 15:17, to stimulate ethical sensibilities relating to gender. These texts present two different perspectives on gender equality. This essay aims to read these texts in order to contribute to the discourse on gender equality in the context of community reconstruction. In order to achieve its goal, two theories will be harnessed, namely canonization and de-ideologization. Considering that canons are ideological in nature,[4] biblical texts need to be de–ideologized.[5] These theories will help to make sense of these texts in view of gender equality. In what follows, these theories will be described and applied to place these texts into perspective. I will then proceed to examine the texts themselves. After examining the texts, a contextual background to the texts will be provided in order to make an informed analysis for application in the reconstruction of our communities. The essay will subsequently propose a theology on gender reformation for the (South) African reconstruction process. Finally, I provide a few closing remarks as summary to the discussion.

CANONIZATION AND DE–IDEOLOGIZATION

With reference to the Old Testament, talking about canon is talking about authoritative Scriptures. Barry A. Jones describes the Old Testament canon as follows:

2. Dryding, "Despite Progressive Laws."

3. Finca, "Decade," 193.

4. Stordalen, "Media of Ancient Hebrew Religion," 24.

5. Farisani, "Use of Ezra-Nehemiah," 141.

> A Christian term for the religious writings of ancient Israel held
> as sacred by Judaism and Christianity. . . Canon in its broader
> sense is the normative functioning of given texts within social
> groups, without regard to the fixed content or exclusive status of
> the texts in use. By this definition, the texts of the OT were em-
> ployed as a fluid, functional "canon-in-the-making" for many
> years prior to their ultimate definition as a fixed and exclusive
> collection.[6]

Terje Stordalen makes useful remarks about the phenomenon of canonization. He refers to what he calls the *canonical ecology*. The major instances in canonical ecology are the *canon* itself, the *canonical commentary*
and the *canonical community*. The canonical community are the believers
who read the canon concerned. They are the people who are guided by the
canon in living out their faith. However, when "historical change alters the
context for interpretation,"[7] the canonical community conjures the old texts
to make new sense without making a radical break.[8] What this means, is
that when historical circumstances change so that the canon cannot provide
satisfactory guidance in the new historical circumstances, the canonical
community will provide a commentary to the canon. The commentary thus
gives relevance to the canon and the canon will provide legitimacy to the
commentary. In this sense both are kept so there is no radical break with
the canon. The commentary will then become canonical and also be part of
the Scriptures together with the canon. Stordalen calls the product of such a
process a *canonical commentary*. Informed by this theory, this essay argues
that Deuteronomy 15:12 and 15:17 are commentary to Exodus 21:7.

Stordalen further remarks that ". . . canons take on ideological functions. . . "[9] and for that reason this essay also draws on the theory of de-ideologization. Following an analysis of the Book of Ezra-Nehemiah, Elelwani
Farisani states the following concerning de-ideologization:

> Having isolated the ideology of Ezra-Nehemiah, this study will
> propose an inclusive reading of this text as opposed to an exclu-
> sive reading. Linked to this is the third point, namely, if African
> biblical hermeneutics has to have an impact in our continent, it
> does not only have to relate the text as is to the African context,
> it must also de-ideologize that particular text in the first place.
> For an unideologised reading may be counterproductive, in that

6. Jones, "Canon of the Old Testament," 215.

7. Stordalen, *Formative Past*, 134.

8. Stordalen, *Formative Past*, 134.

9. Stordalen, "Media of Ancient Hebrew Religion," 24.

instead of supporting and advancing the cause of the poor and marginalized, such a reading may further marginalize the poor by further enslaving them with the "revealed word of God."[10]

In agreement with Farisani, this essay argues that the texts of Exodus 21:7 and Deuteronomy 15:12 and 15:17 need to be de-ideologized in order to avoid further marginalizing of the already marginalized by enslaving them even further with the "revealed word of God." In my own work on de-ideologizing Ezra-Nehemiah, I have described de-ideologization elsewhere as follows:

> The task of de-ideologizing Ezra-Nehemiah is twofold: First, to distinguish the ideology underlying the text, and second, to bring to the fore other ideologies that compete with the dominant ideology in Ezra-Nehemiah.[11]

This is the intent also of this essay, in de-ideologizing these two texts. I set out to reveal the ideologies represented by these two texts and provide the reader with an opportunity to make an informed choice about them. Let us now proceed to examine the respective texts.

EXODUS 21:7 AND DEUTERONOMY 15: 12 AND 15:17

In view of the afore-mentioned theories, close readings of the selected verses now follow. Let us start with Exodus 21:7:

וְכִי־יִמְכֹּר אִישׁ אֶת־בִּתּוֹ לְאָמָה לֹא תֵצֵא כְּצֵאת הָעֲבָדִים:

A possible translation of this verse is as follows: "And if a man sold his daughter as a slave, she shall not go out as male slaves go out." In other words, the conditions of release for male and female slaves are not the same. For male slaves the conditions are as follows: "When you buy a male Hebrew slave, he shall serve six years, but in the seventh he shall go out a free person, without debt" (Exod 21:2). For female slaves, however, the conditions are as follows:

> If she does not please her master, who has designated her for himself, then he shall let her be redeemed. He shall have no right to sell her to a foreign people, since he has broken faith with her. If he designates her for his son, he shall deal with her as with a daughter. If he takes another wife to himself, he shall not

10. Farisani, "Use of Ezra-Nehemiah," 141.
11. Cezula, "De-ideolizing Ezra-Nehemiah," 124.

diminish her food, her clothing, or her marital rights. And if he does not do these three things for her, she shall go out for nothing, without payment of money. (Exod 21:8–11)

What these prescriptions meant, is that slave masters had a right to make female slaves wives or concubines. If they lost interest in them after six years, they could release them for compensation, provided it was not to a foreigner. This, unlike male slaves, who were released for free. Another option was to give the female slave to his son, but then treating her as a daughter. The third option was that he could decide to take her as another wife. In that case, he still had to maintain her marital rights. On these conditions, remarks made by Deborah O'Donnell Setel are worth mentioning:

> In the instance of the daughter sold into slavery, it appears that the measures are intended as more protective than those extended to male slaves. Their effect, however, is to ensure that the captive woman may never leave male control.[12]

The bottom line is this text advocates gender inequality, as male and female slaves are to be treated differently.

With Exodus 21:7 still fresh in our minds, let us turn to Deuteronomy 15:12 and 17b:

כִּי־יִמָּכֵר לְךָ אָחִיךָ הָעִבְרִי אוֹ הָעִבְרִיָּה וַעֲבָדְךָ שֵׁשׁ שָׁנִים וּבַשָּׁנָה הַשְּׁבִיעִת תְּשַׁלְּחֶנּוּ חָפְשִׁי מֵעִמָּךְ:

A possible translation for verse 15:12 is as follows: "If your brother sold to you a Hebrew man or Hebrew woman and the person serves you for six years, in the seventh year then, you shall set the person free."

וְאַף לַאֲמָתְךָ תַּעֲשֶׂה־כֵּן:

Verse 17b could be translated as follows: "And also, to your female slave you shall do likewise."

Deuteronomy 15:12 and 17b are connected to one another by 15:13–17a. It is helpful to also look at these connecting verses, for they detail the conditions. Deuteronomy 15:12 states that both a male and a female slave should be released in the seventh year. Verse 13a introduces the conditions of release. The conditions from verses 13b to 17a are as follows:

1. They shall not be sent out empty-handed.

2. They must be provided for liberally out of the master's flock, threshing floor and wine press.

12. Setel, "Exodus," 38.

3. The motivation for this is that the master, as an Israelite, was once a slave in Egypt and the Lord redeemed him.

4. However, if the slave remains with the master out of their own choice, the master can keep them.

Deuteronomy 15:17b categorically states that what happened to the male slave should happen to the female slave as well. Clearly, here there is gender equality. Although slavery itself is questionable these days, let us deal with this issue in its own context. Slavery in both the selected texts is not the issue at hand—rather, the focus is on the gender dimensions thereof. What we have here, then, is one authoritative text purporting gender inequality, and another gender equality.

What has been illustrated here, is the de-ideologization of both Exodus 21:7, and Deuteronomy 15:12 and 15:17b. The reader now has the opportunity to make an informed decision about each of the texts; for they deal with the same issue, namely the release of slaves. One might argue, though, that the de-ideologization is not comprehensive enough, because Lev 25:39–46 also deals with the release of slaves. There is merit in such a criticism. However, as Adrian Schenker correctly observes, Leviticus "does not treat the manumission of female slaves,"[13] which is the bone of contention for this essay. For this reason, de-ideologization concerning the equality of male and female Hebrew slaves in OT Law is considered to be comprehensive. The discussion therefore continues with the focus on the selected texts from the books Exodus and Deuteronomy.

Considering they are both regarded as authoritative scriptures, how should the contemporary reader deal with this situation? The question might be rephrased as follows: which biblical perspective should the contemporary reader embrace? The gender inequality perspective of Exodus 21, or the gender equality perspective of Deuteronomy 15? This question will be the focus of the conclusion of this essay, where a theology on gender reformation for the (South) African reconstruction process will be proposed.

Before proceeding to the matter of making a choice for one or the other, a few comments on the contextual background of these texts are worth considering.

A CONTEXTUAL BACKGROUND

In the forgoing discussion, and with the framework of de-ideologization, two contrasting biblical perspectives on gender equality were distinguished.

13. Schenker, "Biblical Legislation," 38.

Continuing the discussion with the help of the canonization theory, the reason for these two contrasting biblical perspectives on gender equality will be explored.

The point of departure is the contextual background of the Exodus text. Exodus 21:7 is contained in what is called the Covenant Code. Covenant Code is a name given by scholars to the core legal material in the Book of Exodus; that is, Exodus 21–23. According to Jean-Louis Ska, "the Covenant Code presupposes a society at the heart of which were leaders of 'extended families' who settled the most important conflicts on the local level—that is, in small towns or villages."[14] The extended families were also called the "fathers' houses." Describing a father's house, Nunnally says:

> The "father's house" included the patriarch and his wife, unmarried children, married sons and grandsons with their families, slaves and their families, and resident aliens. This extended family could easily approach 100 members, who resided together in a cluster of dwellings.[15]

If a family could be as large as indicated above, it could well be a social system of some sort on its own. Isaac Mendelsohn's remarks in this regard might lend some merit to this sentiment:

> Like the king who rules over his realm so does the pater familias dominate his household. He is, as the West Semites called him, the *baal* ("owner") of his wives and children. In its infancy the state fought an unceasing battle to restrict the absolute authority of the father who, within his own domain, had the physical power and the legal right to treat his wives and children as he pleased and even to dispose of them as he saw fit.[16]

It is this point that makes Anthony Phillips' description of family law of the time relevant. He argues that family law was "itself best seen as a self-contained section within general customary law," ". . . under the head of the household a very different procedure was adopted," and ". . . under family law the courts had no jurisdiction."[17] Dealing with family law in pre-exilic Israel, he explains why the law of releasing slaves was handled the way it was. It is because only free adult males had legal status. Women, children and slaves were the property of the head of the household, so their protection depended on him and not on the courts. The wrongs inflicted on the

---

14. Ska, *Introduction*, 187–88.

15. Nunnally, "Father's House," 457.

16. Mendelsohn, "Family," 24.

17. Phillips, "Some Aspects of Family Law," 350.

members of his household were not likely to cause any public disorder in the community, like it would in members of other households. "How the head of the household dealt with members of his household who were not free adult males was in general his private affair."[18] When these dependents were no more under his protection, like in the case of widows and orphans, they were understood as being under the special care of God and thus declared objects of charity to the community at large.[19] It is in this context that one should interpret Exodus 21:7. Biblical texts, sometimes, evince something about their social, historical and cultural context of origin. Because women had no legal status and the head of the household was the final authority, the woman slave's fate was in the hands of the household head.

The selected verses from Deuteronomy form part of the Deuteronomic Code. Deuteronomic Code is an academic designation given by scholars to the core legal material in Deuteronomy, namely Deuteronomy 12–26. Schenker offers the following perspective:

> It is usually assumed that Deut. 15.12–18 corrects Exod. 21.2–11, while Lev. 25.39–54 replaces the earlier legislations, both of the Covenant Code and of the Deuteronomic Law, since the three sets of legislation do not seem to be in agreement with each other.[20]

Schenker's statement concerning the relationship of the Covenant Code and the Deuteronomic Code evinces the idea of a canon and a canonical commentary as was expressed above. This essay explicitly asserts that the Deuteronomic Code is a commentary to the Covenant Code. Above was stated that when historical circumstances change to such an extent that the canon cannot provide satisfactory guidance in the new historical circumstances, the canonical community will provide a commentary to the canon. The idea of a change in socio-historical circumstances is discernible in a remark made by Mendelsohn, when he says that "in its infancy the state fought an unceasing battle to restrict the absolute authority of the father who, within his own domain, had the physical power and the legal right to treat his wives and children as he pleased and even to dispose of them as he saw fit."[21] This sentiment is also expressed by Ska:

> In the Deuteronomic Code, the centralization of the cult was accompanied by judicial centralization. The extended family had

18. Phillips, "Some Aspects of Family Law," 350.
19. Phillips, "Some Aspects of Family Law," 350.
20. Schenker, "Biblical Legislation," 23.
21. Mendelsohn, "Family," 24.

to relinquish a large part of its power to the central authority in Jerusalem. Deuteronomy unifies by asserting that Israel constitutes one people with one God and one temple.[22]

The notion of "One People, One God, One Temple" that Ska refers to is extensively elaborated by Gunther Wittenberg when he deals with tithe in Deuteronomy:

> "One Yahweh—one place of worship—one people of God," that was the ideal of the deuteronomic reformers, but the social reality at the time when the reform coalition set about formulating the laws that would reconstitute Israel as the people of God was entirely different. The social crisis which had undermined the fabric of the free peasant community in Israel and Judah since the mid eighth century and which had called forth the prophetic indictments of Amos, Micah and Isaiah, had reached an advanced stage after a century of Assyrian domination at the beginning of the reign of Josiah. In this situation the reformers were intent on finally putting a stop to the disastrous deterioration of the social situation of the poorer members of the peasant community.[23]

In the expression "one people of God," Wittenberg discerns "the concept of equality implying an ethics of brotherhood (sic.) as members of the people of God."[24] This observation is confirmed in Phillips when he says the reason why the female Israelite slave was introduced in the Deuteronomists' legislation (15:12) and thus automatically given freedom like the Israelite male slave, was the extension of legal status to adult Israelite women. He further qualifies by saying that "it is this previous lack of legal status which is the reason for the difference in treatment of male and female slaves in [Exodus] 21.2–11. . . "[25] I agree that there was a conscious change when it is recognized that in Exodus 34:22–24 only men are invited to the Festival of Weeks. However, in Deuteronomy 16:10–12, daughters and female slaves are invited to participate in the joy as well. In accordance with the theory of canonization, I therefore conclude that during the monarchical period the slave laws of the Covenant Code did not resonate well with the principle of "one people of God" and the Deuteronomists thus amended them. Albeit brief, the discussion to this point should suffice to make clear that there are

---

22. Ska, *Introduction*, 188–89.

23. Wittenberg, "Tithe," 94.

24. Wittenberg, "Tithe," 90.

25. Phillips, "Laws of Slavery," 60.

noticeable differences between Exodus 21:7 and Deuteronomy 15:12 and 15:17b.

By way of conclusion, let us wrestle with these different laws toward a proposal for a theology on gender reformation for the (South) African reconstruction process.

AN ETHICAL THEOLOGY ON GENDER REFORMATION

Thus far, two sets of texts were read, and their meanings retrieved. The Exodus text states that a woman slave will not be released like a man slave, and the Deuteronomy text states the opposite. These texts were de-ideologized, that is, it was identified that one advocates gender inequality and the other gender equality. Thereafter, the place of both of these (contradictory) texts in the same canon were explored. Through the theory of canonization, it is possible to determine that the later text is a commentary to the earlier text, due to socio-historical changes. The challenge now is for the contemporary reader, as both texts are canonical. How does one deal with the challenge of gender (in)equality in one's own context without being disobedient to the canon? To be specific to the objective of this essay: how does one formulate a theology of gender if the canon provides two contradictory perspectives? Fortunately, de-ideologization also provides an opportunity to make a choice. It is this choice that I would like to turn to now.

What some readers typically do, is to focus on the one text that resonates with their intentions and to turn a blind eye on the dissenting one. This method is intended to hide self-interest and renders the text a shield to further the interests of the reader. By de-ideologizing, one does not turn a blind eye on the dissenting text, but rather makes a conscious and overt choice against it. In this manner one does not use the text simply as a shield, but also takes responsibility for one's choice. This approach exhibits honesty and transparency which is, in my opinion, a virtuous application of Scripture. This is also an honest acknowledgement of the human element in communicating divine will. Honesty is treasure in divine concerns. Dishonesty, on the other hand, is encapsulated starkly in the following quote:

> According to Proverbs 6:16–19, God hates a lying tongue (17), a devising heart, plans of deception and feet that hurry to run to evil (18), and a false witness who breathes lies and sends out discord between brothers. There are many more proverbs that denounce dishonesty, e.g., Proverbs 11:18, 12:5, 17:4, 24:28, 27:6 and 28:24.[26]

26. Cezula, "The 'Fear of the Lord/God,'" 21–22.

This sentiment is directed to a reader who deliberately ignores a dissenting text and clings to the one that resonates with the reader's concerns. According to this essay, it is in the interest of the divine for the reader to openly declare one's interest in the choice that one makes regarding contradictory texts.

Finally, then, I proceed to my own choice between the two biblical perspectives.

In making my choice I openly declare my personal interest in the choice I make. As an interpreter, it is no longer possible to pretend as if the misfortunes of the victims of irresponsible interpretations of the Bible simply goes unnoticed. This is especially the case for women on the African continent, who continue to be oppressed by means of patriarchal structures, undergirded by patriarchal interpretative choices in biblical interpretation.

From an ethical point of view, I agree with Gerrie Snyman, who states:

> A hermeneutic that remains insensitive to oppressive biblical texts, disempowers the reader to construct a new way of being after apartheid. . . The assumed benevolence masks those texts that are oppressive and its cruelty hides behind the will of God. And doing the will of God is what about every Christian intends to do. It makes one feel good and not evil. I believe apartheid shattered that conviction and we need now a critical sensibility to recognize oppressiveness in biblical texts.[27]

De-ideologizing biblical texts is one dimension of the issue. Additionally, biblical interpreters need to arouse their moral compasses when engaging in biblical interpretation. When readers choose particular biblical perspectives over other competing perspectives, those readers must also remember that they still have an ethical responsibility. How a reader's choice between or among competing biblical perspectives affects other people's lives cannot be the Bible's responsibility, but rather the reader's responsibility. In the face of the reality of competing perspectives in the Bible, the justification that "the Bible says" is no more tenable. Choosing biblical texts that undermine the human dignity of other people when there are other texts affirming such dignity, require more than simply "the Bible says so." In this essay, therefore, I deliberately make a choice for the text of Deuteronomy that acknowledges the dignity of women, over against the text of Exodus that violates such dignity. That being said, what implication does this discussion have for theology in post-apartheid South Africa?

This discussion charges that in post-apartheid South Africa, there is no tenable argument that wants to squarely place responsibility for a gender oppressive theology on the Bible. In the past and the present, gender

27. Snyman, "Collective Memory," 79.

inequality has been plaguing South Africa. Unfortunately, the Bible has also been used to perpetuate this state of affairs. In the discussion above, it was illustrated that the same Bible can also be useful in bringing about genuine and respectful gender equality. Currently, femicide is endemic in South Africa. At least some of the blame can be attributed to gender inequality. Femicide can in no way be considered obedience to God. I therefore propose a theology on gender reformation for the (South) African reconstruction process, that is based on Deuteronomy 15:12, 13a and 17b.

CONCLUSION

Bringing the discussion to a close, I make a few summative remarks. When the first democratic elections took place in South Africa, high hopes for improved circumstances for oppressed social categories in this country were raised. Women were one such social category. However, twenty-seven years later, some changes may have taken place, but conditions have not changed to the satisfaction of those affected. Theology has played a role in shaping different pre-1994 perspectives. Therefore, theology can and should play a fruitful role in the post-1994 reconstruction of society. The theological contribution of this essay was focused on a comparison of Exodus 21:7 and Deuteronomy 15:12 and 15:17. Using de-ideologization, it was established that Exodus 21:7 advocates gender inequality, and that Deuteronomy 15:12 and 15:17 advocate gender equality. Through canonization it was also established that Exodus 21:7 reflected the socio-historical circumstances of its origin. By the same token, the perspective of Deuteronomy 15:12 and 15:17 was a product of the socio-historical changes that had taken place at the time. Recognizing that a contemporary reader is thus faced with a choice between two contradicting theological perspectives, this essay proposes that readers should make ethically responsible choices. It argues that the statement "the Bible says" is no more a sufficient justification for the biblical perspectives that readers prioritize. Subsequently, I made a choice for proposing that the theological perspective on gender equality, as is illustrated in Deuteronomy 15:12 and 15:17, should be selected over and against that of Exodus 21:7.

BIBLIOGRAPHY

Cezula, Ntozakhe S. "De-ideolizing Ezra-Nehemiah: Challenging Discriminatory Ideologies." In *Restorative Readings: The Old Testament, Ethics, and Human*

Dignity, edited by L. Juliana Claassens and Bruce C. Birch, 117–138. Eugene, OR: Pickwick, 2015.

Cezula, Ntozakhe S. "The 'Fear of the Lord/God' in Context of the South Africa We Pray for Campaign." *Scriptura* 116 (2017) 15–26.

Dryding, Dominique. "Despite Progressive Laws, Barriers to Full Gender Equality Persist in South Africa." *Afrobarometer Dispatch* 324 (2019) 2–13.

Farisani, Elelwani B. "The Use of Ezra-Nehemiah in a Quest for a Theology of Renewal, Transformation and Reconstruction in the (South) African Context." PhD diss., University of KwaZulu–Natal, 2002.

Finca, Bongani B. "The Decade: A Man's View." *Ecumenical Review* 46.2 (1994) 191–93.

Jones, Barry A. "Canon of the Old Testament." In *Eerdmans Dictionary of the Bible*, edited by David Noel Freedman et al., 215–17. Grand Rapids: Eerdmans, 2000.

Mendelsohn, I. "The Family in the Ancient Near East." *Biblical Archaeologist* 11.2 (1948) 24–40.

Nunnally, W. E. "Father's House." In *Eerdmans Dictionary of the Bible*, edited by David Noel Freedman et al., 457. Grand Rapids: Eerdmans, 2000.

Phillips, Anthony. "Some Aspects of Family Law in Pre–Exilic Israel." *Vetus Testamentum* 23:3 (1973) 349–61.

——— "The Laws of Slavery: Exodus 21.2–11." *Journal for the Study of the Old Testament*, 30 (1984) 51–86.

Schenker, Adrian. "The Biblical Legislation on the Release of Slaves: The Road from Exodus to Leviticus." *Journal for the Study of the Old Testament* 78 (1998) 23–41.

Setel, Drorah O'Donnell. "Exodus." In *Women's Bible Commentary: Expanded Edition with Apocrypha*, edited by Carol A. Newsom and Sharon H. Ringe, 30–39. Louisville: Westminster John Knox, 1998.

Ska, Jean–Louis. *Introduction to Reading the Pentateuch*. Winona Lake: Eisenbrauns, 2006.

Snyman, Gerrie. "Collective Memory and Coloniality of Being as a Hermeneutical Framework: A Partialised Reading of Ezra-Nehemiah." *OTE* 20.1 (2007) 53–83.

Stordalen, Terje. "Media of Ancient Hebrew Religion." In *Religion Across Media: From Early Antiquity to Late Modernity,* edited by Knut Lunby, 20–36. New York: Peter Lang, 2013.

Stordalen, Terje. *The Formative Past and the Formation of the Future: Collective Remembering and Identity Formation*. Oslo: Novus, 2015.

Wittenberg, Gunther H. "The Tithe: An Obligation for Christians? Perspectives from Deuteronomy." *Journal of Theology for Southern Africa* 134 (2009) 82–101.

9

Paul on Sex

Viable Proposition, Impossible Conundrum, or Simply Queer?

Jeremy Punt

INTRODUCTION: HUMAN SEXUALITY

Paul's stance on gender and sexuality, not unlike other aspects of his writings, often meets with lofty praise or harsh criticism. His views on sex, in particular, has elicited interest to the extent that, ironically, it is matched only by the extent to which Christian groups claim to rely upon Pauline thought for their doctrinal, creedal, and even dogmatic positions.[1] Notwithstanding his letters' far greater concern with other (perhaps not unrelated) matters such as dietary issues, Paul's references to and instructions on sex have attracted a disproportionate amount of interest over the centuries—as far as records in this regard exist.[2] In his first letter, slightly longer than most, directed at the Corinthians, Paul's position on sexuality and sex appears to shift, and eventually oscillates between a seeming unwillingness to accept and affirm human sex on the one hand, and on the other hand, his

---

1. For example, Braaten, *Justification*.
2. For example, Dunning, *Specters of Paul*.

eagerness to construe sex as valued, necessary and unrestricted in contexts such as marriage. Moving beyond conventional dichotomized readings of Paul, queer theory's non-essentialist, post-conventional, binary-resisting, social constructionist view of gender and sexuality shows up Pauline sexuality as—in a word—queer.

Notwithstanding our post-sexual revolution existence, to account for the notion of "sexuality" has never been more urgent: popular (populist) views still often equate sexuality predominantly with a biological, physical or even genital understanding, and within certain church traditions, in an overpowering generative or heteronormative sense at that, all the more worrying in our local context of rampant sexual violence.[3] Such perceptions may have their origin in theological thought or even biblical interpretation. As Bernadette Brooten remarked, while theology today hardly seems to inform discussions on politics or economics, it is ironic that church teachings on gender and sexuality, and family life, are granted remarkable and substantial authority.[4] However, at the same time and courtesy of much research, human sexuality is increasingly, if gradually, understood as "a force that permeates, influences, and affects every act of a person's being at every moment of existence."[5] Rather than seeing sexuality as related to any single aspect of human existence, it is considered to be "at the core and center of our total life response."[6] In the modern context, human sexuality is under-

3. The essentialist perspective ("sex as a natural force, a fixed and unchanging essence that exists prior to and independent of sociocultural arrangements") is increasingly found wanting. In contrast, a (social) constructionist position allows for sexuality to be understood within and according to society and history, and "is susceptible to modification and transformation" (Ellison, *Erotic Justice*, 318). Similar to trends in the USA, in SA the intersection of race ("not a natural, objective category for dividing groups or assigning differentials of power and status, but rather a political and cultural category, institutionalized in systemic patterns of ownership and control of one group over another" (Ellison, *Erotic Justice*, 319–20) with sex/gender issues also leads to fear, suspicion, and intolerance between different racial groups.

4. Brooten, *Love between Women*, 196.

5. The WHO describes sexuality as follows: "Sexuality is a central aspect of being human throughout life and encompasses sex, gender identities and roles, sexual orientation, eroticism, pleasure, intimacy, and reproduction. Sexuality is experienced and expressed in thoughts, fantasies, desires, beliefs, attitudes, values, behaviors, practices, roles, and relationships. While sexuality can include all of these dimensions, not all of them are always experienced or expressed. Sexuality is influenced by the interaction of biological, psychological, social, economic, political, cultural, ethical, legal, historical, religious and spiritual factors" (See "Gender and Human Rights"). Put theologically, "Human sexuality is the concrete manifestation of the divine call to completion, a call extended to every person in the very act of creation and rooted in the very core of his or her being" (Kosnik et al., "Toward a Theology of Human Sexuality," 547).

6. Kosnik et al., "Toward a Theology of Human Sexuality," 547. The further

stood as both an intrapersonal and interpersonal notion of human existence and personhood.

Given modern developments in the understanding of human sexuality, where do the biblical writings, and the Pauline letters, stand in this regard, and how do believers relate interpret these documents? Does one need the Bible for (re)affirming this, for striving toward a perception of sexuality informed by its centrality to human life? Probably not, but the Bible does impact on the lives of millions of believers in SA and around the globe, and has a normative appeal beyond many other apparent authoritative sources, be they scientific, medical or otherwise.[7] "The Bible writes our flesh, its meanings and possibilities."[8] Furthermore, presupposing a static relationship between Bible and bodies is not helpful, since biblical texts are constituted through bodies as sexual and gendered entities, within communities and societal systems at large, and today, read and interpreted, so too. In the NT, the Pauline materials and their interpretation are caught up in this reciprocity, and if nothing else, require a re-consideration of their portrayals of the human dimension of bodily existence and human sexuality, even if very briefly so; but, before approaching Paul, the socio-cultural parameters which framed and informed his letters, deserve our attention.

HUMAN SEXUALITY IN THE 1ST CENTURY AS THE PAULINE LETTERS' CONTEXT

Sexual relationships in the ancient world were governed within the broader social spectrum of a collectivist life by the core values of honor and shame; so too, the isomorphic relation between sexual and social relations ensured that honor was ascribed to the active, penetrating sexual role.[9] Unlike the

---

perspective of Kosnik et al. on sexuality is unfortunately framed heteronormatively as "the way of being in, and relating to, the world as *male* and *female* persons . . . Sexuality is the mode or manner by which humans experience and express both the incompleteness of their individualities as well as their relatedness to each other as male and female" (Kosnik et al., "Toward a Theology of Human Sexuality," 547).

7. And of course, as much as the Bible was (and often still is) seen as "a source that has given rise to values which are fundamentally to be associated with human rights, such as human dignity, freedom, justice and equality" (Vorster, "(E)mpersonating Bodies," 104), the appropriation of the Bible in such matters is at best of times rather complex.

8. Loughlin, "Biblical Bodies," 10.

9. "Male honor is symbolled in the male sexual organs" (Malina, *New Testament World*, 135). And as Lisa Sowle Cahill puts it, "Virtually all sex in the climate out of which the New Testament arose served special social purposes; it seems unexaggerated to say that it was virtually everywhere a symbol of domination" (Cahill, *Sex, Gender, and Christian Ethics*, 152).

relatively recent notion that relationships are built on romance, the ancient pragmatic setting was one where relationships were arranged on behalf of a couple,[10] and sexual relations rendered a biblical world where sexual *acts* were categorized, rather than *people* as happens in modern times. The further hierarchical and patriarchal nature of this world did not envisage sex as primarily an act of fulfilment but rather as an action that one person *did* to another. "[N]o distinction is made in the ancient sources between gender roles (man/woman), sexual orientation (homosexual/ heterosexual/ bisexual), and sexual practice. In those sources, erotic-sexual interaction on the part of people of the same sex is not considered a question of individual identity but a question of social roles and behavior."[11] Such a depersonalized and depersonalizing attitude toward sexuality did not suspend the inextricable links between sexual identity and social and political identity,[12] but rather underscores that the social body preceded the sexual body.

At the same time, concern about matters sexual was neither ultimate nor all-consuming, so that sex for the ancients was morally no more or less problematic than eating and drinking.[13] Regulation of sexual activities existed, in particular to curb harmful effects to society, but without long moral codes of licit or illicit sexual behavior.[14] To some extent the male-biased ancient Greek claim, *"Hetairai* we keep for pleasure, concubines (*pallakai*) for the daily care of our bodies, and wives (*gynaikes*) to procreate children legitimately and to have a trusty guardian of the things inside,"[15] endured in NT times although the extent it was lived up to, typically was mitigated by social, economic and other factors. Still, regardless of the claim's varied uptake, its foundational androcentric and mostly patriarchal sentiments

10. For example, Harris, "'Yes' and 'No' in Women's Desire."

11. Nissinen, *Homoeroticism,* 128. Of the four different forms of same-sex relationships of which all are attested in ancient sources, transgenerational "homosexuality," transgenderal "homosexuality," egalitarian same-sex relationships, and class-distinguished "homosexuality," only the third category plays a significant role in modern society (Nissinen, *Homoeroticism,* 131).

12. "[D]escriptions of sexual relations were dominated by a hierarchical polarization based on the congruence of social status and sexual hierarchy" (Nissinen, *Homoeroticism,* 128).

13. "In the ancient world there were two areas that were of primary concern regarding self–control: sexuality and food" (Moxnes, *Putting Jesus in His Place,* 76).

14. Lambert and Szesnat, "Greek 'Homosexuality,'" 52–56; Nissinen, *Homoeroticism,* 129–30. While "active and passive partners match the distinction between male and female roles," "[s]ame-sex sexual contacts were regarded as a voluntary perversion" (Nissinen, *Homoeroticism,* 128, 130). The notion that "sperm contained the origin of human life" and therefore should not be wasted or used inappropriately (Nissinen, *Homoeroticism,* 130–131), should be noted.

15. Pseudo-Demosthenes, *Against Neaera* 59.122.

prevailed, as did the connection between sex and pleasure as well as the emphasis on marriage and children—and, it should be noted, these aspects were not necessarily connected to one another. Although elite sentiments hardly described the lives of people generally, their anxieties were often the reason for legal arrangements and social systems. So for example were concerns about protecting elite households' *dignitas*, probably the real reason for imperial legislation regulating sexual activity and marital arrangements, extending to all, including free persons and slaves.[16]

Failure to understand how such values and notions functioned in the first century is bound to lead to hasty and misplaced even if well–intended interpretation of biblical texts and theological conclusions. The interpretation of the NT with regard to sexuality has to contend with perceptions about sex in the first century CE that revolved around different models of the human body of which the one-sex model appeared to have been rather influential;[17] different values and value systems informed by honor and shame, framed in a collectivist setting and related to ancient notions such as limited good; and where sex and power were closely associated, and sex often was a penetrative force and tool of power. At the same time, NT authors, including Paul, resisted the imposition of the Torah's purity codes on the new communities of believers, and balked at the idea that adherence to such codes determines the bestowal and reception of God's grace.[18]

---

16. Glancy, *Slavery in Early Christianity*, 27.

17. For example, Laqueur, Thomas W. *Making Sex. Body and Gender from the Greeks to Freud.* Cambridge; London: Harvard University Press, 1990. In modern times, with the two–sex model of human sexuality, the material body that became the primary location for the distinction between men and women usurped the position previously occupied by gender (Vander Stichele, "Like Angels in Heaven," 230). For recent criticism of Laqueur's model as one-sided and generalizing, that both two-sex and one-sex models of the body existed concurrently since antiquity with the rhetorical needs of individual authors determining which one is deployed, see King, Helen. *The One-Sex Body on Trial: The Classical and Early Modern Evidence.* The History of Medicine in Context. Farnham; Burlington: Ashgate: 2013.

18. Countryman, *Dirt, Greed and Sex,* 520–4. In similar fashion, the imposition of the traditional physical purity codes of Western Christianity on communities of faith today, and to moreover pronounce on God's grace, accordingly, is to violate what the NT stands for. However, to deny believers the right to live according to their assumed code of physical purity would be contrary to Paul's respect for strong and weak positions—those who can live faithfully before God without purity codes cannot deny those who rely upon purity codes the right to do so, as much as the latter group cannot insist that the former group also assumes and lives according to the latter group's purity code (Countryman, *Dirt, Greed and Sex,* 520–4).

PAUL AND SEX: VIABLE PROPOSITION

In as far as he is explicit about the topic, sex features for Paul properly within marital life. He formulated circumspect but adamant instructions for marriage in 1 Corinthians 7, presenting sex as important and crucial for married couples.[19] Paul did so in a context where Roman imperial discourse privileged marriage as monogamous and for life. As Herennius Modestinus (mid-third century) put it, Roman marriage was "a life-long partnership, and a sharing of civil and religious rights."[20] With the household seen as basis for empire, the importance of household, the *domus,* in the formation of a Roman's identity,[21] and the household's foundational role as unit of the state,[22] implied a social significance beyond its legal inscriptions. The *lex Iulia de maritandis ordinibus* and the *lex Iulia de adulteriis* 18–17 BCE gave Augustus' so-called moral revolution a legal basis. The purpose of these two Roman laws, as well as the later revision of those in the form of *lex Papia Poppaea* (9CE) was to regulate family sexual moralities.[23] As facilitator of the household with its codes that served as model for the political order, marriage attested to the confluence of political and social significance.[24]

19. "[T]he abiding conceptual and analytical isolation of ancient history as an academic subject" (Scheidel, "Sex and Empire," 282) is the primary reason for the ready acceptance that people in Greek city–states and inhabitants of the Roman *res publica* contracted strictly monogamous marriages although surrounded by polygynous cultures.

20. Modestinus, *Digesta* 23.2.1

21. Saller, "Roman Kinship," 30–4.

22. "The empire itself was envisioned as a great household, and the emperor therefore the 'father of the fatherland', the benefactor or patron of all" (Green, "Crucifixion," 92; Hollingshead, *Household of Caesar,* 109). In the Hellenistic-Roman world city and households could not be separated from each other, and Aristotle already considered cities to be constituted by households and all households to be part of a city (Aristotle, *Politics* 1252a–1253b) (Guijarro, "Family in the Jesus Movement," 119). For example, in the Ptolemaic state, Egypt was the king's estate (*oikos*), with corresponding household terms used for officials (financial manager, *dioikētēs;* submanager, *hypodioikētēs;* steward of an individual district, *oikonomos*) (White, *Apostle of God,* 173–6).

23. While Augustus' aim was to increase the birthrate through encouraging marriage and stable family life, rather than to regulate public morals (Ferguson, *Backgrounds of Early Christianity,* 69), the legislation contributed towards the creation of an environment defined both by patriarchy and domesticity.

24. The laws of family were an important counter-current to laws of the city, although those were generally interpreted to be a subset of laws of the city (Meeks, *Moral World,* 19–39). A larger debate in Hellenistic society concerned the tension between universal justice (by nature) and no justice by nature, the latter which made it a matter all about power, the rule of the jungle or the survival of the fittest. The idealists of the time garnered support for Roman efforts to coordinate just this utopian venture, which implied equity and good order that saw those fit by nature, rule, and those suited by nature to be ruled, submit—in the polis as much as in the household. With Rome as

To briefly digress, the differences in the similar-sounding values and institutions found in the Bible include marriage which did not exclude loving relationships within extended, multi-generational families, but at the same time were predominantly regulated by honor and shame, and patronage and clientage as core values and underpinnings rather than modern notions of primarily care, nurturing, and security.[25] In the first-century culture, where the extinction of groups rather than human over-population was a primary societal threat, sexuality moreover was governed by concerns about fertility and procreation with male domination of women in a hierarchical, patriarchal world taken as an unquestioned given.[26] In the biblical world, gender and sex seem more strongly connected,[27] and feminist biblical scholars have long pointed out that "classic texts and traditions are also a systematically distorted expression of communication under unacknowledged conditions of repression and violence."[28] The dominant male perspective of the texts,

---

the universal polis, the efficiency of her rule underwrote the worthiness and validity of her rule; destined by divine commission to bring nations closer to "one law, eternal and immutable" (Panaetius). Later on, Rome's stature would grow, and the quality of justice obtainable seen as superior to that of autonomous city, since appeal to higher court, even emperor, possible (see, for example, Paul in Acts 25:10–12).

25. The Bible is witness to at least three different kinds of marriage, none of which corresponds to the modern (Western) notion of marriage based on mutual love (Van Aarde in Dreyer, "Homoseksualiteit," 182–3). Van Henten and others have pointed to an even broader spectrum and further differentiated forms of marriage in the Bible (for example, Van Henten, Jan Willem. "The Family Is Not All That Matters. A Response to Esler." In *Families and Family Relations as Represented in Early Judaisms and Early Christianities: Texts and Fictions*, edited by Athalya Brenner and Jan Willem Van Henten, 185–91. Star 2. Deo: Leiden, 2000).

26. To the extent that masculine power was symbolized in the penis, and attested by public statutes (Crossan and Reed, *In Search of Paul*, 258–66). Androcentrism and patriarchy would have found the passive participants in homoerotic acts even more of a threat to the "fibre of society" than women who are considered to be out of place. See Martti Nissinen on the perceived threat of homoeroticism and homophobia as having "more to do with issues of masculinity and femininity than anatomy and psychology" (Nissinen, *Homoeroticism*, 132).

27. Garroway, *Growing Up in Ancient Israel*, 86–9. As an early example of the way in which gender determines and steers sex, is the influence of God's ascribed male gender on his sex: "this becomes all too evident when divinity is used to underwrite certain human orderings, and most notably those that exclude women from certain kinds of power. It is then that we discover that women are not fully human because not really divine—in the way that men are. We discover that gender neutrality is a ruse of male partiality" (Loughlin, "Biblical Bodies," 13). And also, in the words of Teresa Hornsby, "Paul's imaging of God as masculine not only creates gendered ambiguity, particularly for men. . . but engenders the concept of 'sinner' as already more feminine" (Hornsby, "Gendered Sinner," 157).

28. Schüssler Fiorenza, *Rhetoric and Ethic*, 196. Even when one assumes a more neutral understanding of the socio–historical context of a text, it is still "produced

and that "the available sources do not tell the whole truth of the life and reality of ancient people"[29] have to be considered seriously; but, at the same time, "[t]he biblical legacy cannot be reduced to the harsh and repressive strictures of patriarchal custom."[30] Some of these tensions can be observed also in Paul's writings.

For Paul, the link between sex and marriage was not direct, but via property rights, since property rights determined sexuality at the time.[31] Paul's position was that believers through the indwelling of the spirit, became the property of God. Since property rights are in danger of being transferred to another person who is not the owner, intercourse with prostitutes are prohibited (1 Cor 6:12–20). So too, husband and wife have proprietary rights over each other's body, so that reciprocal rights sanction marital sexual relations. Even Paul's renunciation of marriage is explained in terms of property rights, of belonging to God (1 Cor 7:34).[32] This gives perspective to Lisa Sowle Cahill's conclusion "that the biblical literature points toward heterosexual, monogamous, lifelong, and procreative marriage as the normative or ideal institutionalization of sexual activity,"[33] while cautioning against the simplistic equation of sentiments and systems of the past and present.[34] In fact, the adaptation of this morality in different historical contingencies is already evident in some of the NT's so-called divorce texts.

Paul's views in many respects differed vastly from modern notions of sexuality as a non-vital, or an at least equally recreational aspect of human identity, with accompanying notions about the equality of the sexes and genders. Modern views of the natural are established in terms of biology, behavioral sciences and individualist intent, while ancient views focused on societal standards and convention.[35] First century arranged marriages comprising mutual responsibilities and obligations were decidedly

---

rhetorically through selection, classification, and valuation" (Schüssler Fiorenza, *Rhetoric and Ethic*, 196).

29. Nissinen, *Homoeroticism*, 113.

30. Biale, "Sexual Subversions," 374.

31. See also Martin, "Paul without Passion," 201–15 on sexual passion, or the lack thereof, and marriage. Then also, "[t]he notion that the woman is constructed as living gift or donation of herself to the fulfilment of all others' desires and needs—i.e., to make everyone else happy—is an originary myth that is still in need of deconstruction" (Davies, *Black Women, Writing and Identity*, 28).

32. Berger, *Identity and Experience*, 234–5.

33. Cahill, *Sex, Gender, and Christian Ethics*, 330.

34. Importantly, Cahill adds, "I would not say that the biblical texts represent preoccupation with, or indeed much interest in, the justification or exclusion of other sexual expressions" (Cahill, *Sex, Gender, and Christian Ethics*, 330).

35. Nissinen, *Homoeroticism*, 133.

male-focused and -dominated in many respects and are foreign to a world where sex is related to loving relationships, and romantic feelings and sentiment. Moreover, just how viable the proposition of marital sex in the end may have been for Paul, depends on the consideration of his preferred alternative.

PAUL AND SEX: IMPOSSIBLE CONUNDRUM

Paul is often seen as the primary proponent in the Bible to have promoted a negative view of human sexuality, (co-)responsible for postulating the incompatibility between sexual pleasure and sanctity. For Paul, sexuality and service to God were contrasting options, or at the very least, were marked by tension: prayer and sexual relations are mutually exclusive (1 Cor 7:5), and concern for God and the sexual partner come into conflict with one another.[36] He is believed to have advocated eschatological hope in which sexuality and sexual pleasure were explicitly excluded (see Mark 12:25), promoted abstinence from sexual pleasure in anticipation of the future fulfilment (1 Corinthians 7),[37] and dismissed passionate desire for pleasure as contrary to holiness (1 Thess 4:5). So for many, Paul is the instigator of a Christian tradition that for the largest part have posited the eventual incompatibility between sexual pleasure and spirituality or sanctity, where living a sex life or living a divine life become opposites.

Indeed, for Paul sex belonged in marriage (1 Cor 7:5), but his preference for singleness and celibacy is clear, as he emphasized four times in a chapter on marriage: καλὸν ἀνθρώπῳ γυναικὸς μὴ ἅπτεσθαι (1 Cor 7:1; see also 7:7, 32–34). The concern for celibacy invoked a similar concern operative in promiscuity, namely the equation of sexuality with lust or uncontrollable passion.[38] For Paul, sexuality was driven by impulse and needed to be controlled, but the gold standard remained celibacy or not getting married as a way of remaining holy and having unity of commitment. Succumbing to one's sexual impulses, even in marriage, was weakness.[39] Sexuality for Paul, then, was embodied and Paul's rhetoric in scripting the body through celibacy entailed elements both of pushing against Empire and succumbing to

---

36. Berger, *Identity and Experience*, 235.

37. Paul was convinced that "this world as we see it is passing away" (1 Cor 7:31), which can be assumed to have influenced his thoughts on sexuality as well; whether this was the primary point of departure for his views, is a matter of debate.

38. Paul's concern with "lack of self–control" in 1 Cor 7:5, is akin to his encouragement that those "aflame" with passion (1 Cor 7:9) should rather marry.

39. Berger, *Identity and Experience*, 237.

the pull of Empire,[40] but becomes also part of the larger process where bibles script bodies as much as bodies script bibles. As Elizabeth Grosz (emphasis in original) reminds us, the body from a constructivist perspective "must be regarded as a site of social, political, cultural, and geographical inscriptions, production, or constitution. The body is not opposed to culture, a resistant throwback to a natural past; it is itself a cultural, *the* cultural, product."[41] Far from only Paul, in ancient times, a wide range of authors and texts, especially those with a medical inclination, regularly stressed abstinence and bodily discipline in matters of sex, diet, and exercise as laudable ideals.[42] In the first-century society, generally, sex not only implied marriage; marriage required surrender to many and weighty societal expectations and demands.[43] Ergo, privileging the modern view—notwithstanding some exceptions—of sexual renunciation as over the top self-denial or unhealthy rejection of natural impulses, means to be oblivious to the social implications such a position entailed in the first century.

A further contrast is often postulated between the renunciation of sexuality and the traditional position ascribed to Second Temple Judaism as "carnal Israel" where spirituality by definition did not include abstinence from physical life.[44] Celibacy was not considered an option for Jews, but created suspicion "because it was seen as an offense to the divine obligation to procreate (Gen 1:28)."[45] Again matters were not so simple, however, since "singleness and celibacy were part of the role of ascetics, prophets, and vagrant preachers, like John the Baptist, and did not stir up any particular

40. Such ambivalence pertaining to asceticism was nothing out of the ordinary, as Diane Bazell also pointed out: "ascetic practices may function as vehicles for social resistance either by serving to reject them altogether, or by enabling them to be reformed and transformed" (Bazell, "The Politics of Piety," 496).

41. Grosz, *Volatile Bodies,* 23.

42. For example, Punt, Jeremy. "Engaging Empire with the Body: Rethinking Pauline Celibacy." *Journal of Early Christian History* 6(3) (2016) 43–66.

43. Price, "Distinctiveness of Early Christian Sexual Ethics," 24. The social–symbolic ordering of bodies and related gender hierarchies return in Paul's treatment of rebellion against God with reference to same–sex activities (Rom 1:26–27) and his instructions regarding ecclesial organization and authority (1 Cor 11:1–16). The naturalness of vaginal intercourse between men and women mirrored and symbolically enacted what was considered the natural, social hierarchy of men and women in the first century (see, for example, Isherwood and Stuart, *Introducing Body Theology,* 64; Vorster, "(E) mpersonating the Bodies," 118–22). Paul's body theology veers between the radical and conservative, but body stays central in his thought (Isherwood and Stuart, *Introducing Body Theology,* 63–4; see Punt, "Morality and Body Theology," 359–88).

44. Irshai, "Judaism," 413.

45. Nissinen, *Homoeroticism,* 119; see Roetzl, "Sex and the Single God," 238.

speculation."[46] As Daniel Boyarin points out, by the time of the NT, extremely negative views of sexuality were rampant in Judaism, notwithstanding the commandment to propagate.[47] Pauline sentiments, which did not appear to promote an ethic of chastity primarily for the sake of the cult,[48] would not necessarily have been upsetting within first–century Judaism's spectrum of beliefs regarding sexuality.

Paul's sentiments regarding sexuality were in the end not idiosyncratic or vastly different from others of his day. His instructions on sexuality like those of Catullus reflected no personal aspect, anticipated no emotional ties between partners, even if unlike Aristotle he did not ascribe a friendship bond between married partners. While sexuality has become part of personal biographies today, such experiences were not considered important in the development of a love relationship in antiquity. Devoid of sentimentalizing, Paul's presentation of a love relationship between people shows no awareness of an erotic fascination. Instead, given the close relationship between personhood and feelings of shame, Paul addressed in a matter-of-fact way issues like incestuous relationships (1 Cor 5:1–13) and becoming one flesh with a prostitute (1 Cor 6:12–20), since sexuality was a matter of factual or objective concerns.[49] In a referential framework where the Law and faithfulness were aligned, faith was closer to faithfulness than creedal affirmation. Proper sexual behavior was an important way to protect holiness,

46. Nissinen, *Homoeroticism*, 119–20; see Diamond, "'And Jacob Remained Alone,'" 41–64. "[T]he argument that earliest Christianity's derivation from Judaism precluded any originary ascetic impulses has come under increasing scrutiny. With the discovery of the Dead Sea Scrolls and subsequent excavations at Qumran, scholars were forced to register the ascetic way of life that marked this form of Judaism. Despite the presence of a few female skeletons in the cemetery at Qumran, the Qumran community appears to have been composed of male celibates" (Clark, *Reading Renunciation*, 21; see Diamond, "'And Jacob Remained Alone,'" 41–64; however, Roetzl, "Sex and the Single God," 240 calls celibacy at Qumran "strategic and provisional"). See Mary Rose D'Angelo on Philo: "Defining Jewish identity in relation to Roman identity extended to articulating Jewish cultural standards in terms that made them comparable to Roman norms". . ."the virtues shared by the emperors and the Jews in Philo's paradigm [were] 'religion' (εὐσέβεια) and 'self-restraint' (ἐκκράτεια)" (D'Angelo, "Gender and Geopolitics," 65); also Halvor Moxnes for Philo and Josephus describing celibacy positively vs the rabbis who rejected it (Moxnes, *Putting Jesus in His Place*, 86). Roetzl sees Philo's ambivalence as that of a statesman providing offspring while being an ascetic philosopher (Roetzl, "Sex and the Single God," 239).

47. Boyarin, "Body Politic," 460.

48. This practice was not uncommon in the ancient world, for example the Vestal Virgins in Rome; see Braun, "Celibacy in the Greco-Roman World," 24–7.

49. Berger, *Identity and Experience*, 232–4. "Paul's interests are directed not toward the irretrievable preciousness of the moment, but toward the whence and the whither, toward what is of lasting value, not toward the ephemerality of the contingent. And God is the only eternal value" (Berger, *Identity and Experience*, 234).

which was to be achieved and which was always vulnerable. In the Pauline writings, sexual ethics then became a distinguishing aspect of early Jesus communities, framing holiness and dedication to God.[50]

Perhaps not impossible, sex was a conundrum for Paul, as he made an explicit and insistent case for staying celibate and single (1 Cor 7:6–8, 26, 37–38). His preference for celibacy, although he never made it a requirement for all,[51] sat uneasy with the Roman age of domesticity with its legal and other appeals for marital life and propagation.[52] The interpretation of Paul on sex is perhaps the bigger conundrum. The interpretation in Protestant circles in particular of 1 Cor 7's sentiments on celibacy and marriage "as an aberration spurred by particular and temporary historical circumstances,"[53] is unfortunate and irresponsible towards the texts' broader context.[54] Then again, single people were sexual minorities in the first century CE, frowned upon or perceived as different or queer, and often suffered socio-cultural as well as legal pressure, especially since Augustus' attempts to regulate marriage and

50. Koltun-Fromm, *Hermeneutics of Holiness,* 77–96. Various scholars hold other, contextual theological positions, such as that Paul's advocacy of celibacy above marriage (1 Cor 6:12–7:40) was based on his belief about the imminent end of the world, or even addressed as specific reply to an extremist group in Corinth—and that these appeals are not timeless, authoritative teaching that celibacy is somehow superior or always preferred to marriage (see Thatcher, *Liberating Sex,* 17–8).

51. "In spite of his clear preference for celibacy (7:7), Paul refused to offer celibacy as an absolute principle or default position that was required of all believers, that removed all ambivalence from sex, or that papered over the strong powers of eros" (Roetzl, "Sex and the Single God," 24).

52. Roetzl's remark about celibate Syrian Christians in the second and third centuries, "'This margin where they lived as social deviants they turned into a place of radical and revolutionary possibility," applies to Paul as well, as least to some extent (Roetzl, "Sex and the Single God," 246).

53. See Clark, *Reading Renunciation,* 20.

54. "'The early church's enthusiasm for celibacy. . . enabled the use of erotic language and imagery, its spiritualization being underwritten by the celibate's spiritualization of his or her own body through chastisement of its fleshly desires. And when celibacy lost its attraction, and marriage—especially in Protestant Christianity—became more desirable, the homoeroticism involved in men loving a "male" God was secreted away by an increased discernment and destruction of all sodomical bodies. This is why twenty-first century debates about (male) homosexuality and same-sex marriage are so unsettling for the Christian churches" (Loughlin, "Biblical Bodies," 126; see Boyarin, "Body Politic," 459–78). "For those without this gift [with reference to celibacy], Paul considered the satisfaction of desires, so long as it was within the boundaries of the property ethic, entirely appropriate. Any insistence on celibacy for homosexuals as such is, accordingly, contrary to New Testament witness" (Countryman, *Dirt, Greed and Sex,* 522). For a fresh angle on mandatory celibacy for priests, see Kasomo, "The Psychology Behind Celibacy," 88–93.

childbirth. And as for our texts, indications are that most biblical authors were single,[55] and this is where a queer reading may allow for other perspectives.

PAUL AND SEX: SIMPLY QUEER

Ascribing a queer sexuality to Paul is not situated in his apparent if reluctant condonation of sex as long as it is marital sex, or in his enthusiastic if tainted promotion of sexual renunciation amidst Roman domesticity. Pauline sex is queer, first, because the apostle follows biblical tradition. The consequence of inscribing God sexually, or at least ascribing sexuality to God, in the Hebrew Bible already, meant that texts portrayed God in a way that queered the men of Israel, and left them with a choice of having become like women or like men sleeping with men as with women (Lev 18:20). In the NT, divine queerness is related to Jesus Christ too, the offspring of a virgin (Luke 1:26–35) and an imprint of God (Phil 2:6; Heb 1:3). Subscribing to Jesus' parthenogenetic birth leaves him with two X-chromosomes.[56] Although first-century audiences undoubtedly would have understood it differently given the dominance of an androcentric physiology,[57] does Jesus' virgin birth imply—to use our categories—a sex reversal to a male phenotype, or a savior with an inter-sexual rather than male identity?[58]

Paul, however, was not merely regurgitating scriptural traditions or refurbishing Jewish notions for Gentile Jesus-followers. The move away from conventional dichotomized readings of Paul as either for or against sex, allows for applying queer inquiry's non-essentialist, post-conventional, binary-resisting, social constructionist views of gender and sexuality.[59] Us-

55. Hanks, *Subversive Gospel*, 148–9, 177, 182.

56. Extrapolating the notion of a dual-genderedness is important, also given the importance of invoking parthenogenetic birth, or at least, divine sonship, for many other important figures of the first century. See also Crossan, John Dominic, and Jonathan L. Reed. *In Search of Paul. How Jesus's Apostle Opposed Rome's Empire with God's Kingdom. A New Vision of Paul's Words and World.* New York: HarperSanFrancisco, 2004; and White, John L. *The Apostle of God. Paul and the Promise of Abraham.* Peabody: Hendrickson, 1999.

57. For example, Laqueur, *Making Sex*.

58. Other indications of queering gender are in the reference to Epimenides for example, a "gay shaman" from Crete (sixth century BCE) who is quoted twice, and favorably, in the New Testament (Acts 17:28; Titus 1:12–13). Clement of Alexandria ascribed the references, which is different from the original in not being in poetic metre or even the expected dialect, to Epimenides (poet from Crete, c. 600 BCE); however, as the plural (ποιητῶν, poets) in Acts 17:28 suggests, others Stoics may also be included in the reference, such as Aratus' *Phaenomena* 5; or even Cleanthes' *Hymn to Zeus*.

59. For example, Cheng, "Contributions from Queer Theory."

ing a queer lens of course adds positionality if not bias, as much as any other theoretical perspective. As with other hermeneutical approaches, a queer reading of Paul raises the question whether it is the texts' suitability for the method, rather than the other way around, that renders Paul's approach to human sexuality, queer. Paul's perspective on sexuality revolves around the notion of being at someone else's disposal. Analogous to his extension of justification language from the metaphysical to the interpersonal realm (Rom 13:7–8), Paul also transfers the notion that human beings are slaves of God (Rom 6:16–23), to interpersonal, sexual relations (1 Cor 7:4, 32–34). As Berger explains, the slavery motif has a number of consequences: the relationship with God moves toward the center; the highest of all relationships (with God) is built on the lowest rung of social relationships (slaves); the status-conscious Hellenistic world is challenged by a different standard of evaluation; and, the slavery motif overrides the possible use of a friendship, not to mention egalitarian, perception.[60] Such perceptions were poised to challenge the conventional, binary and essentialist notion of sexuality in the first century, and also in the twenty first century.

In Paul's letters, the followers of Jesus are queered in various instances and the list is long. "If only at a symbolic level, all Christian men are queer."[61] Women were included among Jesus' brothers (Rom 8:28–29), and in the later Pauline tradition, men became brides of Christ (Eph 5:29–32). Beyond binary gender constructions, the whole (female) church is "to grow in every way into him who is head" (Eph 4:15).[62] Cross-dressing metaphors receive new, positive meaning (Rom 13:14, see Col 3:9–10), father Abraham is redefined through motherhood (Gal 4:21–5:1), a transgendered Paul becomes a mother giving birth (Gal 4:19),[63] and male-female polarities

---

60. Berger, *Identity and Experience*, 235–37.

61. Loughlin, "Biblical Bodies," 24.

62. In the middle ages, female mysticism was one consequence of exclusion of women brought on by increased clericalism, which again was the result of increased ecclesial activity through the sacraments, relics, and others to deal with the body and suspicions against it. Female mysticism fed of deeply embodied, erotically charged encounters between women and Christ. Women in the middle ages "subverted the patriarchal association of fleshiness with femaleness by obtaining bodily knowledge of Christ in their own flesh" (Isherwood and Stuart, *Introducing Body Theology*, 69).

63. Maybe even more interesting is that Paul's self-claimed transgenderedness hardly evoked comments from biblical scholars. Studies by, for example, Beverly R. Gaventa ("Maternity of Paul," 189–201) emphasize the maternal metaphor and its significance rather than the transgression of gender lines; but see Martyn (*Galatians*, 424–31); and Osiek ("Galatians," 333–37). Paul often claimed fatherhood of the congregations, too (e.g., 1 Cor 4:14–15).

are listed as a dichotomy to be overcome (Gal 3:28).[64] In Galatians, where the supra-masculine sign of circumcision was the discourse marker and symbol par excellence, "his shamefully 'unmanly' boasting of weakness as something to be imitated (4:12–15), his rejection of male honor and image games (5:26;6:12), his nasty remark concerning castration, and his model of a 'household of faith' without patriarchal authority (6:10)," scripts Pauline sexuality as positively queer.[65] Situated in a tradition where holiness (not to be confused with salvation) can be achieved through obedience to the Torah, Paul saw faith as obedience or faithfulness required from people.[66] As noted above, for Paul appropriate sexual behavior served to keep holiness, ever so vulnerable, intact. It is understandable, then that in the Pauline writings, the deployment of sexual ethics was used to underscore the distinctive nature of early Jesus communities, particularly for how Paul framed holiness and dedication to God.

CONCLUSION: PAUL'S (QUEER) RELEVANCE FOR CONTEMPORARY REFLECTION

This was a preliminary and all too brief foray into exploring the contribution of the Pauline letters to modern day theological concerns about sex. The inherent duality of sexuality, at once a physical drive as well as an affective, spiritual experience, and the endless repercussions of this relationship have never ceased to fascinate humankind. Cahill's remark that "(t)wentieth-century Americans are no more or less obsessed with sex than our predecessors; it is only that our obsessions take different forms," reaches beyond the USA.[67] Dismissing the notion that the ethics of the NT, being irretrievable and in any case non-replicable, amounts to their irrelevancy, Countryman maintains that these, admittedly context-bound, ethical models indeed have value for today. "The spiritual function of the Bible's antiquity

---

64. While Paul shows no particular concern about women or slaves in this letter, Gal 3:28 nevertheless has implications for them. See D'Angelo, "Gender Refusers," 158.

65. Kahl, "No Longer Male," 49; see also Mollenkott, "Crossing Gender Borders," 192–93.

66. The further and related discussion on how *porneia* functions in the Pauline letters cannot be discussed here. On the history of the concept, see Gaca, *The Making of Fornication*; on its use and function in incipient and early Christianity, see Harper, "Porneia"; and more specific to Rom 7:7–25, see Gundry, *The Old Is Better*. For Paul, the significance of transgressing boundaries is perhaps best visible in his use of a vice list, as for example in 1 Cor 5:10–11 where various (stereotyped!) vices in various spheres of life are all connected by their lack of control.

67. Cahill, *Sex, Gender, and Christian Ethics*, 326.

is rather to relativize the present, to rule out in advance the notion that things can only be as they are."[68] Cahill goes one step further and suggests, "[t]he most important biblical contribution to a Christian ethics of sexual activity and of relationship between the sexes is the placement of morality within the life of the faith community."[69] Indeed, in communities of faith the lasting and paradigmatic value of Pauline exhortations (also) on sexuality is confirmed, acknowledging them as attempts to formulate responses that were faithful to the teaching and life of Jesus, reflecting antecedent Jewish traditions and reigning first-century worldviews, and appropriate to circumstances of the early Jesus-follower communities. Of all rescue attempts concerning Pauline morality, none is probably seen to be more challenging or to have such potentially disastrous consequences to his interlocutors, as the sexual ethics and morality of the Pauline letters. However, the relevance of Paul and sex for today's communities of faith is probably not in the first instance situated in the extrapolation of specific sexual morals.[70] Rather, in the same way that religion is a queer thing,[71] it is the queerness that remains the lasting significance of the Paul and sex–connection and calls for further hermeneutical and theological exploration.

BIBLIOGRAPHY

Bazell, Diane M. "The Politics of Piety: Response to the Three Preceding Papers." In *Asceticism*, edited by Vincent L. Wimbush and Richard Valantasis, 493–501. Oxford: Oxford University Press, 1998.

Berger, Klaus. *Identity and Experience in the New Testament*. Translated by Charles Muenchow. Minneapolis: Fortress, 2003.

68. Countryman, *Dirt, Greed and Sex,* 516. Beyond the importance of concrete acts of human sexuality, Pauline body theology reaffirms for our context the significance of attitude as well, the "pattern or habit over the isolated instance" and "the intersubjective and social over the abstract and individual." "Contemporary theologians are once again insisting that any attempt to evaluate the moral object of an action apart from motive and circumstances is necessarily incomplete and inadequate" (Kosnik et al., "Toward a Theology of Human Sexuality," 553).

69. Cahill, *Sex, Gender, and Christian Ethics,* 330. Cahill is in any case of the opinion that the biblical notions on morality need to be supplemented by three other reference points for Christian ethics; namely, the religious tradition of the Christian community, philosophical accounts of humanity, and empirical studies of human life (Cahill, *Sex, Gender, and Christian Ethics,* 328).

70. "So much Christian theology is conducted not in the present but in the past. This is particularly evident in Christian sexual discourse, which tends to revolve around trying to find a way of reconciling contemporary understandings of sexuality and gender with the tradition" (Stuart, "Sex in Heaven," 195–96).

71. With reference to Stuart et al., *Religion Is a Queer Thing*.

Biale, David. "Sexual Subversions in the Bible." In *Sexuality: A Reader*, edited by Karen Lebacqz and David Sinacore-Guinn, 373–88. Pilgrim Library of Ethics. Cleveland: Pilgrim, 1999.

Boyarin, Daniel. "Body Politic among the Brides of Christ: Paul and the Origins of Christian Sexual Renunciation." In *Asceticism*, edited by Vincent L. Wimbush and Richard Valantasis, 459–78. Oxford: Oxford University Press, 1998.

Braaten, Carl E. *Justification: The Article by Which the Church Stands or Falls.* Minneapolis: Fortress, 1990.

Braun, Willi. "Celibacy in the Greco–Roman World." In *Celibacy and Religious Traditions*, edited by Carl Olson, 21–40. Oxford: Oxford University Press, 2008.

Brooten, Bernadette J. *Love between Women: Early Christian Responses to Female Homoeroticism.* Chicago: University of Chicago Press, 1996.

Cahill, Lisa Sowle. *Sex, Gender, and Christian Ethics.* Cambridge: Cambridge University Press, 1996.

Cheng, Patrick S. "Contributions from Queer Theory." In *The Oxford Handbook of Theology, Sexuality, and Gender*, edited by Adrian Thatcher, 153–72. Oxford: Oxford University Press, 2014.

Clark, Elizabeth A. *Reading Renunciation: Asceticism and Scripture in Early Christianity.* Princeton: Princeton University Press, 1999.

Countryman, L. William. *Dirt, Greed, and Sex: Sexual Ethics in the New Testament and Their Implications for Today.* Philadelphia: Fortress, 1988.

Crossan, John Dominic, and Jonathan L. Reed. *In Search of Paul: How Jesus's Apostle Opposed Rome's Empire with God's Kingdom: A New Vision of Paul's Words and World.* New York: HarperSanFrancisco, 2004.

D'Angelo, Mary Rose. "Gender and Geopolitics in the Work of Philo of Alexandria: Jewish Piety and Imperial Family Values." In *Mapping Gender in Ancient Religious Discourses*, edited by Todd Penner and Caroline Vander Stichele, 63–88. Biblical Interpretation Series. Leiden: Brill, 2007.

———. "Gender Refusers in the Early Christain Mission: Gal 3:28 as an Interpretation of Gen 1:27b." In *Reading in Christian Communities: Essays on Interpretation in the Early Church*, edited by Charles A. Bobertz and David Brakke, 14:149–73. Notre Dame: University of Notre Dame Press, 2002.

Davies, Carole Boyce. *Black Women, Writing and Identity: Migrations of the Subject.* London: Routledge, 1994.

Diamond, Eliezer. "'And Jacob Remained Alone': The Jewish Struggle with Celibacy." In *Celibacy and Religious Traditions*, edited by Carl Olson, 41–64. Oxford: Oxford University Press, 2008.

Dreyer, Yolanda. "Homoseksualiteit: Die Kerk, Die Tradisie En Die Bybel—Homofobie En Sarkofobie En Die Evangelie." *Hervormde Teologiese Studies* 60.1–2 (2004) 175–205.

Dunning, Benjamin H. *Specters of Paul: Sexual Difference in Early Christian Thought.* Philadelphia: University of Pennsylvania Press, 2011.

Ellison, Marvin M. *Erotic Justice: A Liberating Ethic of Sexuality.* Louisville: Westminster John Knox, 1996.

Ferguson, Everett. *Backgrounds of Early Christianity.* 2nd ed. Grand Rapids: Eerdmans, 1993.

Gaca, Kathy L. *The Making of Fornication: Eros, Ethics, and Political Reform in Greek Philosophy and Early Christianity.* Hellenistic Culture and Society 40. Berkeley: University of California Press, 2003.

Garroway, Kristene Henriksen. *Growing Up in Ancient Israel: Children in Material Culture and Biblical Texts.* ABS 23. Atlanta: SBL, 2018.

Gaventa, Beverly R. "The Maternity of Paul: An Exegetical Study of Galatians 4:19." In *The Conversation Continues: Studies in John and Paul, in Honor of J Louis Martyn,* edited by Robert T. Fortna and Beverly R. Gaventa, 189–201. Nashville: Abingdon, 1990.

"Gender and Human Rights." *World Health Organization.* https://www.who.int/reproductivehealth/topics/gender_rights/sexual_health/en/.

Glancy, Jennifer A. *Slavery in Early Christianity.* Minneapolis: Fortress, 2006.

Green, Joel B. "Crucifixion." In *The Cambridge Companion to Jesus,* edited by Markus Bockmuehl, 87–101. Cambridge Companions to Religion. Cambridge: Cambridge University Press, 2001.

Grosz, Elizabeth. *Volatile Bodies: Towards a Corporeal Feminism.* St. Leonards: Allen and Unwin, 1994.

Guijarro, Santiago. "The Family in the Jesus Movement." *Biblical Theology Bulletin* 34 (2004) 114–21.

Gundry, Robert H. *The Old Is Better: New Testament Essays in Support of Traditional Interpretations.* Tübingen: Mohr Siebeck, 2005.

Hanks, Tom. *The Subversive Gospel: A New Testament Commentary of Liberation.* Translated by John P. Doner. Cleveland: Pilgrim, 2000.

Harper, Kyle. "Porneia: The Making of a Christian Sexual Norm." *Journal of Biblical Literature* 131.2 (2012) 363–83.

Harris, Edward M. "'Yes' and 'No' in Women's Desire." In *Sex in Antiquity: Exploring Gender and Sexuality in the Ancient World,* edited by Mark Masterson, Nancy Sorkin Rabinowitz, and James Robson, 298–314. London: Routledge, 2014.

Hollingshead, James R. *The Household of Caesar and the Body of Christ: A Political Interpretation of the Letters from Paul.* Lanham: University Press of America, 1998.

Hornsby, Teresa J. "The Gendered Sinner in Romans 1–7." In *Gender, Tradition and Romans: Shared Ground, Uncertain Borders,* edited by Christina Grenholm and Daniel Patte, 143–66. Romans through History and Cultures Series. New York: T&T Clark, 2005.

Irshai, Ronit. "Judaism." In *The Oxford Handbook of Theology, Sexuality, and Gender,* edited by Adrian Thatcher, 413–31. Oxford: Oxford University Press, 2015.

Isherwood, Lisa, and Elizabeth Stuart. *Introducing Body Theology.* Cleveland: Pilgrim, 1998.

Kahl, Brigitte. "No Longer Male: Masculinity's Struggles behind Galatians 3.28?" *Journal for the Study of the New Testament* 79 (2000) 37–49.

Kasomo, Daniel. "The Psychology Behind Celibacy." *International Journal of Psychology and Behavioral Sciences* 2.4 (2012) 88–93.

King, Helen. *The One-Sex Body on Trial: The Classical and Early Modern Evidence.* The History of Medicine in Context. Farnham: Ashgate, 2013.

Koltun-Fromm, Naomi. *Hermeneutics of Holiness: Ancient Jewish and Christian Notions of Sexuality and Religious Community.* Oxford: Oxford University Press, 2010.

Kosnik, Anthony, et al. "Toward a Theology of Human Sexuality." In *Sexuality: A Reader*, edited by Karen Lebacqz and David Sinacore-Guinn, 544–62. Pilgrim Library of Ethics. Pilgrim: Cleveland, 1999.

Lambert, Michael, and Holger Szesnat. "Greek 'Homosexuality': Whither the Debate?" *Akroterion* 39.2 (1994) 46–63.

Laqueur, Thomas W. *Making Sex: Body and Gender from the Greeks to Freud*. Cambridge: Harvard University Press, 1990.

Loughlin, Gerard. "Biblical Bodies." *Theology and Sexuality* 12.1 (2005) 9–27.

———.*Queer Theology: Rethinking the Western Body*. Malden: Blackwell, 2007.

Malina, Bruce J. *The New Testament World: Insights from Cultural Anthropology*. Rev. ed. Louisville: Westminster John Knox, 1993.

Martin, Dale B. "Paul without Passion: On Paul's Rejection of Desire in Sex and Marriage." In *Constructing Early Christian Families: Family as Social Reality and Metaphor*, edited by Halvor Moxnes, 201–15. London: Routledge, 1997.

Martyn, J. Louis. *Galatians*. New York: Doubleday, 1997.

Meeks, Wayne A. *The Moral World of the First Christians*. Louisville: Westminster John Knox, 1986.

Mollenkott, Virginia Ramey. "Crossing Gender Borders: Towards a New Paradigm." In *Body and Soul. Rethinking Sexuality as Justice–Love*, edited by Marvin M. Ellison and Sylvia Thorson-Smith, 185–97. Cleveland: Pilgrim, 2003.

Moxnes, Halvor. *Putting Jesus in His Place. A Radical Vision of Household and Kingdom*. Louisville: Westminster John Knox, 2003.

Nissinen, Martti. *Homoeroticism in the Biblical World: A Historical Perspective*. Minneapolis: Fortress, 1998.

Osiek, Carolyn. "Galatians." In *The Women's Bible Commentary*, edited by Carol A. Newsom and Sharon H. Ringe, 333–37. Louisville: Westminster John Knox, 1992.

Price, Richard M. "The Distinctiveness of Early Christian Sexual Ethics." In *Christian Perspectives on Sexuality and Gender*, edited by Elizabeth Stuart and Adrian Thatcher, 14–32. Grand Rapids: Eerdmans, 1996.

Pseudo-Demosthenes. *Orations 59: Against Neaera*. Loeb Classical Library 351. Translated by A. T. Murray. Cambridge: Harvard University Press, 1939.

Punt, Jeremy. "Engaging Empire with the Body: Rethinking Pauline Celibacy." *Journal of Early Christian History* 6.3 (2016) 43–66.

———."Morality and Body Theology in Paul: Parameters for a Discussion." *Neotestamentica* 39.2 (2005) 359–88.

Roetzl, Calvin J. "Sex and the Single God: Celibacy as Social Deviancy in the Roman Period." In *Text and Artifact in the Religions of the Mediterranean Antiquity: Essays in Honour of Peter Richardson*, edited by Stephen G. Wilson and Michel Desjardins, 9:231–48. Studies in Christianity and Judaism. Waterloo: Wilfred Laurier University Press, 2000.

Saller, Richard P. "Roman Kinship: Structure and Sentiment." In *The Roman Family in Italy: Status, Sentiment, Space*, edited by Beryl Rawson and Paul Weaver, 7–34. Oxford: Humanities Research Centre, 1999.

Scheidel, Walter. "Sex and Empire. A Darwinian Perspective." In *The Dynamics of Ancient Empires: State Power from Assyria to Byzantium*, edited by Ian Morris and Walter Scheidel, 255–324. Oxford: Oxford University Press, 2009.

Schüssler Fiorenza, Elizabeth. *Rhetoric and Ethic: The Politics of Biblical Studies*. Minneapolis: Fortress, 1999.

Stuart, Elizabeth. "Sex in Heaven: The Queering of Theological Discourse on Sexuality." In *Sex These Days: Essays on Theology, Sexuality and Society*, edited by Jon Davies and Gerard Loughlin, 1:185–204. Studies in Theology and Sexuality. Sheffield: Sheffield Academic Press, 1997.

Stuart, Elizabeth, et al. *Religion Is a Queer Thing: A Guide to the Christian Faith for Lesbian, Gay, Bisexual and Transgendered People*. Cleveland: Pilgrim, 1997.

Thatcher, Adrian. *Liberating Sex: A Christian Sexual Theology*. London: SPCK, 1993.

Van Henten, Jan Willem. "The Family Is Not All That Matters: A Response to Esler." In *Families and Family Relations as Represented in Early Judaisms and Early Christianities: Texts and Fictions*, edited by Athalya Brenner and Jan Willem Van Henten, 185–91. Leiden: Deo, 2000.

Vander Stichele, Caroline. "Like Angels in Heaven: Corporeality, Resurrection, and Gender in Mark 12:18–27." In *Begin with the Body: Corporeality Religion and Gender*, edited by Jonneke Bekkenkamp and Maaike De Haardt, 215–32. Leuven: Peeters, 1998.

Vorster, Johannes N. "(E)mpersonating the Bodies of Early Christianity." *Neotestamentica* 34.1 (2000) 103–24.

White, John L. *The Apostle of God: Paul and the Promise of Abraham*. Peabody: Hendrickson, 1999.

10

How Far Does God's Violence Go?

John's Jezebel in Conversation with Rape Culture

Nina Müller van Velden

VIOLENT CONTEXTS, VIOLENT TEXTS

The prevalence of rape culture in societies across the globe has increasingly received attention over the past few years—including the South African society. According to the UN Women website,

> (R)ape culture is the social environment that allows sexual violence to be normalized and justified, fueled [*sic*] by the persistent gender inequalities and attitudes about gender and sexuality. Naming it is the first step to dismantling rape culture.[1]

A core component of rape culture is sexist, gender-biased and patriarchal language and discourse. The absurd notion that females are inferior objects to be sexually desired, conquered and even harassed if necessary, for the satisfaction of male pleasure, is embedded in language, slurs, comments and opinions which propagate and enforce such abusive ideas and,

---

1. See "16 Ways," para. 2.

ultimately, actions.[2] Moreover, there is often an intrinsic violent undertone to such discourses.[3]

Sexist and patriarchal language and discourse, prevalent in societies across the globe, have various sources. In a fairly traditional, conservative and religious society such as South Africa, where most persons identify as Christians and/or participates in the Christian faith tradition,[4] the influence of the Bible as a core faith document on issues of gender and sexuality should not be underestimated.[5] Such influence—even if religious—deserves to be interrogated, given the war on the bodies of girls, women, and gender non-conforming individuals in South Africa: a country which has the shameful reputation of having some of the highest statistics of gender-based violence, sexual violence, and rape in the world. This does beg the question: how is that that social contexts informed to a large extent by a religion—which should in principle contribute to moral formation and values such as human dignity, love for the neighbor, and care for the stranger (all of which can be biblically validated)—is marked by abuse and violence in its crudest form possible?

2. Within rape culture, heteronormativity serves as a bar of measure for all persons, irrespective of individual sexual identities. Consequently, the stigmatization, victimization, and abuse of persons identifying with the LGBTIQA+ or queer community (collective and non-derogatory terms for people who do not fit themselves into the category of heterosexuality or an heterosexual understanding of being male or female) form part of rape culture. In an extreme form, this is portrayed by what is known as "corrective rape"; a form of rape whereby a person not conforming to heterosexuality is raped in order to "correct" their "deviant" sexual desires, expression, and/or relations.

3. The interwoven relationship between violence, violent crime, and sexual violence in the South African society is complex and can be analyzed from a range of positions: historical, sociological, political, psychological, religious, etc. South African scholars Rachel Jewkes and Louise du Toit have made insightful contributions towards research on sexual violence, specifically then also rape, in the South African context, where these complexities are explored in more detail. See for example Jewkes, "Intimate Partner Violence," 1423–29; Jewkes and Abrahams, "Epidemiology of Rape," 1231–44; and Du Toit, "Phenomology of Rape," 253–74.

4. The General Household Survey (GHS), 2015 concluded that 86 percent of South Africans are affiliated with the Christian religion. Statistics South Africa, "General Household Survey, 2015" 27–8. The 2016, 2017, and 2018 (latest) reports do not include the category of religious affiliation and observance.

5. The ongoing debate in, for example, the Dutch Reformed Church (DRC) (the largest Afrikaans reformed church in South Africa) on the full acceptance, participation and ordination of LGBTIQA+ persons, and more recently also permission for DRC clergy to conduct the solemnization of civil unions of same-sex couples, is a case in point. Central to the ongoing discussions and debates in various contexts (in and outside of the DRC), are the few biblical texts in the Old and New Testaments which refer to so-called "homosexuality" (the term preferred by most contemporary translations) and the manner in which to interpret them.

In such a context, the Bible as a core faith document finds itself in a particularly precarious position, precisely for the fact that its texts are by no means neutral in terms of gender and sexuality. Rather, it has originated, been written, compiled and canonized in patriarchal, heteronormative environments, favoring the position of a hierarchically constructed world in which male and all things male are favored.[6] Thus, a contemporary society already dominated by sexist, patriarchal, gender-violent language and behavior, is further influenced (and in some cases sustained, promoted and idealized) by a primary religious source document which mirrors such unjust attitudes and worldviews—at least, to a large extent.

As a New Testament biblical scholar, I have a keen interest in the role of interpretation of Christian writings to promote human dignity and inclusion in contemporary settings and societies, particularly with regard to gender and sexuality. Therefore, I constantly ask myself: how might one engage with biblical texts in a manner that can question or challenge contemporary injustices pertaining to gender and sexuality, rather than en*force* it (in all the senses of the word)—even when the latter might appear to be the only option? No single hermeneutical approach or lens has yet satisfactorily provided an all-round fail-proof solution, although feminist and gender critical lenses have brought me further along the road than where I was a few years ago.

Even difficult and unsettling conversations need to begin somewhere. A hermeneutical starting point for a dialogical engagement with biblical texts, gender, and sexuality, could be to acknowledge in some form or the other (and at least by way of introduction) the three worlds of a biblical text.[7] However, even when that may have been done in great detail, there are certain biblical texts that remain problematic, specifically when viewed from a feminist or gender critical perspective.[8] One such example is the Book of Revelation.

6. This is of particular concern for feminist biblical scholars, who have been the leading voices in highlighting this characteristic and broader reality of the Christian biblical and canonical tradition.

7. These three worlds are the world behind the text, the world within the text, and the world in front of the text. The world behind the text refers to the socio–historical and socio–cultural contexts within which a text originated; the world within the text has as focus the literary aspects and contexts of a text; and the world in front of the text refers to the contexts of readers and reader communities, past and present. Depending on the text and the specific focus of the interpretation at hand, one world might sometimes enjoy prevalence above another.

8. The feminist biblical scholar, Phyllis Trible, aptly refers to "texts of terror" when referring to four lesser-known narratives of women in the Hebrew Bible which are characterized by cruelty, violence, and the silence of God. She explores the role of the often-neglected narratives of Hagar, Tamar, an unnamed concubine, and the daughter of Jephthah in not only religious settings of the Jewish and Christian faiths, but also in biblical-scientific research (*Texts of Terror*, 1984).

The Book of Revelation is no stranger to criticism from biblical scholars, especially in feminist critical (and more recently, gender critical) circles.[9] Female gendered discourse, imagery and metaphors are hardly employed positively.[10] At best, female characters appear to serve more often than not a male agenda, making appearances at strategic moments and then disappearing again, once the task has been completed.[11] What is interesting, is that many feminist and gender critical scholars choose to focus on the female characters and characterization of the Book of Revelation. What is subsequently often found lacking, is a focus on the manner in which the character of Godself is part of this gendered, violent agenda; that is, the characterization of God as the one who initiates and actively participates in a male-dominant victory—and then doing so in explicitly violent terms— over the all too familiar characterization of the female evil.[12]

9. Noteworthy scholars include Elizabeth Schüssler Fiorenza, Tina Pippin, Paul Duff, David Barr and Stephen Moore. The essays contained in the edited volume of Amy-Jill Levine and Maria M. Robbins, *A Feminist Companion to the Apocalypse of John,* 2009 provide an insightful overview of recent feminist and gender critical engagements with the Book of Revelation.

10. The ultimate sinful and evil enemy character in the Book of Revelation is that of the promiscuous female, namely the whore Babylon, described in great detail in Rev 17:1–6. She resembles promiscuity, lust and fornication in all possible ways. The kings of the earth have given themselves over to her, the inhabitants of the earth have become drunk on the wine of her indecencies (17:2); she sits on a bright red animal with blasphemous names and seven heads and ten horns (17:3); she wears purple and bright red clothing and adorns herself with gold, gemstones and pearls (17:4); in her hand she holds a gold cup filled with promiscuity, the impurity of her indecency (17:4); on her forehead she has written the name "Great Babylon," meaning the mother of the indecent and promiscuous people of the earth (17:5); she is drunk on the blood of the faithful, of those who have witnessed to Jesus (17:6). The promise of her destruction is described almost with a sense of glee (Rev 17:15–18), followed by the cruel and vicious realization thereof in Rev 18:1–8.

11. In Rev 12:1–17 the vision of the woman clothed in the sun and the dragon is described. At the point of the woman delivering the male–child, destined to rule over all the nations, a ferocious and bloodthirsty dragon stands before the woman. As soon as she gives birth to the child, he plans to devour it. Once the male–child does see the light, he is snatched away to God and his throne. The woman, who has just given birth to the future ruler of all nations, flees to a place in the desert prepared by God. There she will have to remain for 1260 days.

12. Ironically enough, when viewed from a feminist and gender critical perspective, the Christian Bible seems to support this type of gendered narrative even on a meta-level, when considering both the literary "start" and "finish" as a whole. The creation narratives of Genesis give way to a portrayal of female Eve as an evil seducer to whom the fall of humankind can be ascribed (see Gen 3, especially 3:13)—an interpretation further strengthened in the memories of early Jesus communities when Eve is mentioned by name in a Pauline letter (2 Cor 11:3) and in a pastoral letter (1 Tim 2:13). In the Book of Revelation, the realization of the promised new creation is possible once

For the purpose of this discussion, I focus on a specific pericope in the Book of Revelation where such characterization of Godself is seemingly present, namely Rev 2:18–29. I make a deliberate choice for an exploration of the world *within* the text, with a specific focus on the violent and sexual narrative language used (albeit metaphorically) to describe both the manner in which the female character Jezebel has apparently conducted herself and exerted influence, and the resultant punishment by the character Son of God (2:20–23). I offer an attempt at a close (yet by no means exhaustive) reading of the pericope in dialogue with various commentators. In an attempt to make sense of this type of (sexually) violent narrative, I will subsequently provide some comments on the literary dimension of the Book of Revelation.[13]

This exploration is done specifically in light of rape culture as the world *in front of* the text, as well as my own location as a female, gender critical biblical scholar, and Christian believer.[14] Thus the essay will conclude where it started: what to make of the explicit language and imagery of a biblical text, such as this specific one, which appears to allow for and validate (sexually) violent behavior by Godself, when read within a contemporary context which is marked by unacceptably high levels of sexual abuse and violence whilst also being deeply influenced by the Bible as an authoritative religious source document.

CLOSE READING OF REVELATION 2:18–29 (20–23): ENCOUNTERING A (SEXUALLY) VIOLENT DEITY?

Rev 2:18–29 contains the fourth of seven letters to the churches of Asia, namely to the church (ἐκκλησία) in Thyatira. According to Rev 1:1, these letters have been written by the servant John in obedience to the command

---

Babylon, yet again an evil female seducer, is finally destroyed. What place does this offer women, if at all, in the New Jerusalem?

13. In broad lines I approach the pericope from a narrative critical perspective, dealing with the text "as is" and recognizing the manner in which an implied author (John) has created characters and characterization to serve a specific plot. This essay, thus, does not suggest in any way that God is literally and/or inherently a violent (or even sexually violent) deity, who acts in (sexually) violent ways towards humankind. Rather, the focus is on the manner in which Godself is characterized (as Son of God) in this narrative in opposition to the character Jezebel, and the effect such type of characterization might evoke in contemporary contexts.

14. The world behind the text is not a primary concern in this essay, although that is not to say that it is irrelevant. The world in front of the text serves as a conversational springboard "into" and "out of" the text itself, with a primary focus on the sexually violent South African landscape.

of the voice he heard behind him (Rev 1:10-11, 1:19), spoken by One like the Son of Man (Rev 1:13).

In general, though with slight variations, the messages to the churches follow a rather typical pattern, namely: an address to the angel of the church, followed by a description of Christ; words of praise and/or admonition and condemnation; an exhortation; a call to hear; and a promise to the one who will conquer.[15] This typical pattern is quite easily distinguishable in the fourth letter.

For the sake of the theme of this discussion, the focus of the close reading will be on Rev 2:20-23, with brief comments on the content of verses 18-19 and 24-29.

For the first and only time in the Book of Revelation, the title "Son of God" (ὁ υἱὸς τοῦ θεοῦ) is used in Rev 2:18.[16] The description of his eyes and feet (ὁ ἔχων τοὺς ὀφθαλμοὺς αὐτοῦ ὡς φλόγα πυρός, καὶ οἱ πόδες αὐτοῦ ὅμοιοι χαλκολιβάνῳ) (2:18) reminds one of the vision in Rev 1:9-20.[17]

Initially, the church of Thyatira is praised for their works, namely their love, faithfulness, service and perseverance, and their recent behavior which is even better than before (2:19). However, immediately after follows the contrast, the troubling issue at hand, introduced by a "but" (ἀλλά) at the start of 2:20.

The criticism offered toward this ἐκκλησία is aimed at their toleration of Jezebel, a woman who calls herself a prophet and is teaching and beguiling the servants of the Son of God to practice fornication and to eat food sacrificed to idols (2:20).[18] The name Jezebel hints back at the name of the wife of Ahab, king of Israel, who was famous for influencing Ahab to worship other gods (1 Kings 16:31).[19] She was known as an opponent of the

---

15. Reddish, "Revelation," 100.

16. Van Hartingsveld, *Openbaring van Johannes*, 27; Groenewald, *Openbaring van Johannes*, 57.

17. Aune, *Revelation 1–5*, 202.

18. The symbol-laden Book of Revelation shows here too its true colors. The name "Jezebel" most likely does not refer to the name of an actual prophetess in the Thyatira church called Jezebel, but rather serves as symbol of one acting as a female prophet in the footsteps of the historical Jezebel (according to tradition, at least).

19. Aune, *Revelation 1–5*, 203; Koester, *Revelation*, 298. The story of Jezebel is narrated in 1 Kings 18–21 and 2 Kings 9, and her actions include the following: a campaign to kill the prophets of Yahweh (1 Kgs 18:4, 13); her support of 450 prophets of Baal and 400 prophets of Asherah (1 Kgs 18:19); an attempt to kill Elijah (1 Kgs 19:1–3); the framing of Naboth, who was consequently stoned to death (1 Kgs 21:1–16); and eventually the death of Jezebel during a revolt fomented by Elisha, when her opponents hurled her from an upper-story window, after which she was eaten by dogs on the street (2 Kgs 9:30–37). Even though Jezebel is accused of "harlotries and sorceries" (2 Kgs 9:22), nothing in the preceding narrative supports such charges. One can,

true prophet Elijah, who was a zealous critic of idolatrous compromise with the religion of Baal—exactly that which she had encouraged. Ahab's marriage to Jezebel (1 Kings 16:31; 21:25) resulted in apostasy from the service of the one true God, Yahweh, just as Balaam had led Israel astray.[20]

The Christian community at Thyatira are collectively responsible for tolerating "their" Jezebel in their midst and allowing her teachings which have led them to go astray: specifically, by indulging in sexual immorality and eating meat sacrificed to idols. Thus, she is linked to the Great Whore of Babylon, with whom the nations of the world have fornicated (14:8; 17:2; 18:3; 19:2).[21]

Some commentators are of the opinion that the reference to πορνεύω should be understood metaphorically rather than literally within a context of sexual slander levelled at opponents by ancient writers,[22] as well as the use of the word as metaphor for unfaithfulness to God.[23]

The Son of God makes it clear that this woman has had time to repent from her wrongdoings (καὶ ἔδωκα αὐτῇ χρόνον ἵνα μετανοήσῃ, καὶ οὐ θέλει μετανοῆσαι ἐκ τῆς πορνείας αὐτῆς) (2:21); the warning was given with judgment initially withheld, so that repentance might come.[24] Sadly, this was not

---

therefore, conclude that they are metaphors for abandoning the worship of Yahweh (Aune, *Revelation 1–5*, 203).

20. Keck, *New Interpreter's Bible*, 581.

21. Aune, *Revelation 1–5*, 204.

22. For example, Aune, *Revelation 1–5*, 204; Rowland, "Book of Revelation," 581; Koester, *Revelation*, 299. In the publication titled, *Unprotected Texts. The Bible's Surprising Contradictions about Sex and Desire*, Jennifer Wright Knust devotes an entire chapter (Chapter 4, "Sexual Politics") to the use of sexual slander in biblical texts as a means to distinguish between "us" and "them"; the *true* people of God, and the so-called opponents, be they apparent insiders or obvious outsider opponents. She contends that the sexual language and biblical imagery describing religious purity or impurity have far too often been misinterpreted as literal descriptions of behavior, resulting in a Christian ethic of sexuality which is not only biblically unsound, but unrealistic and even harmful at times. Knust, *Unprotected Texts*, 2011.

23. Koester, *Revelation*, 288–89 traces the metaphorical understanding of πορνεύω to the history of Israel, noting that their covenant relationship with God was like a marriage. Therefore, relationships with other gods were compared to prostitution and adultery, as is seen in Hosea 1:2; Isaiah 1:21; Jeremiah 3:1–14; and Ezekiel 16:15–22. Moreover, the comparison of Israel's worship of other gods to sexual infidelity was a poignant indicator of polytheism (Lev 20:5; 1 Chr 5:25). At times, idolatry and immorality were mentioned together, with the sense that one contributed to the other, but immorality is also a metaphor for worship of deities other than God (Exod 34:15–16; Deut 31:16; Judg 2:17). In the Book of Revelation, the critique includes both traditional Greco–Roman religions and the imperial cult.

24. Koester, *Revelation*, 289.

the case for Jezebel or those who continued to be deceived by her. Therefore, judgment will come.

And judgment does come, threefold, in no uncertain terms: the Son of God will *throw* Jezebel on *a bed*; He will afflict those who fornicate with her with *great tribulation*, if they do not repent; and He will *kill "her children"* with the plague (own emphasis) (ἰδοὺ βάλλω αὐτὴν εἰς κλίνην, καὶ τοὺς μοιχεύοντας μετ᾽ αὐτῆς εἰς θλῖψιν μεγάλην, ἐὰν μὴ μετανοήσωσιν ἐκ τῶν ἔργων αὐτῆς· καὶ τὰ τέκνα αὐτῆς ἀποκτενῶ ἐν θανάτῳ·) (2:22–23a).

The word κλίνη ("bed" or "couch") plays on several aspects of meaning, namely a bed used for resting, for guild–banqueting, or for sickness.[25] Koester unpacks the various aspects of meaning as follows: 1) Jezebel's idolatrous actions are compared to immorality and adultery, which were actions committed in bed; 2) eating meals held in honor of a deity often took place in a reclined position on a couch, also called a κλίνη, linking the eating of food offered in sacrifice to other gods with religious (metaphorically sexual) infidelity; 3) as an idiomatic expression, βάλλω εἰς κλίνην could mean to cause someone to contract a severe illness, creating symmetry in divine judgment: Jezebel teaches it is acceptable to "go to bed" with other deities in the sense of religious adultery, whereby judgment on her will be to be put to bed with illness; 4) people might die in bed and ancient funerary monuments often pictured dead persons reclining on a κλίνη as a person would do at a banquet.[26]

> Working with all four meanings, Revelation likens festive dining on a couch to sexual infidelity in bed, while intimating that it is a form of religious infidelity, which will lead to being put to bed through sickness and death.[27]

Or, as Johnson ominously puts it:

> On a bed she sinned, and on a bed she will suffer. . .[28]

Worth noting, though, is that some commentators prefer to only mention the meaning of κλίνη related to the sickbed.[29] This is particularly interesting given the verb detailing the manner in which Jezebel will find herself on the bed, namely by means of the verb βάλλω, that is by (literally) being "thrown." According to the narrator, God says that He will *throw* her on a

25. Johnson, *Writings*, 1146.

26. Koester, *Revelation*, 299.

27. Koester, *Revelation*, 299

28. Johnson, *Writings*, 1146.

29. Examples include Aune, *Revelation 1–5*, 205; Van Hartingsveld, *Openbaring van Johannes*, 28; Reddish, "Revelation," 102; and Groenewald, *Openbaring van Johannes*, 59.

bed (own emphasis), in itself quite a strong action which serves to indicate power and control by the protagonist. This prophetess will not merely be "put" to bed or "nudged" towards a bed; no, she will find herself in a helpless position of disempowerment when the judgment takes place.[30]

The same verb extends to the action of judgment against those who have committed "adultery" with her (καὶ τοὺς μοιχεύοντας μετ' αὐτῆς). Adultery is used here as a metaphor for violating a covenant relationship with God; therefore, as Jezebel faces severe suffering (necessarily "sickness"?), her followers are warned of "affliction." These two judgments are parallel to one another.[31] Final punishment of τὰ τέκνα αὐτῆς ("her children") in the form of ἀποκτενῶ ἐν θανάτῳ (often simply translated as "death," but possibly also referring to "plague" or "sickness") will take place, should her followers not respond to the affliction with repentance. Using the description "children," likens her disciples or followers to the children of an adulteress, in contrast to the faithful ones who are the children of God.[32] Thus, in no uncertain terms, drastic action will be taken against Jezebel and her followers who do not repent, which will cause much pain and ultimately death.

This judgment will be the evidence that God is omniscient (καὶ γνώσονται πᾶσαι αἱ ἐκκλησίαι ὅτι ἐγώ εἰμι ὁ ἐραυνῶν νεφροὺς καὶ καρδίας) (2:23), the One who examines minds (literally "kidneys") and hearts, and all will be judged according to their works (καὶ δώσω ὑμῖν ἑκάστῳ κατὰ τὰ ἔργα ὑμῶν). Therein lies the promise of fair judgment: good works of the righteous will not go unnoticed but will evoke praise and reward, and evil works of opponents will be punished.[33]

The violent descriptions of the condemnation and imminent judgment(s) in these verses are followed by much more palatable calls for perseverance, obedience and the promise of victory and reward (verses 24–29) to the church of Thyatira, and the letter ends as it started: on a fairly positive note. This optimistic start and finish places yet even more emphasis on the contrasting and threatening violent judgment against Jezebel and "her children."

30. Noteworthy is the manner in which various popular English Bible translations present the phrase ἰδοὺ βάλλω αὐτὴν εἰς κλίνην: "Behold, I will cast her into a bed" (King James Version); "Indeed I will cast her into a sickbed" (New King James Version); "Behold, I will throw her onto a sickbed" (English Standard Version); "So I will cast her on a bed of suffering" (New International Version); "Behold, I will throw her on a bed of sickness" (New American Standard Bible); "Take note: I will throw her on a bed [of anguish]" (Amplified Bible); "And so I will throw her on to a bed" (Good News Bible).

31. Koester, *Revelation,* 300.

32. Koester, *Revelation,* 300.

33. Koester, *Revelation,* 300.

MAKING (LITERARY) SENSE OF SUCH
A VIOLENT NARRATIVE

In terms of the theme of this essay, it is especially the one-and-a-half verses of Rev 2:22–23a that are troubling: the forceful throwing of a female presented as a prostitute on a bed (or couch) by a male, followed by some form of physical punishment and suffering;[34] the warning to her adulterers of great affliction that will come their way as a means to cease their sexual and idolatrous misconduct before final judgment; and the threat of infanticide aimed at the children of Jezebel, should they not stop their unfaithful behavior. Might one close your eyes and hear this narrative without knowledge of the context and source thereof, it sounds all too familiar; as if but yet another story of suffering of one of thousands of South African women (and her children) affected daily by gender-based and sexual violence.

Taking one step back and reminding oneself that this is, indeed, a biblical text in which an author was attempting to convey a particular message to a specific audience, the narrative does not necessarily become more acceptable, but perhaps a little more understandable. Or does it?

The literary genre of the Book of Revelation, namely apocalyptic literature, is hugely influential in terms of the type of language, imagery and characterization found in it. Although not purely apocalyptic in a technical literary sense, it can be considered an apocalyptic writing in a broader sense.[35] Of specific interest for the pericope under discussion are the characteristics of judgment, visions, symbolism and a dualistic worldview.

By offering a summary of the broader narrative of the Book of Revelation, Selvidge touches on some these characteristics:

> The contents of Revelation reveal a seer who claims to have had a vision from God. He describes a titillating blood-and-guts adventure story of combatants who are struggling for power over the earth. His God is on the winning side. His God uses

34. Marshall, "Gender and Empire," 22, 25–6.

35. Apocalyptic literature generally has the following characteristics: narrative form, pessimistic view of the future, emphasis on the end times, transcendence of this world, deterministic view, pseudonymity, dualism, symbolism, unveiling of visions, revelation of secrets, and an element of judgment (Du Rand, "Openbaring aan Johannes," 220–224). The Book of Revelation does not adhere to all the characteristics in this list, but the resemblance is sufficient enough, in spite of its unique presentation, to be considered apocalyptic literature by the majority of commentators. In a thematic sense the Book of Revelation identifies itself as an ἀποκάλυψις, namely as a revelation, in Rev 1:1. More specifically, it is the revelation of and about Jesus Christ. For a detailed overview of apocalyptic literature, see Collins, *Apocalyptic Imagination*, 1998; Rowland, *Open Heaven*, 1982; and Collins, *Early Christian Apocalypticism*, 1986.

whatever means is necessary to win. All forces who oppose his
God are accused and doomed to a hideous annihilation. No one
survives the violent power of the writer's God except those who
agree with his point of view. In the end, even the heavens and
the earth must be destroyed to make room for a new, pure universe under a theocratic rule (Rev 20).[36]

For an implied audience who find themselves in a situation of oppression, persecution and imminent danger, such a narrative of spectacular
and triumphant victory of Good over Evil—set within a familiar religious
framework of the monotheistic rule of God—offers hope and motivation
for perseverance, faithfulness and obedience to God until the promised day
of judgment arrives.[37] Considering the pericope of Rev 2:18–29 it makes
sense that an almighty and all-powerful God would warn, and ultimately
offer judgment on any person or group who attempts to derail from fidelity
to Him alone—in the most severe forms possible. This was not an objective
matter; rather, it was loaded with subjective feelings and emotions. Clinical
and sterile imagery would not suffice.

Collins suggests that the author of the Book of Revelation deliberately made use of specific narrative techniques to create an emotional effect amongst his audience—knowing full well in what (highly emotional)
situation/s they found themselves in. These are namely: presentation of the
Apocalypse as an authoritative, true and trustworthy revelation of heavenly
origin; reinterpretation of prophecy and of other texts in the Jewish Bible
read as prophecy; and use of traditional symbols in the composition of alle-
gorical narrative. By using these narrative techniques, the author attempted
to deal with the thoughts, attitudes and feelings of the audience—feelings of
powerlessness, lack of control, and fear.[38]

The author thus created and constructed the narrative of the Book of
Revelation in such a manner as to comfort the (initial) audience with familiar themes, imagery and content. For such an audience it made sense to hear

36. Selvidge, *Exploring the New Testament*, 352.

37. As stated earlier, the focus of this essay is not the world behind the text. There
is, however, no lack of research available on it. Through the years great effort has been
made by scholars to explore the socio-historical and socio-cultural contexts of the Book
of Revelation. In popular culture, the symbolism of the Book of Revelation continues to
provide ample inspiration for book series, video clips, and movies—typically with little or
no regard for these contexts. Subsequently, many contemporary lay readers of the Book of
Revelation are completely unaware that this writing was not, in the first instance, written
as a prophecy for "how the world will end." For introductory scholarly comments on the
historic dimension of this writing, see e.g., Johnson, *Writings*, 1999; Court and Court,
New Testament World, 1990; and Selvidge, *Exploring the New Testament*, 2003.

38. Collins, *Crisis and Catharsis*, 145–52.

that the victory and new life promised by the plot and symbols will be realized in dramatic fashion, but only on the other side of suffering and death.[39]

EMBRACING VIOLENT TEXTS—OR NOT?

The challenge for contemporary readers of this narrative is that precisely such a text which might have offered comfort and hope to the initial audience, has at the very least, the potential for the opposite effect in our day and age—especially then in a society marked by such high instances of sexual violence in all its forms.

Might I suggest that the way in which translators have, in many cases, opted for the translation of κλίνη to an idiomatic "sickbed" is one way of trying to numb the discomfort the gendered violence of the narrative might generate? Is it, in our day an age, perhaps easier to fathom a narrative in which God extends judgment in illness language, rather than in language which might evoke ideas of violence in sexual terms? Is it, maybe, too crude an image for contemporary readers to imagine God in the role of a (sexually) violent male, who purposefully throws a woman on a bed as punishment for her promiscuous and adulterous behavior, threatening to kill her children if they do not stop their relations with her? Is this a narrative which is perhaps too familiar in our own sexually violent context, and ultimately too unholy to relate even to God Almighty?

The question then is—especially for the South African context where the Bible holds a particular position of authority given the religious affiliation of the majority of its members—what should be done with this narration? One option would be to simply ignore it, or another to merely emphasize its ancient context and its literary features genre and leave it at that. However, inasmuch as such options could still be viable in academic settings, it will likely not sit well in many contemporary religious settings.

I want to suggest that this narration—in all its explicit violence, and its problematic (and unfortunately familiar) hierarchical gender characterization of powerful male versus deceitful and subsequently helpless female and children—could create a space for dialogue on the role of religion and the interpretation of religious texts, in societies marked by rape culture. As such, the text extends an invitation for critiquing, posing questions, putting lived experiences on the table, and collectively seeking wisdom. This could provide much needed life-seeking alternatives to the types of interpretative engagement often prevalent in religious communities, which simply shut down conversation or which guard against any critical engagement with biblical texts.

39. Collins, *Crisis and Catharsis*, 152.

Such an option is, of course, not necessarily the popular one. It is open-ended, does not have a "right answer" in mind at which to "arrive," and will likely put difficult questions and conversations on the table for those who are regarded as "qualified" to give religious guidance on the interpretation of biblical texts. Yet, this could be the gift of such an option: to at least start having discussions on rape culture, sexual violence, and the role of religion and biblical interpretation in the South African society—an alternative desperately needed given the discomfort, avoidance or downright ignorance thereof in many church settings in our country.

As such, this narrative may become a way for a deeply religious society such as South Africa to speak out, to say much louder, "No more!" No more of this type of conquering, no more of this type of violence, no more support of this type of portrayal of God who sides with and participates in patriarchy, sexism and abuse. "No more!" Exactly that which the larger narrative of the Book of Revelation promises to communities in dire circumstances of hopelessness.

BIBLIOGRAPHY

Aune, David E. *Revelation 1–5. Word Biblical Commentary Volume 52.* Dallas: Works Books, 1997.

Collins, Adela Y. *Crisis and Catharsis: The Power of the Apocalypse.* Philadelphia: Westminster, 1984.

Collins, Adela Y. ed. *Early Christian Apocalypticism: Genre and Social Setting. Semeia* 36. 1986.

Collins, John J. *The Apocalyptic Imagination. An Introduction to Jewish Apocalyptic Literature.* 2nd edition. William B. Eerdmans: Grand Rapids, 1998.

Court, John M. and Court, Kathleen M. *The New Testament World.* Cambridge: Cambridge University, 1990.

Du Rand, Jan A. "Die Openbaring aan Johannes: Inleiding en Teologie,." In *Handleiding by die Nuwe Testament VI. Die Johannesevangelie; Hebreërs tot Openbaring; Inleiding en Teologie,* edited by A.B. du Toit, 219–314. Pretoria: NG Kerkboekhandel, 1988.

Du Toit, Louise. "A Phenomenology of Rape: Forging a New Vocabulary for Action." In *(UN)Thinking Feminist Debates in Contemporary South Africa,* edited by Amanda Gouws, 253–274. Burlington: Ashgate, 2005.

Groenewald, E.P. *Die Openbaring van Johannes.* Kaapstad: NG Kerk–Uitgewers, 1986.

Jewkes, Rachel. "Intimate Partner Violence: Cause and Prevention." *The Lancet* 359 (2002) 1423–29.

Jewkes, Rachel and Abrahams, Naeema. "The Epidemiology of Rape and Sexual Coercion in South Africa: An Overview." *Social Science and Medicine* 55 (2002) 1231–44.

Johnson, Alan F. "Revelation." In *The Expositor's Bible Commentary. Abridged Edition. New Testament,* edited by Kenneth L. Barker and John R. Kohlenberger, 1125–31. Grand Rapids: Zondervan, 1994.

Johnson, Luke T. *The Writings of the New Testament. An Interpretation. Revised Edition.* Minneapolis: Fortress, 1999.

Keck, Leander E, ed. *The New Interpreter's Bible. Volume Twelve.* Nashville: Abingdon, 1998.

Knust, Jennifer W. *Unprotected Texts. The Bible's Surprising Contradictions About Sex and Desire.* New York: HarperCollins, 2011.

Koester, Craig R. *The Anchor Yale Bible. Volume 38A. Revelation.* New Haven; London: Yale University, 2014.

Levine, Amy–Jill. and Maria M. Robbins, eds. *A Feminist Companion to the Apocalypse of John.* London; New York: T&T Clark, 2009.

Marshall, John W. "Gender and Empire: Sexualized Violence in John's Anti–Imperial Apocalypse." In *A Feminist Companion to the Apocalypse of John,* edited by Amy–Jill Levine and Maria M. Robbins, 17–32. London; New York: T&T Clark, 2009.

Rowland, Christopher C. "The Book of Revelation." In *The New Interpreter's Bible. Volume Twelve,* edited by Leander E. Keck, (page numbers missing). Nashville: Abingdon, 1998.

Rowland, Christopher. *The Open Heaven. A Study of Apocalyptic in Judaism and Early Christianity.* London: SPCK, 1982.

Reddish, M.G. 2000. "Revelation." In *Mercer Commentary on the Bible. Volume 8. General Epistles and Revelation,* edited by Watson E. Mills and Richard F. Wilson, 93–128. Macon: Mercer University, 2000.

Selvidge, Maria J. *Exploring the New Testament. Second Edition.* Upper Saddle River: Prentice Hall, 2003.

Statistics South Africa. "General Household Survey, 2015." http://www.statssa.gov.za/publications/P0318/P03182015.pdf.

Trible, Phyllis. *Texts of Terror: Literary-feminist Readings of Biblical Narratives.* Minneapolis: Fortress, 1984.

Van Hartingsveld, L. *Die Openbaring van Johannes. Een Praktische Bijbelverklaring. Tekst en Toelichting.* Kampen: JH Kok, 1984.

"16 Ways You Can Stand against Rape Culture." *UN Women,* November 18, 2019. https://un-women.medium.com/16-ways-you-can-stand-against-rape-culture-88bf12638f12.

SECTION 3

Ethical Reflections

11

Revisiting the Church's Moral Authority on Sexual Ethics

Reform or Retreat?

Tanya van Wyk

INTRODUCTION: THE CHURCH'S MORAL AUTHORITY—CONFUSION, PROTEST AND IGNORANCE

After being inundated with revelations that boys and teenagers were being sexually abused by priests and after admissions of guilt by the Roman Catholic Church trickled in,[1] the world bore witness to yet another admission by

1. The Roman Catholic Church's history with regard to sexual abuse spans decades. Reports started to trickle in during the 1980s, and by the 1990s it had garnered public attention in countries like Australia, Canada, Ireland, and the United States. In the introduction of their book, Frank Bruni and Eleanor Burkett have stated that a report was written in 1985 by several prominent Catholics, "that accurately gauged the depth and implications of the looming crisis . . . most Church leaders decided to simply ignore it" (Bruni and Burkett, *The Gospel of Shame*, xviii). By 2001, Pope John Paul II started to acknowledge and apologize. In 2008 and in 2010, Pope Benedict XVI apologized and denounced the abuse by church authorities (Wynne-Jones, "Pope's Apology"). In 2018, Francis first accused the victims of fabricating the allegations, however later in that year he apologized for his statements (Noack, "Pope Admits Error") and convened a meeting at the Vatican to be held in early 2019 to discuss the prevention of sexual abuse in the Catholic Church.

Pope Francis in February 2019 about the sexual abuse of nuns by priests, which has been taking place for years.[2] In March of 2019, the North Gauteng High Court in South Africa set aside the Dutch Reformed Church's (DRC) decision on gay marriages. In 2015 the DRC decided to accept gay marriages, allowing ministers to perform such unions and effectively giving their blessing to gay people in the Church. This decision was however controversially overturned one year later by some of the DRC's officials, stating that homosexuality and same-sex unions do not meet Christian guidelines.[3] This was almost a year (March 2018) after the South African Anglican Church publicly acknowledged that it was facing allegations of sexual abuse by some of its priests, which took place during the 1970s and 1980s.[4]

It is not an understatement to say that the Christian church has had a difficult relationship with human sexuality over almost 2000 years.[5] To be more specific, the Christian church has attempted to keep a strict hold on human sexuality by way of sole proprietorship of moral authority on human sexuality.[6] For the church, the connection of sex to Christianity has apparently been a self-evident one.[7] Members of the Christian church, spread out over different denominations and traditions across the world, have reacted differently to the church's problematic relationship with human sexuality. There has been both "shouting and silence."[8] This relates to attempts at fixing a moral code that would be universally valid, as well as a renewed emphasis on what may be considered as "sexual sin." This in turn is based on the notion that moral teaching and reading the Christian bible is straightforward.[9] However, there are also loud calls for discussions about sexuality and sex that are morally engaged and affirmative: "The conventional Christian framework of 'celibacy in singleness, sex only in marriage' is being explicitly contested by many inside and outside the church who no longer abide by that moral code."[10] The response is a mixture of acceptance, ignorance, frustration, and defiance.

This mixture of responses is echoed by my experience of teaching courses on (Christian) sexual ethics and ecclesiology to theology students

---

2. Poggioli, "After Years of Abuse."

3. See "Dutch Reformed Church Loses Court Battle Over Same-Sex Unions."

4. See "SA Anglican Church Sex Abuse Scandal."

5. Ellison, *Making Love Just,* 3–4; Farley, *Just Love,* 17–56.

6. Ellison, *Making Love Just,* 3–6.

7. Wiesner-Hanks, *Christianity and Sexuality,* 1.

8. Ellison, *Making Love Just,* 3.

9. Vardy, *The Puzzle of Sex,* xi–xiii.

10. Ellison, *Making Love Just,* 4.

at a South African public university since 2010. When students are asked about their opinions about the role of the church with regard to human sexuality and sexual ethics, their answers are more often than not contradicting or vague. It is often expressed that the church is probably not as inclusive as its Gospel witness attests, and that church membership and attendance in some cases is not appealing—yet at the same time it is expressed that the church is an institution which teaches principles to people. Other responses have indicated other contradictions, namely that the church is both organic ("the body of Christ") and static (with set, dogma-style rules) and that the church should not tell people what to do, yet it provides good life lessons. It could be that these contradictory or confused responses are indicative of the paradoxical nature of the church itself.

Even though students are at times extremely critical of the church—specifically during lectures on ecclesiology—when it comes to the topic of human sexuality, students almost revert to a complete opposite framework and they argue that the church, even though it might have lost its way to some measure, should provide ethical guidelines and be a moral leader. When asked about what those guidelines should look like, the responses are often contradictory too, stating that the church should provide space for inclusive discussion, but the church should also protect heterosexual marriage as the true and correct form of human relationships. It seems there is either unhelpful criticism or total confusion with regard to the church's moral authority in general and with regard to human sexuality in particular. This was also illustrated by a speaker at a Reproductive Health Conference hosted by the Faculty of Theology of Stellenbosch University in 2018. She told the audience about how she would want to become a surrogate mother for her sister's child. Chaos ensued in her church denomination, because she is a single woman and the church could not establish if her deed would be a praiseworthy act of Christian charity, or if it would be an immoral sexual sin to have a baby out of wedlock.

This type of contradiction, confusion and criticism is mostly related to diverse hermeneutics and readings of the Christian bible. However, in my 2009 Master's thesis, I argued that the church's problem with its approach toward human sexuality, specifically homosexuality, was an ecclesiological problem, not one of biblical interpretation.[11] This implies that the church's difficult relationship with human sexuality can be linked to something other than debates regarding biblical hermeneutics. In the thesis, I specifically explored the way in which the church perceives the

---

11. Van Wyk, "Rol wat 'n Ekklesiologie Speel," 10–19; see also Van Wyk and Buitendag, "Die Eenheid van die Kerk," 2.

relationship between two of its identity markers or marks of the church, namely unity and catholicity and how this influences the church's understanding and approach toward homosexual people. In this contribution it is investigated whether another one of those classic marks of the church (or *notae ecclesiae*) of the church, namely holiness, can influence the church's ecclesiology and in turn have an impact on the church's own interpretation of its moral authority on issues of human sexuality, as well on how others view the church's moral authority. In its simplest sense, the holiness of the church denotes "being set apart," being different."[12] But what does this mean with regard to the church's moral authority?

I will discuss this in the paragraphs that follow. First, I will look at historical aspects of the church's stance on human sexuality or sexual ethics and the way the church has exercised moral authority, before turning to the notion of holiness in general and how it is related to the church, and how it might relate to the integrity of the church and its conduct. Finally, I will return to the question of whether the church should retreat or reform with regard to "authority" on matters of human sexuality.

HISTORY OF OBSESSION: THE CHRISTIAN CHURCH'S ATTEMPT AT REGULATING HUMAN SEXUALITY

Throughout much of Christian church history, the church's teachings about the human body, (with a focus on women's bodies), sensuality, sexual intimacy and the so-called correct ordering of gender and sexual relations have been negative. "In the popular mind of Christian-based culture, sex is an alien and dangerous force to be contained. . . sin is defined in essentially sexual terms, above all as a loss of control over the body and capitulation to sexual desire."[13] Daniel Maguire has traced this back to the beginning of the Constantinian era and the establishment of a "pelvic theology" which entailed an obsession with sexual control.[14] Peter Vardy describes the early Christian church's position on human sexuality as an "obsession about sex"[15] which resulted in human sexuality being regulated severely. Adultery and so-called homosexual acts were treated as analogous to murder and carried similar sentences.[16] The ratio of punitive measures toward sexual offences to other offences, like murder and theft was approximately 4:1 (for every one

12. McGrath, *Christian Theology*, 373.

13. Ellison, *Making Love Just*, 4.

14. Maguire, "Shadow Side," 38–39.

15. Vardy, *The Puzzle of Sex*, 52.

16. Price, "Distinctiveness," 261; cf. Vardy, *The Puzzle of Sex*, 52.

rule or law governing theft or murder there were four relating to "sexual" offences). In fact, Christians were more concerned about repressing the body's
need for food, sleep and sexual urges than anything else—including pagan
ascetics.[17]

Vardy illustrates how the early church position is a culmination of a
patriarchal interpretation of the content of the Hebrew Scriptures (and specifically the creation stories)[18] about sexual relations, sexual intercourse and
childbearing.[19] Vardy emphasizes the era of Augustine (354–430 CE), drawing a distinguishing line between everything before and after Augustine
because "Augustine was responsible for turning a generally negative attitude
to sex which arose from a desire to maintain the identity of the growing
Christian Church into a negative attitude based on theological principles."[20]
Augustine's position reflected ideas of the Greek philosopher Plato (430–
340 BCE) and the Jewish philosopher Philo of Alexandria (25 BCE–40 CE)
on the dualistic nature of a human being and the general degenerative state
of the body as opposed to the higher good of the soul.

In this regard, the early Christian church gradually developed a binary
understanding of human sexuality, which was utilized to divide human sexual acts into the categories of "normal" and "deviant." A deviant expression
of sexuality would be anything outside of what the church recognizes as normal or biblically sanctioned. A binary understanding of sexuality can however be traced back also to the interpretation of the apostle Paul's writings.
He was not necessarily negative towards sex itself, as long as it does not lead
you to commit sin. He was more positively inclined toward marriage, not as
a "holy sanctified union, instituted by God," but rather for the same reason,
namely that human beings are weak and easily tempted, and that it would be
better to release sexual energies within marriage than outside it.[21] Together,
Paul, Augustine's neo-Platonic theology, and Philo's Jewish philosophy had a
profound influence on the development of Christian thought about how the

17. Radford-Ruether, *Christianity and the Making of the Modern Family*, 36; see also
Brown, *The Body and Society*.

18. The interpretation of the creation stories of the Christian Bible had a particularly devastating effect on the role and position of women in the church and society
and the prescription of gender roles. The story of Eve's so-called temptation of Adam in
the Book of Genesis was one of the main foundations on which Christian theologians
and leaders had built their understanding of sexuality, God's will for the relationship
between men and women, and very specifically, the subservient position of women.
Radford-Ruether, *Women and Redemption*, 59; cf. Vardy, *The Puzzle of Sex*, 10.

19. Vardy, *The Puzzle of Sex*, 3–42.

20. Vardy, *The Puzzle of Sex*, 53; cf. Radford-Ruether, *Christianity and the Making of
the Modern Family*, 45–46.

21. Vardy, *The Puzzle of Sex*, 46.

celibate state or unmarried state was spiritually superior to being married. This resulted in a growing pejorative stance toward sex which was considered vulgar and evil in itself.[22] Philo had maintained that the sole purpose of sex was procreation and Augustine merely tolerated sexual desire (which he considered to be an evil) since it was necessary for procreation.[23] This mixture of philosophy and theology culminated in the formation of natural law during the Middle Ages, as developed particularly by Thomas Aquinas (1226–1274), the Roman Catholic theologian who utilized the philosophy of Aristotle. Aristotle's philosophy was empirically based and focused on the purpose (*telos*) of all things. Something had to be utilized or someone had to act in accordance to their designated purpose. From this he derived the "purpose" of human sexual organs, which was procreation only. Aquinas's natural law resulted in church teachings that regarded any aspect of sexuality which does not ascribe to a natural pattern of purpose as deviant, sinful and therefore punishable. This had meant for example that birth control, masturbation and homosexual deeds were considered an evil, because all of these contravened the purpose of sex organs.

In a context where sex was only understood in terms of the purpose of procreation, marriage was a type of remedy against sin,[24] because the evil of sex could be tolerated within a marital bond and could aid one to not succumb to sexual desire. Within this framework however, Philo still condemned sexual relations during a woman's "infertile period" and considered women to be objects of pleasure and instruments of evil.[25] According to Augustine, marriage could alter the desire for sex to become a desire for children.[26] One important and long-lasting result of the connection made between sex, procreation and marriage is that marriage became a heteronormative overemphasis for the "correct" ordering of sexual relationships in general and the relationship between a man and a woman in particular.[27] Due to the above mentioned mixture of influences, marriage became a sacrament in the Roman Catholic Church and consequently, divorce became a punishable offence.

---

22. Radford-Ruether, *Women and Redemption*, 63–73.

23. Augustine argued that sex for procreation, together with marriage and gender differentiation, was part of God's original plan (see Augustine, *The Literal Meaning of Genesis*, in Taylor, *Ancient Christian Writers*, 41–42).

24. Augustine, *On the Good of Marriage*.

25. Cf. Philo's *De Opificio Mundi*; Vardy, *The Puzzle of Sex*, 49.

26. Augustine, *On the Good of Marriage*.

27. Botha and Dreyer, "Shifting Ecclesial Perspectives."

In the Reformed tradition, Martin Luther de-sacramentalized marriage[28] and placed it within the sphere of the world and the sphere of relationships.[29] However, Luther kept to Augustine's emphasis on the (sexual) roles of man and woman, based on his interpretation of the Genesis creation narratives.[30]

The other remedy against the sin of sex was to remain celibate,[31] which in turn had an immense influence on the Catholic Church's history and consequently also the church's history of sexual abuse because there is evidence of a psychological link between the suppression of sexuality and sexual violence.[32] Refraining from sex in the form of being celibate or a virgin was the precursor to how virginity and celibacy came to be associated with the holiness of the church (specifically with regard to the morality of its members), which will be discussed in more detail below.

In her work about Christianity, sexuality and the early modern world, Merry Wiesner-Hanks explores Christianity and the regulation of sexual attitudes and activities from the years 1500 to about 1750. Although there occurred many shifts in the geographical areas she conducted the study about—Europe and areas that were being colonized by Europe—like new ideas about the body, changes in marriage patterns and a greater symbolic importance attached to sexuality, all centered on new ways to control people's sexual lives:[33]

> Christianity had an impact on the regulation of sexuality not only though the actions of the church officials and the ideas of theologians, but also through the actions and ideas of lay people, from monarchs to ordinary individuals. . . [this includes] individuals or groups who described their actions as Christian or held a position of authority within a Christian denomination or a state where the official religion was Christianity.[34]

28. Cf. Pelikan, *Luther's Works*.

29. Botha, "Verskuiwing van Teologiese Denke."

30. Pelikan, *Luther's Works*; cf. Botha, "Verskuiwing van Teologiese Denke," 115–16.

31. Thatcher, *Marriage After Modernity*, 137.

32. Cf. Bruni and Burkett, *Gospel of Shame*; Vardy, *The Puzzle of Sex*, 103–16.

33. Wiesner-Hanks, *Christianity and Sexuality*, 2–3.

34. Wiesner-Hanks states that the use of the term "sexuality" in reference to the church's stance of matters sexual is considered problematic because "sexuality" was not understood during those early centuries and even during the 1500s until the 1750s in the way it is considered today. She states that people had sexual desires and wrote about ways in which people engaged in sexual actions—but these were not necessarily regarded as expressions of sexuality (Wiesner-Hanks, *Christianity and Sexuality*, 3). In this regard, one must be careful to use sexuality in an anachronistic fashion, as is many times done with regard to debates about how the Bible supposedly prohibits

THE HOLINESS OF THE CHURCH AND
THE CHURCH'S MORAL AUTHORITY

It was the Nicene creed of 381 CE that professed the church to be "one," "holy," "catholic," and "apostolic." This is the oldest ecumenical definition of the identity and characteristics by which the Christian church may be recognized. Traditionally, the assertion of the holiness of the church as one of the *notae ecclesiae* faced the same tension between theory and empirical praxis as the other marks of the church. This relates to how the church could be regarded as holy when its history as an institution points to the sinfulness of both the church and its members.[35] One way was to relate the holiness of the church to the empirical holiness of its members. This led to the exclusion of members who were considered to have lapsed from these set standards of sanctity, as (for example) was the core issue of the Donatist controversy[36] in which lapsed bishops could not perform sacraments and were regarded as "outside" the church. The other way to deal with the seemingly contradictory nature of the holiness of the church was to regard the holiness of the church as an eschatological reality, which meant that the contemporary "sinfulness" of the church will be purified "on the last day."[37]

From the church's historical obsession with regulating sex based on the conviction that sex and sexual desire is evil, it follows that the Christian church would have connected the notion of holiness to being "set apart" in the sense of "purity" or being unblemished, with the emphasis on virginity and celibacy.[38] Thus the Christian church connected the notion (or self-understanding) of its moral authority in matters sexual to its understanding of holiness.

According to Ellison,[39] the imperial approach to Christian sexual morals which originated in the Constantinian era and in many cases still exert influence today, is shaped by three assumptions: 1) moral truth is located in the past—in a tradition which was shaped and defined by patriarchy; 2) any theological discourse about sexuality can proceed in an abstract

---

homosexuality (cf. Waetjen, "Same-Sex Relations in Antiquity"; Seitz, "Sexuality and Scripture's Plain Sense"). I take her point, however in this contribution, "sexuality" is used in reference to the way the Christian church developed an over-emphasis on matters sexual and labelled it a Christian sexual ethic. It is used in relation to the question about the Church's authority to continue to do so.

35. McGrath, *Christian Theology*, 373.

36. McGrath, *Christian Theology*, 358–60.

37. McGrath, *Christian Theology*, 373.

38. Radford-Ruether, *Women and Redemption*, 63–77.

39. Ellison, *Making Love Just*, 5.

way—which is devoid of recognizing contextual changes and challenges; and 3) people telling their narratives or speaking out about their moral struggles are too subjective—which rests on the idea that one can offer a "pure" ethic untainted by one's interests.

In decades-long debates by the Christian church about homosexuality and the church's struggle to acknowledge its complicity in covering up sexual abuse, these three assumptions have led to the church's moral authority being questioned. Historically, the church has functioned as a major source of moral authority. According to the ethicist Louise Kretzschmar, this has been the case for both individual Christians and wider society.[40] The church has exercised its moral authority as a social institution, as was the case during the Middle Ages when the Roman Catholic Church exercised spiritual and temporal authority in Europe. This was the result of a Constantinian model which saw the church and state unified. For a while, the balance of power shifted towards the church, which had the power to make and unmake monarchs. The church held moral sway over the social-religious lives of millions of people.[41] This authority was situated in the Church's control of baptism, marriage and burial and its' influence over education, law, arts and even medicine.

After the Reformation, the unity of church and state had been broken and there was a social, political and economic rivalry between church and state that lead to the onset of secularization. Modern science, democracy and the industrial revolution contributed to the Christian church's diminished moral power. The church's authority had become indirect (not direct) and its moral judgement ignored. Today, church authority is communicated to most Christians through their local community or church. Local churches (or congregations, communities) do not always just pass on the major ideas or influences of the larger, universal church. These church communities are shaped by their locations and the societies they are part of. Kretzschmar states that some communities, however, have sought escape from their larger social responsibilities within the community and are propagating a privatized form of the Christian faith.[42] She defines "privatization" in this regard as the limitation of the gospel to the private spiritual concerns of the individual. A privatized understanding of the message of the Gospel is a-contextual because it professes that salvation and or reconciliation is about our relationship with God alone and not about our relationship with

---

40. Kretzschmar, "Ethics in a Theological Context," 13.

41. Kretzschmar, "Ethics in a Theological Context," 13.

42. Kretzschmar, "Ethics in a Theological Context," 14.

each other and the Other. A privatized gospel "fails to bring about holistic spiritual renewal. . . or to promote ecclesiastical or social transformation."[43]

Kretzschmar argues that our moral values are influenced by the church—as an institution and as a force in a local community—and the influence of the church can be positive or negative, depending on the particular circumstances, individuals and groups involved. In my opinion, it comes down to the church's integrity.

MORALITY: HOLINESS AS INTEGRITY

For the feminist theologian of praxis, Denise Ackermann, "holiness" is primarily concerned with concrete reality and the way one assumes responsibility for living in the world.[44] In her book titled *Surprised by the Man on the Borrowed Donkey*, she recounts how hard it was for her to think or talk about holiness, out of trepidation of regarding herself "holier than thou" and trying and failing to attain a state of perfection or a sense of having arrived—ways in which holiness are many times regarded. Eventually she accepted according to her—the biblical truth—that she was holy, made in the image of God and living a life directed to God. This is a paradoxical holiness, in which one lives and confesses simultaneously the broken human condition and the triumph of God's grace.

Traditionally, holiness denotes a sense of awe, mystery and the sacred and is attributed to God, rather than human beings. And yet, Ackermann states that holiness is rooted in the Incarnation: how Christ is-with-us and therefore too in the way in which Christ's holiness was recognized: a carpenter's son, friend of sinners and outcasts and crucified as a criminal.[45] Jesus "was born and died on days that were not then holy, but were made holy by the way he lived them."[46] She describes moments that she has glimpsed holiness in others:

> I remember the patient beauty of an old *gogo* (grandmother) in
> a shack, holding a spoon to the mouth of a child with cerebral
> palsy; the loving care of friends for a little daughter with Down's
> syndrome; the courageous resolve in the eyes of a member of the
> Black Sash in the face of a police armored vehicle in the 1980s;

43. Kretzschmar, "Ethics in a Theological Context," 14.

44. Ackermann, *Surprised by the Man*, 107.

45. Ackermann, *Surprised by the Man*, 101.

46. Ackermann, *Surprised by the Man*, 106.

and the dignity accorded to homeless people by a friend who runs a night shelter.[47]

Holiness is lived—it is an embodied spirituality that encompasses both the personal and communal human response to God. Holiness is embodied by sharing material goods, offering hospitality, standing for justice and making relationships of friendship and trust. Holiness is about striving to reflect the Image of God and being-for-others—transcending the self. Holiness, then, is not about being set apart as unblemished and distinct from "sinners." "*Living into* your holiness takes courage and humility, because it is an act of love for the sake of Jesus. . . to live into holiness is to live in God's love and to *be* God's love here in the world."[48]

Ackermann's understanding of holiness resonates with Leo Koffeman's understanding of holiness—and it is very far removed from connecting holiness with celibacy and virginity (purity) as the basis of Christian morality of the church. The church historian Leo Koffeman argues that the integrity of the church should be linked directly to its holiness.[49] In this regard, the word/notion "holiness" in reference to the church should be replaced with "integrity" every time one comes across it. In this way, "holiness" is not a hierarchical distinction mark between the church "and the rest of the world." Holiness cannot provide the church with an uncritical foundation for regulating human sexuality. It does not provide those inside the church with a stick for proverbially hitting those outside the church. If the holiness of the church is understood as its integrity, then the church might be able to reign in the derisive sentiments about its reputation and conduct. According to Koffeman, the church's holiness has institutional consequences. It is about the church being reliable and trustworthy. I would argue the integrity of the church should at least include:

- the way the church's conduct corresponds with the church's confession
- the way the sacraments are a realization of inclusivity
- the way the church is a community
- the way in which the church translates the indicatives of the identity of the church (the marks/identity markers of the church) into imperatives in the twenty-first century.

Being moral and having "moral authority" is indeed closely connected with the church's holiness, but only if holiness is understood as "being set apart"

47. Ackermann, *Surprised by the Man*, 109.

48. Ackermann, *Surprised by the* Man, 123, 131.

49. Koffeman, *In Order to Serve*, 217; cf. Dreyer, "Church, Mission and Ethics," 4.

by the way one lives with integrity. For the church, this entails the way it embodies God's love in the world in service of the wellbeing of humanity. In this regard, to be "moral" is to live with integrity, which means a way of life as a response to the "inclusive summons to all of us to be whom we truly are—people in the image of God."[50] This is what should set the Christian church apart and this is what could provide the basis of what Ellison describes as a "just" sexual ethics,[51] that is, a Christian sexual ethics that is formulated and practiced within the framework of justice:

> . . . the imperial and patriarchalised Christian tradition has obscured the central place of justice in biblical faith. . . Pursuing a comprehensive justice includes critiquing sexual injustice with its interlocking components of sex-negativity, compulsory heterosexuality and sexualized violence. Beyond critique, justice making involves the constructive movement to create the conditions of respect and well-being that would make it possible for all people to thrive.[52]

CONCLUSION: RETREAT OR REFORM FOR THE CHURCH?

In 1994, John de Gruchy described mixed feelings toward the identity and calling of the church:

> The word "church" conjures up a variety of different and often conflicting images. For some people, "church" has a very negative connotation: an authoritarian, patriarchal and conservative institution which cramps the Spirit of Christian freedom, joy and witness: an instrument of colonialism; or a legitimator of apartheid. For such reasons people have often expressed a preference for Christianity rather than "churchianity," for Jesus of Nazareth, but not the church of Christendom. There are other people, however, for whom the church is the indispensable womb within which their faith has been born and nurtured. For them, the church, despite its faults, is something essentially positive, a community of faith, hope and love without which Christianity would be inconceivable.[53]

---

50. Ackermann, *Surprised by the Man*, 107.

51. Ellison, *Making Love Just*, 93–97.

52. Ellison, *Making Love Just*, 6.

53. De Gruchy, "Christian Community," 125.

These remarks can easily be applied to sentiments about the Christian Church's moral authority on issues of human sexuality.

Terry Eagleton is of the opinion that the real moral dilemmas today can be summarized with the phrase "trouble with strangers," as "living with the neighbor" is the overarching challenge for many people in the world today.[54] It comes down to the same phenomenological problem: binary thinking leads to a struggle with otherness and diversity, whether it be knowledge, people or morality. By its simplest definition, morality is "being for the Other."[55] If the church could clarify and seriously take up its role with regard to "being for the Other," it might be possible for the church to be a non-regulatory moral partner in coping with the complexity of reality and sexuality. If not the church, then the law?

For the sociologist Zygmunt Bauman, law alone is not sufficient to help humanity face the challenges of an ever-changing world.[56] In his work on political theology, Dirkie Smit re-iterates this and says it is a question whether the law is sufficient for a humane society and whether the law can embody and guarantee love, that is, change the hearts and minds of people.[57] Jürgen Moltmann has argued that one of the main ways through which we could create, sustain, and live a shared value orientation is through the holiness of the church.[58] In terms of the integrity of the church, the church still could reclaim its moral authority if it is willing to reform and seriously consider its integrity in the twenty-first century. One of the key aspects of its reformation would be the reconception of a nonbinary approach to human sexuality, which would entail recognition of how human spirituality, biology, physiology and psychology mutually influence one another—and that the human person is more than the sum total of the different sections. It would entail the recognition that aspects like sexual and gender identity exist on a sliding scale, a continuum, where these identities are dynamic and not static.[59] The biggest challenge of the church in this regard, remains, being for the Other.

According to Bauman and Donskis, evil is not merely confined to war, violence or unrest.[60] They argue that evil more often than not today reveals itself in everyday insensitivity to the suffering of others, an inability

---

54. Eagleton, *Trouble with Strangers.*

55. Bauman, *Individualized Society,* 175.

56. Cf. Smit, "Justice as/and Compassion?," 113.

57. Smit, "Justice as/and Compassion?," 109–28.

58. In Naudé, "Marks of the Church," 286–88.

59. *Diversity in Human Sexuality,* 16–23

60. Bauman and Donskis, *Moral Blindness,* 10–1.

(or refusal) to understand them and the turning away of one's ethical gaze, immorality meaning to turn away from the other.[61] This constitutes a moral blindness. The church (and religion) should not regulate human sexuality, but it cannot turn away from the fight against evil and it may not become numb to the suffering of others. It could still be the greatest partner in humanity's fight against evil and the broken human condition and therefore I would not want to see the church "retreat," but rather "reform."

BIBLIOGRAPHY

Ackermann, Denise M. *Surprised by the Man on the Borrowed Donkey*. Cape Town: Lux Verbi, 2014.

Aquinas, Thomas. *Summa Theologica*. 2 vols. Translated by Fathers of the English Dominican Province. Notre Dame: Benzinger Brothers, 1981.

Aristotle. *Metaphysics*. Translated by J. H. McMahon. New York: Prometheus, 1991.

Augustine. *The Literal Meaning of Genesis*. Edited and translated by John H. Taylor. New York: Newman, 1982.

———. "On the Good of Marriage." In *Treatises on Marriage and Other Subjects*, translated by Charles T. Wilcox, 9–54. Washington, DC: Catholic University of America Press, 1999.

Bauman, Zygmunt. *The Individualized Society*. Cambridge: Polity, 2001.

Bauman, Zygmunt, and Leonidas Donskis. *Moral Blindness: The Loss of Sensitivity in Liquid Modernity*. Cambridge: Polity, 2013.

Botha, Annelie. "Verskuiwing van Teologiese Denke oor die Huwelik vanaf Luther tot Vandag." In *Nadenke oor 500 jaar se Reformatoriese teology*, edited by Natie van Wyk, 113–30. Cape Town: AOSIS, 2017.

Botha, Annelie, and Yolanda Dreyer. "Veranderende Perspektiewe op Seksualiteit en die Huwelik in 'n Postmoderne Kerk." *HTS Theological Studies* 69.2 (2013).

Brown, Peter. *The Body and Society: Men, Women, and Sexual Renunciation in Early Christianity*. New York: Columbia University, 1988.

Bruni, Frank, and Elinor Burkett. *A Gospel of Shame: Children, Sexual Abuse and the Catholic Church*. New York: HarperCollins, 2002.

De Gruchy, John W. "Christian Community." In *Doing Theology in Context: South African Perspectives,* edited by John W. De Gruchy and Charles Villa-Vicencio, 125–38. New York: Orbis, 1994.

Dreyer, Wim. "Church, Mission and Ethics. Being Church with Integrity." *HTS Theological Studies* 72.1 (2016). https://hts.org.za/index.php/hts/article/view/3163.

"Dutch Reformed Church Loses Court Battle Over Same-Sex Unions." *E-News Channel Africa*, March 8, 2019. https://www.enca.com/news/court-overturns-dutch-reformed-church-stance-same-sex-unions.

Eagleton, Terry. *Trouble with Strangers: A Study of Ethics*. Oxford: Wiley-Blackwell, 2009.

Ellison, Marvin M. *Making Love Just: Sexual Ethics for Perplexed Times*. Minneapolis: Fortress, 2012.

61. Cf. Bauman, *Individualized Society*.

Farley, Margaret. *Just Love: A Framework for Christian Sexual Ethics.* London: Continuum, 2006.

Koffeman, L. J. *In Order to Serve: An Ecumenical Introduction to Church Polity.* Berlin: Lit Verlag, 2014.

Kretzschmar, Louise. "Ethics in a Theological Context." In *Doing Ethics in Context. South African Perspectives,* edited by John W. De Gruchy and Charles Villa-Vicencio, 2–21. Maryknoll: Orbis, 1994.

Maguire, Daniel C. "The Shadow Side of the Homosexuality Debate." In *Homosexuality in the Priesthood and the Religious Life,* edited by John Boswell and Jeannine Gramick, 38–42. New York: Crossroad, 1989.

McGrath, Alister E. *Christian Theology: An Introduction.* 6th ed. Oxford: Wiley Blackwell, 2017.

Naudé, Piet. "The Marks of the Church in South Africa Today. In Dialogue with Jürgen Moltmann on His 80th Birthday." In *Pathways in Theology: Ecumenical, African, and Reformed,* edited by Piet Naudé, 279–94. Stellenbosch: SunMedia, 2015.

Noack, Rick. "Pope admits 'grave error,' apologizes for not believing Chilean sex abuse victims." *Washington Post,* December 4, 2018. https://www.washingtonpost.com/news/worldviews/wp/2018/04/12/pope-admits-grave-error-apologizes-for-not-believing-chile-sex-abuse-victims/.

Pelikan, Jaroslav. *Luther's Works.* Vol. 1. Saint Louis: Concordia, 1958.

Poggioli, Sylvia. "After Years Of Abuse By Priests, #NunsToo Are Speaking Out." *WPSU,* March 18, 2019. https://radio.wpsu.org/post/after-years-abuse-priests-nunstoo-are-speaking-out.

"Pope sends first e-mail apology." *BBC,* November 23, 2001. http://news.bbc.co.uk/2/hi/europe/1671540.stm.

Price, Richard M. "The Distinctiveness of Early Christian Sexual Ethics." *Heythrop Journal* (1990) 257–76.

Radford-Ruether, Rosemary. *Christianity and the Making of the Modern Family.* London: SCM, 2001.

———. *Women and Redemption: A Theological History.* Minneapolis: Fortress, 1998.

Seitz, Christopher. "Sexuality and Scripture's Plain Sense: The Christian Community and the Law of God." In *Homosexuality, Science and the "Plain Sense" of Scripture,* edited by David L. Balch, 177–96. Grand Rapids: Eerdmans, 2000.

Smit, Dirk J. "Justice as/and Compassion?: On the Good Samaritan and Political Theology." In *Considering Compassion. Global Ethics, Human Dignity and the Compassionate God,* edited by Frits de Lange and Juliana C. Claassens, 109–28. Eugene, OR: Pickwick, 2018.

"SA Anglican Church Sex Abuse Scandal: Four Victims Come Forward." *Times Live,* March 22, 2018. https://www.timeslive.co.za/news/south-africa/2018-03-22-sa-anglican-church-sex-abuse-scandal-four-victims-come-forward/.

Thatcher, Adrian. *Marriage after Modernity.* New York: New York University Press, 1999.

Van Wyk, Tanya. "Die Rol wat 'n Ekklesiologie Speel in die Verstaan en Hantering van Homoseksuele Persone met Besondere Verwysing na die NHKA." MTh thesis, University of Pretoria, 2009.

Van Wyk, Tanya, and Johan Buitendag. "Die Eenheid van die Kerk in Gedrang." *HTS Theological Studies* 66.1 (2010). https://hts.org.za/index.php/HTS/article/view/908.

Vardy, Peter. *The Puzzle of Sex.* London: HarperCollins, 1997.

Waetjen, H. C. "Same-Sex Relations in Antiquity and Sexuality and Sexual Identity in Contemporary American Society." In *Biblical Ethics and Homosexuality*, edited by Robert L. Brawley, 87–102. Louisville: Westminster John Knox, 1996.

Wiesner-Hanks, Merry. *Christianity and Sexuality in the Early Modern World: Regulating Desire, Reforming Practice*. Abingdon: Routledge, 2010.

Wynne-Jones, J. "Pope's apology: 'You have suffered grievously and I am truly sorry.'" *Telegraph*, March 20, 2010. https://www.telegraph.co.uk/news/worldnews/europe/vaticancityandholysee/7489455/Popes-apology-You-have-suffered-grievously-and-I-am-truly-sorry.html.

12

Swipe Right for Love
Social Media and the Born-Free Generation

Ashwin Afrikanus Thyssen

INTRODUCTION

Soon after 31 October 1517 (when Martin Luther had nailed his ninety-five theses to the door of Wittenberg Cathedral) the Latin *solas* became the creedal statements that captured the heart of the Protestant Reformation. These are: *sola Christus, sola Deo Gloria, sola Scriptura, sola gratia,* and *sola fide.* I contend that the ecumenical church, both locally and globally, finds itself in a similar moment; a sexual reformation is presently afoot. Yet, the zeitgeist has an alternative agenda to that of the Protestant Reformation. In this time the theological creedal statements of the present sexual reformation may be *quod sic corpus, quod sic amor, quod sic experientia.* More plainly stated: yes body, yes love, yes experience.

This creedal statement (an affirming "yes" as opposed to an exclusivist "only") sets the tone of the sexual reformation underway and offers guidance for the logic of this essay. Briefly, this essay sets out to prioritize the importance of social media in the lives of the "born-free" youth. That is, the generation of South Africans born around and after 1994. This generation may also be considered as part of those termed Millennials (Generation Y);

born between the 1980s and late 1990s. At present, public theology plays a significant role in South Africa's religious imagination; as such, this discussion places these concerns within the discipline of public theology. While it marginally draws from body, feminist and queer theologies, this is done in order to uncover the contours of the sexual reformation taking place. This means the contribution of these disciplines will be analyzed using the lenses of public theology.

What, then, is public theology? Drawing from David Tracy's *Analogical Imagination*, public theologians consider the public dimension of Christian theology and how this impacts church, academy and society. "The premise of public theology is that the discourse does not remain within a rarefied community of academic theologians, which would only be self-serving."[1] Public theology, of course, draws from various schools of thought—notably, Catholic Social Teaching, the Social Gospel Movement and Political Theology. In South Africa, the rise of public theology follows the advent of democracy; when the need arose to formulate a theological paradigm that could attend to the challenges of conceptualizing a secular democracy theologically.[2] Yet, public theology is not without its limitations in the South African theological academy. This essay, therefore, employs public theology as tool of analysis while recognizing these limitations and critiquing them.

Three objectives are pursued in this essay. First, it attempts to capture a working definition of social media, in relation to the youth (Millennials or Generation Y) who are queer. Throughout this essay, "queer" is used as shorthand referring to those people who identify as lesbian, gay, bisexual, transgender, intersex, asexual and all sexual minorities. Queer may also refer to gender identities not acknowledged within the heteronormative gender binary (man/woman); therefore, including those who identify as gender non-binary and gender non-conforming. Second, it tries to articulate how the sexual reformation is already afoot, at least on social media. Third, an effort will be made to account for the impetus this reformation has for theology and the church, and what is required in our time.

As all religious reflection, this essay is very much rooted in my own experience of sexuality and the Christian faith. Following black feminist thought, it is also helpful to note that this reflection is informed by the author's intersectional identity; as a black, cis-gender gay man. These identity markers—perhaps even hermeneutical lenses—frame my consideration of social media and the role it plays in the lives of South Africa's youth, who comprise 20 million (that is, 35.7 percent) of the population.

---

1. Day and Kim, *Companion to Public Theology*, 11.
2. Koopman, "Public Theology," 150.

It should be noted that the term "born-free" is not without contestation. Since 2013 much critique has been offered of this designation of the youth, by the post-1994 establishment. This is eruditely explored in Malaika wa Azania's publication, *Memoirs of a Born-Free*. While those born around and after 1994 are born after the legal demise of apartheid, it would do well to note that material conditions continue to hold the black majority captive.[3] Further, in a lecture delivered in May 2019, Lovelyn Nwadeyi calls into question the politicizing of the generation born around and after 1994, by virtue of employing the term "born-free."[4] As such, I reject the term "born-free"; opting instead for "youth." To be sure, the term "youth" does present itself to be problematic; even so, its use seems more apt for the present discussion.

Further, it is needful to note, this essay took final form months after the International Association of Athletics Federation's (IAAF) discriminatory ruling regarding Caster Semenya.[5] Moreover, in 2019 the academic article, "Age- and education-related effects on cognitive functioning in Colored South African women" was retracted by the journal *Aging, Neuropsychology and Cognition*.[6] In the article the authors argued that "colored" women have lower cognitive functioning; thus, racializing cognition and contributing to pseudo-scientific research. It is important to note this article, as it attempts to assert the value of "colored" women's cognition in post-1994 South Africa, thus including queer women. On 28 September 2019 the celebrity and choreographer Somizi Mhlongo married his husband Mohale Motaung, which many followed on social media, and some considered to be immense progress for the queer community.[7] More recently, on 23 October 2020, President Cyril Ramaphosa signed the Civil Union Amendment Bill into law, which prevents marriage officers of the state from refusing to conduct civil unions based on conscience.[8] The reason for this amendment, of course, is because it impeded on the rights of queer people to access civil unions. I am intentional about listing these events: in quite a profound way they inform the social imagination of South Africa's queer youth. Moreover, through social media these events shape the lives of these youths and their religious reflection.

3. Cronje, *Born Free but Still in Chains*, 1.
4. Nwadeyi, "Born Frees and Democracy."
5. Middlebrook, "New Ruling."
6. Terblanche et al., "Retracted Article."
7. Igual, "Congratulations!"; Kesa, "WATCH."
8. Seleka, "Same-Sex Marriages."

DEFINING THE SEXUAL AND FINDING LANGUAGE

There is no doubt that progress is being made regarding the recognition queer rights—both their promotion and protection. The abbreviation LG-BTIQA+, in its varied forms, is becoming all the more increasingly used, particularly by the mainstream media. Churches, too, are joining in the conversation; albeit rather late, and tainted by their conservatism and much preferred "family values" rhetoric.[9] As such, workable definitions are in order to make sense and create meaning.

In 2011, making sense of my sexuality, I Google searched the question: "Am I gay?" Unsurprisingly, the screen lit up with thousands of sources, all of which sought to provide me with an answer. I was not unique in my search for an answer; other youths like me also followed suit. Some would perform searches about being "lesbians"; others about being "transgender." With Caster Semenya being the subject of media reporting at the time, some would search about being "intersex." In all, performing these Google searches afforded many of my generation the opportunity to come to terms with our sexuality and identity.

All of this communicates that my generation, those born post-1994, is a generation which has had access to the internet and social media for as long as we can remember. Mine is a generation partly nurtured by auntie Google and her civil union partner Facebook. Of course, we ought not forget my friend—their gender non-binary child—Instagram. "These technologies have changed us. They have given us potential for communication and interaction that we did not previously possess" writes Miller and Costa.[10] Access and use of these media platforms have assisted the youth in making sense of their gender and sexuality. Even so, youth's access to these various platforms remains predicated on economic class and geographical location. Therefore, this analysis may be limited to those youth closest to the urban centers.

What, then, is social media? To answer this question, it is needful to remind oneself of the traditional two forms of communication: first, public broadcast media; and second, private dyadic communication.[11] With the development of the internet, the dividing line between public and private would become blurred. Social media is still constantly being developed:

> We define social network sites as web-based services that allow individuals to (1) construct a public or semi-public profile

9. Van der Walt, "LGBTIQA+."
10. Miller et al., *How the World Changed Social Media*, 1.
11. Miller et al., *How the World Changed Social Media*, 2.

within a bounded system, (2) articulate a list of other users with whom they share a connection, and (3) view and traverse their list of connections and those made by others within the system. The nature and nomenclature of these connections may vary from site to site.[12]

With this expansive definition of social network sites, one cannot but think of platforms such as Facebook and Twitter. "The majority of Internet users aged 15–25 (80%) and 26–35 (84%) use the Internet to access social media."[13] This, then, underscores the important relationship the youth have with social media; thus, requiring further research. Moreover, this may also suggest that research into the interplay between religion and social media is worthwhile.

In 2018 the digital marketing company VetroMedia found that Facebook remains the leading social media platform, having 16 million users; a total of 29 percent of the South African population.[14] Following this was Twitter (at 8 million users) and Instagram (at 3,8 million users).

The landscape of online dating in South Africa is no different. In 2017 Kaspersky Lab found that 31 percent of South Africa utilize online dating platforms. These are the likes of Tinder, Badoo and Grindr (the latter which is primarily used by gay men). Yet interestingly, only 10 percent report to using these platforms with the intention of finding an intimate partner.[15] This is compared to half (50 percent) of whom are using these platforms for fun. It would seem, then, that many are swiping right simply for pleasure and enjoyment. It, then, appears as if social media affords the youth the language and symbols with which to make sense of their real-life world. I contend that it is no different for their gender and sexuality.

DECONSTRUCTING THE SEXUAL REFORMATION

The question may indeed be asked: why make this claim? What evidence suggests that youth, via their access to the internet and social media, are conceptualizing their sexuality on new and profound terms? I attribute this to the silent sexual reformation presently afoot. Currently the online streaming company Netflix allows users access to no fewer than 134 queer-themed

---

12. Boyd and Ellison, "Social Network Sites," 211.

13. Gillwald, *State of ICT in South Africa*, 98.

14. See "A Glimpse of South Africa's Social Media Landscape."

15. See "The Ugly Truth."

films. This means that no fewer than 139 million individual users have access to these films, at the time of writing.[16]

In 2018 the technology company Google advocated for queer rights via the #ThisIsFamily campaign.[17] On its website, Google narrated the stories of various queer families, presenting different compositions of families that are not considered "traditional." Google also went further: it offered users the opportunity to add their own narratives to this campaign. As a result, Google contributed to normalizing the manifold forms families take.

In 2017 the choreographer Somizi Mhlongo took to Instagram, to lament the homophobia of a guest preacher at the Grace Bible Church.[18] This was met by much support on various social media platforms, most notably Twitter. Further, this act of lamentation on the part of Mhlongo contributed to an environment in which churches could be held accountable (albeit for a while) for their practices of homophobia.

All this suggests that perhaps the sexual reformation will not be televised in the traditional sense. Rather, it will be found in cyberspace. This reformation is narrated and archived by South Africa's "black Twitter," critiqued by those who are woke, and led by Instagram influencers. Moreover, this sexual reformation is intersectional.

For some theorists, this sexual reformation is predicated on the notion of worldmaking. Worldmaking is the active conceptualizing and constructing of the world; to create it habitable for human occupation. Building on this idea, Nakayama and Morris suggest: "Queer worldmaking takes place in all kinds of places, at all different times, involving all kinds of people, who work toward creating a different world. It is not a strategic plan, organized by anyone, but a bottom-up engagement with the everyday."[19]

If you think the Christian church has not been too impacted by this sexual reformation, closer investigation proves otherwise. On 8 March 2019 the Pretoria High Court ruled the Dutch Reformed Church's 2016 decision on same-sex relationships unlawful and invalid.[20] In 2016, the Dutch Reformed Church reversed its 2015 decision which afforded the licensing of queer ministerial candidates and the recognition of their civil unions. Thus, the 2016 decision sought to change it back to the previous status quo, which denied queer members licensing and a refusal to recognize their civil unions.

---

16. Fiegerman, "Netflix."

17. Google, "#ThisIsFamily | Google Pride 2018."

18. Nemakonde, "Somizi Storms Out."

19. Nakayama and Morris, "Worldmaking and Everyday Interventions," v.

20. See "Kerksaak"; Mitchley, "High Court Scraps Dutch Reformed Church decision."

Leading up to and throughout the court case; the #WhyDiscriminate campaign sought to familiarize the broader public with the civil suit via social media. By 21 August 2018, Stellenbosch University's Faculty of Theology had pledged its support for this campaign. I posit that even this protest action was a sign of the current sexual reformation. This campaign sought to garner the support of social media users, inviting them to post photos of themselves wearing t-shirts bearing the colorful print "love is love." Further, the administrators of the campaign's Facebook page were three students of theology; two who identified as gay, and one who considered herself a straight ally.[21]

In March 2019, the New York-based Union Theological Seminary sought to raise visibility of queer people of faith. This followed the United Methodist Church's decision to vote against the embracing of queer persons. The visibility-raising campaign was done under the banner and hashtag #QueerFaith. Like #WhyDiscriminate, Union posted the photos and stories of thirty-five of its students and staff who identify as queer. Further, they invited social media users to share their stories using this hashtag. Union dedicated the project to those who grew up in a church that is not affirming; to those who have been told that who they love or how they as identify is sinful; who were taught that God rejects them; who struggle to fully love themselves—in all of their God-given beauty.[22] This, no doubt, took the American and global seminary communities by surprise.

It seems clear, queer worldmaking is being done—yet this is on the terms dictated by those who self-identify as queer, giving little or no regard to the respectability of conservatism. The sexual reformation we thus perceive, attempts to create a social order that is more loving and just. The *solas* (or creedal statements) here endorses and centers bodies, loves and experiences. It seeks to do away for the heteronormative regime which renders the lives of queer people religiously superfluous.

DEEPENING THE SEXUAL REFORMATION

Given this discussion, there is no doubt that some form of sexual reformation is happening. Recognizing the work of the people—the *leitourgia*, perhaps— the present moment nudges the church and theological academy to deepen this reformation by offering a response. Given the importance of social media in the lives of South Africa's youth, the church and academy must attend to what implications this may have for the integration of faith and sexuality.

21. Collison, "Theology Students Back Queer Rights."
22. Perry, "Queer Faith."

Anita Cloete rightly notes: "The availability of advanced technology is therefore reshaping what it means to be human. . . It could further be argued that technology has its own set of values and is transforming the very nature of being human as it impacts the way we think about ourselves."[23] The church and academy must present the public with sense making tools that not only assist, but also allow for the progress of the sexual reformation already underway.

This suggests the need for the church and theology to grapple most urgently with social media (and the Internet at large). The approach Cloete prefers is that of "mediatization": the recognition that social media is part of our society, affecting all of us—while still maintaining the independence and autonomy of this media.[24] Cloete probes us further: "What embodiment means within a digital culture seems to be one of the most important areas in need of theological reflection."[25] Even so, embodiment transcends mere physicality.

This, then, brings us to embodied theology. I contend that the best response of the church and theology would be one that centers lived experiences. That is, an approach that centers of intersectionality and corporeality. The church and academy are not without help; already within the corpus of theological thought there are aids to assist us.

For decades now, a great body of works have been produced under the varied banners of feminist, body and queer theologies. These paradigms are, in my view, helpful to the present discussion. Feminist and womanist approaches remind us of the importance of intersectionality, and the need for an adequate analysis of power. Body theology makes the audacious claim that one's body is the landscape of faith. Thus, corporeality plays an all-important role in theologizing. Queer theology ferments these outlooks by inviting the religious to consider "queer" as all-embracing, transgressive and boundary-erasing.[26] It should not stop there, though: Althaus-Reid reminds us of to go beyond neat-and-nice theological formulations. Rather, we are required to be *indecent*. Perhaps, then, it would do us well to consider the present sexual reformation as duly "indecent."[27]

Of late, ironically via Instagram, I have become aware of yet another paradigm—that of activist theology. Using their Instagram account, the "Transqueer Latinx" gender non-binary theologian Robyn Henderson-Espinoza

---

23. Cloete, "Living in a Digital Culture," 1.

24. Cloete, "Living in a Digital Culture," 2.

25. Cloete, "Living in a Digital Culture," 6.

26. Cheng, *Radical Love*, 9–10.

27. Althaus-Reid, *Indecent Theology*, 1.

advocates for this new paradigm. Henderson-Espinoza, along with others, launched the Activist Theology Project, which flowed out of their own research. True to its name, the vision of Activist Theology is to be a project that "exists to shift culture and mindset in such a way that we can all hear, feel, and experience the world midwife hope and possibility for a more loving world of radical difference."[28] This, I believe, is yet another invaluable resource theology offers as response to the current sexual reformation.

Discursive Limits, Public Theology, and the Sexual Reformation

Any theology must meet the unique demands of society, church and academy—as conceptualized by David Tracy.[29] Thus, a public theological analysis of this sexual reformation may prove telling. Public theology draws on numerous streams (not least the Social Gospel Movement, and theologians such as Reinhold Niebuhr, Dietrich Bonhoeffer, and Martin Luther King, Jr.). Given these streams of thought, public theology may offer quite a significant contribution to this sexual reformation.

In the contemporary South African public theological imagination, no regard is afforded to issues pertaining to human sexuality. Public theology continues to remain the intellectual home of cis-gender heterosexual men, who determine both its present focus and future. In the recent publication *African Public Theology*, only two women theologians contributed to this work. I argue that this highlights the problem present in the field of public theology. Moreover, we ought to question why women and queer theologians choose not to use public theology as helpful theological framework. Given these discursive limits, this essay attempts to draw from the resources of public theology to analyze the sexual reformation at work within the South African and global societies.

For McIntosh "matters of race, gender and sexual equality are highly significant areas of engagement for public theology."[30] Informed by a public theological paradigm, the sexual reformation may articulate its concern most clearly in the public sphere, when considering itself as making a contribution to both church and academy. Reflecting on the challenges that beset public theological discourse, McIntosh notes: "A constructive methodology for the future of public theology has to begin by looking at who is included in its canon and where it finds its theology."[31] Therefore, the use of a public

28. See the website, https://activisttheology.com/.

29. Tracy, *Analogical Imagination*, 3–5.

30. McIntosh, "I Met God, She's Black," 300.

31. McIntosh, "I Met God, She's Black," 318.

theological paradigm must acknowledge its limits, while still employing it as a critical tool. Even with its problems, the scholarship public theologians offer may be quite helpful to make sense of the present sexual reformation.

Still, this public theological paradigm must be foregrounded in a feminist ethic, as noted by Althaus-Reid and Isherwood who argue:

> One of the many strengths of feminist theologies has always been the ability to include many voices within the debate. . . This is not the same thing at all as having no method and no cohesion, it is, however, about creating space for diverse voices to express what they experience about the divine among and between us. It is about respect and an overwhelming belief that the divine cannot be contained by any one group whoever they may be and however blessed and sanctioned they believe themselves to be.[32]

Centering such a feminist ethic allows those whom the heteronormative public render voiceless an opportunity to give articulation to their lived experiences.

A Theological Response to the Sexual Reformation

Offering a response to the current sexual reformation, these theological approaches are no doubt helpful. But, unlike the Protestant Reformation, this time this reformation is not clerical in leadership—rather, it is people-led. This time, it is *intersectional*, it is *embodied* and it is *indecent*. In "this time," the church is called to respond to a reformation it did not initiate. Formulating a response, I propose a three-pronged approach for the church and the theological academy—a response drawing from various disciplines yet buttressed on public theology.

First, the church would have to attend to normalizing a culture of *accountability*. For much of our ecclesial history, the institute of the church has exercised considerable power, and only in recent decades has this been called out to account. This intersectional reformation will not accommodate the pervasive hetero-patriarchy so endemic in the church. This is most visibly seen in the protest offered by Somizi Mhlongo and the #WhyDiscriminate campaign.

Second, *redress* must be prioritized. The current sexual reformation does not seek a mere seat at the table. Instead, it seeks the redesign of the present table, which bell hooks terms, "imperialist white supremacist

32. Althaus-Reid and Isherwood, *Controversies in Feminist Theology*, 1.

capitalist [hetero-] patriarchy."[33] This call to redress seeks to put an end to the ableism and ageism that prevails within the church and theological academy. Netflix, Google and advances in the legal framework, in this sense, have been pointing us toward redress.

Third, this sexual reformation prioritizes *visibility*. It should no longer be strange for queer persons to attend our churches. Rather, our faith communities ought to be "houses of prayer for all people." This means, more pointedly, churches must admit to ministry those who are queer, without any restrictions; and that the unions of queer couples ought to be recognized. Union Theological Seminary displayed this call to visibility through the campaign #QueerFaith.

This approach—which centers accountability, redress and visibility— attempts to weave together the differing and divergent strands of feminist, body and queer theology. It seeks to account for the form that the sexual reformation is taking in the three publics of society, church and academy. Moreover, it would rightly recognize the important role social media plays in deepening the work of this sexual reformation. I submit, public theology will only be a helpful and relevant analytical tool if and when it accounts for queer people's lived experiences. Failure to do so would render this theological discipline irrelevant and oppressive to queer people.

CONCLUSION

In a nation where 35.7 percent is considered youth, of whom at least eighty percent use social media, research into social media and its theological implications ought to be pursued. Ours is a time of social influencers who, to some degree, exercise tremendous power over the lives of the youth. As such, the zeitgeist calls church and the academy to respond to the signs of the sexual reformation already taking place.

Throughout this essay, I have intentionally argued for a sexual reformation, as opposed to a sexual revolution. The reason, I contend, is that the church and theological academy are best suited to respond to challenges when its own vocabulary is utilized, while still allowing for nuance. Thus, the essay considers reformation to be a theological concept that deserves much more exploration, especially in relation to that which is sexual.

While this reformation is already a reality, it invites us to something more expansive. In eschatological terms, theologians consider this undefined "more" as the "not yet." Perhaps it is at this juncture where theology may assist the church: by providing an intersectional, embodied and

33. Hooks, "Understanding Patriarchy," 4.

indecent praxis; further, by prioritizing the values of accountability, redress and visibility. Doing this, we may indeed deepen the impact of the sexual reformation.

There is no doubt that the Gutenberg Press contributed to the advancement of the Protestant Reformation; in like manner social media does indeed contribute to the current sexual reformation. Then, like now, it was a public affair; therefore, in this time a public theological engagement is required. However, given the discursive limits of public theology, this engagement must draw from the insights of body, feminist and queer theologies.

Earlier I noted that the creedal formula of our sexual reformation is different. The solas of the sixteenth century are simply not helpful in our day. The present creedal agenda is clear: *quod sic corpus, quod sic amor, quod sic experientia*. Yes bodies, yes love, yes experience. This focus on bodiliness, love and human experience—no doubt—gives preference to intersectionality, corporeality and indecency. For the first time the bodies, loves and experiences of queer youths are prioritized via social media. This, then, is the very heart of the current sexual reformation.

BIBLIOGRAPHY

Agang, Sunday B., et al. *African Public Theology*. Bukuru: HippoBooks, 2020.

Althaus-Reid, Marcella. *Indecent Theology: Theological Perversions in Sex, Gender and Politics*. London: Routledge, 2000.

Althaus-Reid, Marcella, and Lisa Isherwood. *Controversies in Feminist Theology*. London: SCM, 2007.

Boyd, Danah M., and Nicole B. Ellison. "Social Network Sites: Definition, History, and Scholarship." *Journal of Computer-Mediated Communication* 13.1 (2007) 210–30.

Cheng, Patrick S. *Radical Love: An Introduction to Queer Theology*. New York: Seabury Books, 2011.

Cloete, Anita L. "Living in a Digital Culture: The Need for Theological Reflection." *HTS Teologiese Studies/Theological Studies* 71.2 (2015) 1–7.

Collison, Carl. "Theology Students Back Queer Rights." *Mail & Guardian*, August 10, 2018. https://mg.co.za/article/2018–08-10–00-theology-students-back-queer-rights/.

Cronje, Frans. *Born Free but Still in Chains: South Africa's First Post-Apartheid Generation*. Johannesburg: Institute for Race Relations, 2015.

Day, Katie, and Sebastian Kim. "Introduction." In *A Companion to Public Theology*, edited by Sebastian Kim and Katie Day, 1–21. Leiden: Brill, 2017.

Fiegerman, Seth. "Netflix adds 9 million paying subscribers, but stock falls." *CNN Business*, January 18, 2019. https://edition.cnn.com/2019/01/17/media/netflix-earnings-q4/index.html.

Gaum, Laurie. "The #WhyDiscriminate movement could be the spark plug for the NG Kerk to reclaim credibility." *Daily Maverick*, August 2, 2018. https://www.

dailymaverick.co.za/opinionista/2018–08-02-the-whydiscriminate-movement-could-be-the-spark-plug-for-the-ng-kerk-to-reclaim-credibility/.

Gillwald, Alison. *The State of ICT in South Africa*. Cape Town: Research ICT Africa, 2018.

Google. "#ThisIsFamily | Google Pride 2018." YouTube video. June 4, 2018. https://www.youtube.com/watch?v=cfIVNX6dqVM&ab_channel=Google.

Helena, Jacobie M. "Waarom sou die Kerk Diskrimineer? Vra Student." *Kerkbode*, March 9, 2018. https://kerkbode.christians.co.za/2018/09/03/waarom-sou-die-kerk-diskrimineer-vra-studente/.

Hooks, Bell. "Understanding Patriarchy." *ImagineNoBorders*, August 9, 2015. https://imaginenoborders.org/pdf/zines/UnderstandingPatriarchy.pdf.

Igual, Roberto. "Congratulations! Somizi ties the knot in spectacular wedding." *Mamba Online*, September 30, 2019. https://www.mambaonline.com/2019/09/30/congratulations-somizi-ties-the-knot-in-spectacular-wedding/.

"Kerksaak: lees volledige uitspraak hier." *Kerkbode*, March 8, 2019. https://kerkbode.christians.co.za/2019/03/08/kerksaak-lees-volledige-uitspraak-hier/.

Kesa, Deepa. "WATCH | Somizi and Mohale's extravagant wedding: Mzansi reacts." *TimesLIVE*, September 20, 2019. https://www.timeslive.co.za/tshisa-live/tshisa-live/2019–09-30-watch-somizi-and-mohales-extravagant-wedding-mzansi-reacts/.

Koopman, Nico. "Public Theology in the Context of Nationalist Ideologies: A South African Example." In *A Companion to Public Theology*, edited by Sebastian Kim and Katie Day, 150–163. Leiden: Brill, 2017.

McIntosh, Esther. "I Met God, She's Black." In *A Companion to Public Theology*, edited by Sebastian Kim and Katie Day, 298–324. Leiden: Brill, 2017.

Middlebrook, Hayley. "New Ruling Prevents Caster Semenya From Defending 800-Meter World Championship Title." *Runner's World*, July 30, 2019. https://www.runnersworld.com/news/a28556020/caster-semenya-ruling-world-championships/.

Miller, Daniel, et al. *How the World Changed Social Media*. London: UCL Press, 2016.

Mitchley, Alex. "High Court scraps Dutch Reformed Church decision against same-sex marriages." *news24*, March 8, 2019. https://www.news24.com/news24/SouthAfrica/News/high-court-scraps-dutch-reformed-church-decision-against-same-sex-marriages-20190308.

Nakayama, Thomas K., and Charles E. Morris, III. "Worldmaking and Everyday Interventions." *QED: A Journal in GLBTQ Worldmaking* 2.1 (2015) v–viii.

Nemakonde, Vhahangwele. "Somizi storms out of Grace Bible Church over homosexuality remarks." *Citizen*, January 22, 2017. https://citizen.co.za/lifestyle/1404845/somizi-storms-out-of-grace-bible-church-over-homosexuality-remarks/.

Nwadeyi, Lovelyn. "Born Frees and Democracy—Freedom and Responsibility." *L&N Advisors*, 2018. https://www.lovelynnwadeyi.com/post/born-frees-and-democracy-freedom-and-responsibility.

Perry, Benjamin, ed. "Queer Faith." *Union*, March 12, 2019. https://utsnyc.edu/queer-faith/.

Seleka, Ntwaagae. "Same-sex marriages protected as Ramaphosa passes the Civil Union Amendment Bill into law." *news24*, October 23, 2020. https://www.news24.com/

news24/SouthAfrica/News/ramaphosa-passes-the-civil-union-amendment-bill-into-law-20201023.

Terblanche, Elmarie, et al. "Retracted Article: Age- and Education-Related Effects on Cognitive Functioning in Colored South African Women." *Aging, Neuropsychology, and Cognition* 27.3 (2019) 321–37.

Tracy, David. *The Analogical Imagination: Christian Theology and the Culture of Pluralism.* New York: Crossroad, 1981.

"The Ugly Truth about Tinder and Online Dating in South Africa." *BusinessTech,* October 22, 2017. https://businesstech.co.za/news/mobile/205888/the-ugly-truth-about-tinder-and-online-dating-in-south-africa/.

Van der Walt, Charlene. "LGBTIQA+ is 'n happy sambreel." *Kerkbode,* October 23, 2018. https://kerkbode.christians.co.za/2018/10/23/lgbtiqa-is-n-happy-sambreel/.

"A Glimpse at South Africa's Social Media Landscape in 2018." *VetroMedia,* January 31, 2018. https://vetro.mu/south-africas-social-media-landscape/.

wa Azania, Malaika. *Memoirs of a Born Free: Reflections on the Rainbow Nation by a Member of the Post-Apartheid Generation.* New York: Seven Stories, 2018.

13

A Practical-Theological Consideration of Infertility[1]

Natalia Strydom

INTRODUCTION

In the denomination where I hold office (the Dutch Reformed Church), congregation members do not speak openly about infertility. It is rather a silent matter, and a silent struggle for those involved. Quite often the minister is not even informed about the struggle of infertility or, when it is known to him or her, they are not fully equipped to counsel and assist the couple.

A practical-theological consideration of infertility—such as the one offered in this essay—benefits greatly from the perspectives of contextual theology. One of the claims that contextual theology makes is that it is an epistemological break from traditional theologies. David Bosch argues that one of the features of contextual theologies is that theology (spirituality) can only be practiced *with* persons who hurt. Furthermore, Bosch places an

1. This essay is based on my unpublished thesis, titled "Infertility a Female Problem?: Engaging with Narrative theory and Biblical Narratives in Pastoral Care for Infertile Couples," completed in 2019 at the University of Stellenbosch as partial fulfillment of the requirements for the Masters of Theology (Practical Theology).

emphasis on *doing* theology, since performance is more far-reaching than just "knowing or speaking."[2] It dares us to move from "*being* right to *doing* right."[3] When academics, ministers and pastoral counselors contribute to the understanding of the crisis of infertility, they become doers—contributors—in the process of healing.

As noted by Gravett and Müller, "(m)eaningful healing resists the pursuit of only individual and personal healing and rather recognizes the interlocking of social, political and religious forces and the challenge to bring healing to people's lives on multiple levels."[4] Healing cannot only be an individual endeavor of the couple involved, because this will simply perpetuate the cycle of stigmatized comments, and unwanted questions and accusations which is present in the range of social networks in which they find themselves. It requires a range of spaces in which healing can take place—also in the context of the church.

In this essay I proceed with a practical-theological consideration of infertility in two parts. First, I offer a brief overview of the complexity of the matter of infertility and the emotional crisis that it causes for (heterosexual) couples. Second, I provide practical considerations for three church settings in view of such experiences for couples: the pulpit; the counseling office; and the broader life of the congregation.

INFERTILITY AND STIGMATIZATION

According to the World Health Organization (WHO), one in four heterosexual couples in developing countries are affected by infertility.[5] Research by the WHO shows that infertility and sub-category fertility leaves a large number of people in distress. An individual is classified as "infertile" when they are trying to have children, without success, and have consequently consulted with a medical practitioner concerning their procreative abilities. The WHO (according to the WHO-ICMART revised glossary)[6] defines infertility as "a disease of the reproductive system defined by the failure to achieve a clinical pregnancy after 12 months or more of regular unprotected sexual intercourse."[7]

2. Bosch, *Transforming Mission*, 424.

3. Kotzé and Kotzé, *Telling Narratives*, 7.

4. Gravett and Müller, "Poetic Song of Hester," 2.

5. See "Fertility and Infertility."

6. ICMART refers to the International Committee for Monitoring Assisted Reproductive Technologies.

7. See "Revised Glossary."

This organization has calculated that more than 10% of women suffer from infertility—"women who have tried unsuccessfully and have remained in a stable relationship for five years or more." According to the WHO, the burden in men is unknown. The WHO categorizes infertility as a health problem, and they state further that infertility, especially in women, is categorized as the fifth uppermost "global disability."[8] Other published research findings indicate that infertility affects both male and female on an equal level (and at much higher levels than indicated by the WHO): 35% of men, and 35% of women.[9] In my opinion, the WHO fails to reckon with male infertility as a cause to primary or secondary infertility.

Infertility can lead to stigmatization. Although perhaps not obvious to everyone, those who have struggled with infertility can attest to this:

> When people interpret infertility and consequently ostracize people and treat them differently or do not create a welcoming space for people with this problem, it leads to a social problem with far-reaching effects.[10]

Perhaps unfairly, it is women who are the most stigmatized because of infertility, but it is also a serious problem for men.[11] Moreover, in my own research, I have found that the studies of infertility have unfairly focused more on women than on men when considering the crisis of infertility of the couple.

Moss and Baden suggest that infertility should not only be studied from a medical perspective but also from a cultural, religious, biological and gender viewpoint.[12] Infertility as a subject is generally approached from a female perspective. There are, however, a few researchers that acknowledge that the reality presents itself that male infertility problems are just as likely to contribute or influence the infertility of the couple.[13] Subsequently, I argue that both men and women can experience health, social, economic and spiritual problems as a result of infertility.

8. See "Fertility and Infertility."

9. Culley et al., "Where are all the Men?"; Daniluk and Webb, "End of the Line," 6.

10. Strydom, "Infertility a Female Problem?," 14.

11. Vähäkangas, *Christian Couples*, 1.

12. Moss and Baden, *Reconceiving Infertility*, 4.

13. Culley et al., "Where are all the Men?"; Skakkebæk et al., "Pathogenesis."

INFERTILITY—AN INVISIBLE, GENDERED DISABILITY?

To say that infertility is a disability—as is done by the WHO—is a loaded statement. It signifies a physical inability, namely, to conceive babies. However, as noted by Moss and Baden, "this inability, and the lived experience that stems from it, is less easily defined than it might initially appear."[14] It is saddening that the real stories of infertility is often overseen not only in family circles, but also in faith communities and in society as a whole.

Supposing that we argue that infertility is a disability, Moss and Baden warns that we should be cautious that it is an "invisible disability."[15] A further note of caution relates to the naming itself: by labelling infertility as a disability, the already existing range of reasons—including social, economic and religious reasons—that only half of suffering infertile individuals have sought medical or counseling services, is likely further aggravated. If infertility is viewed as a disability, it asks of us to consider the cultural ideas and investigate the social context from which we make these diagnoses that we use to understand the physical, cognitive and emotional differences that exist between humans—and how we "story" them in different ways.

A prominent notion with which women are continuously confronted, is that all women are maternal, and have the need to bear children. When unable to produce offspring, especially in a society where higher value is placed on fertility and child-rearing, the social alienation may increase even more. The assumptions made about childless women (Dykstra and Hagestad adds "men") is that it was by choice and they are often labelled as selfish, bitter, "*un*-maternal," career-driven, pleasure-seeking, self-indulgent, and lacking a sense of responsibility.[16]

Childless women are labelled far more than men in our society.[17] Most commonly, the same labels are not given to men who are childless. It is often assumed that it is due to the career-driven wife's choice that the "poor man" is left childless, or when infertility is suspected, it would be accepted that the wife is the infertile one.[18] Dykstra and Hagestad remarks that childless couples are perceived as problem cases or deviations from the norm—not only by the social community, but also throughout the academic research field.[19]

14. Moss and Baden, *Reconceiving Infertility*, 2.

15. Moss and Baden, *Reconceiving Infertility*, 2.

16. Dykstra and Hagestad, "Roads Less Taken," 1284.

17. Dykstra and Hagestad, "Roads Less Taken," 1278; Moss and Baden, *Reconceiving Infertility*, 6.

18. Moss and Baden, *Reconceiving Infertility*, 8.

19. Dykstra and Hagestad, "Roads Less Taken," 1284.

Cooper-Hilbert remarks that applying a gender lens when considering specifically infertility as an issue, it is clear that gender does indeed place a magnifying glass on the "pain and confusion" of both of the partners.[20] In my own research I found that, although infertility can be a shared experience between both partners, and where both male factor and female factor infertility is evident, it is not to say that infertility can be treated like most other illnesses where gender is irrelevant: in this case, the experience for each partner is different due to the quintessence of maleness and femaleness.[21]

It seems that both historically and in modern times, male infertility specifically has often been a taboo subject. Researchers such as Culley et al. remarks that this might be due to the fact that infertility is seen to be "operationalized" in female bodies. Although men also have the desire to be a parent and carry the concern or experiences of the crisis of infertility, they are often left out of the picture. Their concerns are silenced and stigmatized.[22]

Since experiencing firsthand both male and female factor infertility in our own journey as a couple, I became more empathic about the silence of men in their sharing of the infertility crisis. Both partners in a couple suffer, although they may express it in different ways.

When counseling a couple, there are two conversation partners: the husband and the wife. It is possible that either male infertility or female infertility—or both—might be the cause of their struggle to fall pregnant. However, the largest amount of research papers focused on infertility point to studies which solely focus on women's experience of the infertility crisis, and much more guidance is given on the coping tactics advocated for women. This is in stark contrast to the few studies focusing exclusively on both genders. Consequently, I agree with Culley et al: "What interests me is that recent studies with more sophisticated proposals show that men show equal amounts of distress."[23] Given that "(t)he crisis of infertility is a heavily psychological crisis where social support is often needed," it is worrisome that there is such an absence of support structures and resources for couples on this painful journey.[24]

20. Cooper-Hilbert, *Infertility and Involuntary Childlessness*, 64.

21. Cooper-Hilbert, *Infertility and Involuntary Childlessness*, 65; Webb and Daniluk, "End of the Line," 9.

22. Culley et al., "Where are all the Men?," 226.

23. Culley et al., "Where are all the Men?," 227.

24. Vähäkangas, *Christian Couples*, 14.

INFERTILITY IS AN EMOTIONAL CRISIS

Berger et al. remarks that infertility is an experience where you are faced with "struggle, loss, failure, stressors, painful experiences and an emotional roller coaster."[25] It is a multi-complex crisis with many different feelings, that I can attest to personally. Infertility also entails a relational dimension as it confronts and disturbs on an individual as well as communal level of the couple.[26] The infertility struggle can affect the marital dynamics when communication tools are lacking. This could further have an impact on the intimacy levels of the couple. The experience of powerlessness affects the couple on many different levels of their livelihood.[27]

In the midst of this extreme crisis, medical experts (e.g., doctors and infertility specialists) first meet the couple:

> Most couples visit these professionals with high expectations that the statistics will not include them and that this is only a minor setback in the achievement of the pregnancy and "hoped-for" child or children.[28]

It is often assumed that all couples should procreate and generate offspring. Therefore, a deep emotional response such as a deep sense of loss is quite probable.[29] The couple is essentially grieving about something they never had. Vergin elaborates on this very specific experience of grief as experienced by an infertile couple: "The couple who are not able to have a child, or to have as many children as they want are a couple who have suffered a loss."[30] This is further intensified by being an "intangible" loss.[31]

The psychologist, pastoral counselor and perhaps family members are most likely to be included after a medical diagnosis. By then the couple has been confronted on different levels and to extreme extents of the crisis of infertility. Only on this level they might begin to consider getting help and seeking some form of intervention to cope with this crisis:

> It is typically at this point that the minister or pastoral counselor will become part of the journey. Many couples would have journeyed in silence about their infertility struggle without

25. Berger et al., "Women's Experience of Infertility," 60.

26. Berger et al., "Women's Experience of Infertility," 60–61.

27. Gieselor-Devor, "Pastoral Care," 355.

28. Strydom, "Infertility a Female Problem?," 112.

29. Atwood and Dobkin, "Storm Clouds," 389.

30. Vergin, *Infertility*, 100.

31. Gieseler-Devor, "Pastoral Care," 356.

necessarily including the pastor/minister or counselor from the beginning.[32]

However, the pastor/minister is better equipped for such a role than he/she may think: "(p)erhaps more than any other professional, the minister has extensive and extended personal contact with persons who have suffered significant losses. The gradual resolution of infertility is a grief process."[33]

At the same time, it must be noted that it is of importance for the pastoral care counselor to be informed about the specific emotional turmoil that the crisis of infertility presents. Menning—who laid the foundation on the theory of grief in the infertility process—illustrates the resemblances with the grief process that Kübler-Ross (1969) laid down.[34] Counselors have a role to communicate with couples in such a way that they are educated about their feelings, since it is only through understanding that meaningful progress can be made. The safe space that is created in a counseling environment is one where they do not need to be cautious of judgement. Keylor and Apfel especially highlight this notion as a prerequisite for men to be able to verbally express their emotions.[35]

Atwood and Dobkin distinguish three phases of the infertility crisis: first (and at the most obvious level), the physical toll of infertility; second, the emotional response, and third, resolution. The second phase, response, is mostly negative and begins to surface in the form of experiences such as "isolation, alienation, guilt, low self-esteem, grief and depression."[36] Keylor and Apfel add feelings of hopelessness and helplessness to this list, and note that it often further numbs the couple.[37] Daniluk and Webb list the emotions of denial, devastation, shock, numbness, anger, disbelief and depression,[38] and Atwood and Dobkin are of the opinion that the primary emotions for both genders are shame, feelings of deviance, and fear of labelling as a failure.[39] In their research, Watkins and Baldo found that the following emotions also surface: "inadequacy, anxiety, stress, fear of spousal rejection, devastation, rage, loss of control, feeling cheated, frustration, moodiness,

---

32. Strydom, "Infertility a Female Problem?," 112.

33. Vergin, *Infertility*, 100.

34. Clarke et al., "Continuity and Discontinuity," 103.

35. Keylor and Apfel, "Male Infertility," 71.

36. Atwood and Dobkin, "Storm Clouds," 388–94.

37. Keylor and Apfel, "Male Infertility," 69.

38. Daniluk and Webb, "End of the Line," 13.

39. Atwood and Dobkin, "Storm Clouds," 389.

fatigue, disappointment and loneliness."[40] Such a tremendous emotional crisis is all the more amplified by the reality that the infertile couple often suffer in silence, with the counselor as the sole creator of a listening space.

In the second phase, the couple and the counselor venture to begin to make meaning out of the crisis through utilizing the narrative tool of deconstruction. The social idea that the only form of parenthood is through biological reproduction is investigated. Deconstruction further entails "the construction of a new identity consonant with the infertility information which for many is psychologically the most difficult and stressful undertaking of the grieving process."[41] The counselor fulfills a crucial role during this challenging phase. He/she helps the couple to deconstruct social ideas by asking and prompting questions that may help the individuals to move forward in their journey.

There is no particular time frame allocated to dealing with the crisis of infertility and the resolution thereof, and the counselor should be cautious not to rush the process. It may also be that the couple get "stuck" in a specific phase. It is also possible that the couple may decide that they cannot live as a couple with this diagnosis of infertility, and subsequently decide to separate. On the other hand, if the couple make the decision not to separate, they will experience a fresh sense of empowerment in due course.[42]

INFERTILITY IS A COUPLE'S CRISIS

Wischmann and Thorn argue that both partners are confronted with variable degrees of "loss-orientation and restoration-orientation styles of coping." However, it would seem that often one person in the couple (woman) is grieving the loss, while at the same time, the other (man) needs to rewrite the reproductive story in order to restore meaning and hope for the future.[43] O'Donell notes that although infertility is a couple's problem, the problem of infertility treatment is experienced in the roles of "observer and participant."[44] Since each one is confronted with their own unique emotions it often leads to confusion as to how to support the spouse.[45]

---

40. Watkins and Baldo, "Infertility Experience," 397.

41. Atwood and Dobkin, "Storm Clouds," 393–94.

42. Atwood and Dobkin, "Storm Clouds," 394.

43. Wischmann and Thorn, "(Male) Infertility," 237.

44. O'Donnell, "Making Room," 29.

45. Cooper-Hilbert, *Infertility and Involuntary Childlessness*, 65.

Cooper-Hilbert says more research is needed to establish whether men and women grieve in a comparable way or whether great differences can be seen in their suffering. He adds, however, that

> the research also needs to neutralize gender bias by targeting both men's and women's issues more equitably and to explain differences in reactions with the context of differences in how the genders respond, rather than attributing reactions necessarily to differences in feelings.[46]

Of importance in considering that infertility affects both partners, irrespective of who is biologically at fault, is Anderson's viewpoint that "the reality of loss is not gender-specific."[47] Both partners suffer loss—even if the significance of the loss may be different and may vary from one person to another due to the value attributed to the loss. It is a mistake to think that men do not suffer the loss symbolized by infertility. Therefore, the critical departure point in pastoral narrative counseling is the acknowledgement that the man, just as much as the woman, dreamt about being a parent. As Neuger remarks, "(w)hen men become aware that their dreams will not be realized, they experience intrapsychic or internal loss that is difficult to mourn because, in order to talk about the loss, they have to talk about the dream."[48] As a pastoral counselor the task is to listen and assist the couple in verbalizing the loss. However, Anderson warns, "(i)t is fruitless for caregivers to strive to make men grieve like women."[49] Every individual should be invited and given the liberty to grieve in a way that resembles them.

This particular awareness is highlighted by Petok as he addresses the gender role conflict when in counseling. According to Petok, "there is evidence that men with higher gender role conflict have greater negative attitudes toward counseling services and are less likely to seek those services."[50] Cholette goes even further to say that "recognition, respect and acknowledgement of grief as a valid response of a bereaved father, is an intricate part of caring and lays the central foundation in establishing a therapeutic-healing relationship with the father and his family."[51]

Atwood and Dobkin summarizes the goal of counseling of couples facing the crisis of infertility as follows: ". . . to help couples, separately and as a

---

46. Cooper-Hilbert, *Infertility and Involuntary Childlessness*, 67.

47. Anderson, "Men and Grief," 222.

48. Neuger, *Care of Men*, 220.

49. Anderson, "Men and Grief," 222.

50. Petok, "Infertility Counseling," 263.

51. Cholette, "Through the Eyes of a Father," 36.

couple, deconstruct the fertility crisis, to move to the acceptance stage, and then, through *languaging* with the couple, to help them to construct a new reality around their marriage and children."[52] When the couple approaches the counselor it is primarily out of the need for coping with the crisis, therefore at this point they have already constructed an idea regarding the problem of infertility. Therefore, the task of the counselor is to begin unpacking their problem-story in such a way that deconstruction can take place.

INFERTILITY COUNSELING FROM A PASTORAL NARRATIVE COUPLE'S APPROACH

Neuger provides a helpful "toolkit" for a counselor to assist the couple to regain the power over their life-story. According to her, these five tools—the five Rs—are vital processes in feminist-oriented pastoral counseling. These are also theologically encouraged as they seek to help build authenticity and power for counselees and "for a culture struggling to resist patriarchal and *kyriarchal* forces that destroy its members."[53]

What follows is a list and explanation of how the Rs can be engaged within the counseling journey.[54]

The first R is "remembering." The couple is invited to remember a time when there was not the experience of powerlessness or the crisis of infertility. Thereby the couple begin to explore the tools or characteristics they already possess to help them cope and move forward. This is necessary, considering that often the problem or crisis blocks their memory.

The second tool is "reframing." This provides the opportunity for the couple to explore the factual and truthful elements of their story, but then goes further to venture toward new perspectives. In this manner the couple can start to make meaning of the content of this story. The task of the counselor is to assist the couple in providing fresh viewpoints on the problem or crisis that they are facing, and to establish new meaning rather than being "stuck."

Third is "reversing," with the aim of leading the couple to better clarity. By means of a feminist lens, Neuger "reverses the great reversals of patriarchy" to assist the counselor and the couple to acknowledge the role of patriarchal standards especially for women. A reversal of patriarchal standards will represent a great truth for women's lives. Yet at the same time, it should

---

52. Atwood and Dobkin, "Storm Clouds," 397.

53. Neuger, *Counseling Women*, 142.

54. Neuger, *Counseling Women*, 143–47.

be acknowledged that the patriarchal value of masculinity causes both men and women much pain.

"Re-imagine" is a tool used by the narrative counselor to help the couple dream up or imagine a new preferred reality in which they can see and utilize new choices. Neuger elaborates that "the integrative power of imagination allows new narrative possibilities to emerge that come out of authentic self-experience and yet takes the various contextual realities of the woman's life into consideration."[55]

The fifth tool is "re-story," to discover stories that have been hidden or not yet discovered. Some stories included in the infertility crisis experience of the couple may be so prominent as a problem story that the couple cannot see the other possibilities to the story as well. By utilizing language, a new reality can be created and built to bring about change; "(i)t is through *languaging* in therapy that persons define and experience reality."[56]

During the counseling process the role is not only primarily that of listening, but rather listening in such a way that skills are unlocked: skills such as metaphors, deconstruction, imagination, externalization, and so forth. Not only will this minimize the extent of the crisis, but it will also empower the couple to create a new preferred story.[57] Although the couple has not acquired the birth of a biological child, for which they had wished for, the counselor can guide them to at least make meaning of this crisis in their lives and how they can move forward toward the future. Thereby "the narrative regains a sense of continuity and meaning, which can be communicated to the self and to others in ways that lead to a more abundant and faithful life."[58] The process enables the couple to reach a point of sense in their self-narratives, which prior to the counseling process had no sense of meaning at all.[59]

Vergin profoundly describes the point of conclusion of the counseling journey for the couple with the following acknowledgement: "One's awareness of infertility never really disappears, but eventually it can and must be accepted and lived with. This can be called the experience of surrender."[60]

---

55. Neuger, *Counseling Women*, 142.

56. Atwood and Dobkin, "Storm Clouds," 396.

57. Atwood and Dobkin, "Storm Clouds," 396–402.

58. Neuger, *Counseling Women*, 147.

59. Atwood and Dobkin, "Storm Clouds," 395.

60. Vergin, *Infertility*, 108.

WHAT CAN CLERGY AND MINISTERS LEARN FROM THIS?

"Just as Eli the priest did not understand Hannah's plea for a child, church and ministry leaders often miss the cry from women and couples in their congregations."[61] Feske goes on to say that the couple who are struggling with the crisis of infertility, the trauma of a miscarriage (or multiple miscarriages), and/or who are on the unsure road of adopting can be further hurt and traumatized when they get "disillusioned with their places of worship, thinking they can receive help."[62] Feske lists three concerns or warnings to the local church community: one, the isolation and loneliness felt by these individuals in family-centered churches; two, the need for both individual and institutional recognition of their pain and grief; and three, the ability of congregants and religious professionals to offer informed and sensitive forms of comfort and support which speak to the particularities of these losses.[63]

Ministers, pastors and counselors can create a safety net for these couples by being informed about infertility and the different experiences that accompany this emotional crisis, as detailed above. Lawson's clarification of what the main goal of counseling the infertile couple is, can serve as foundation: "The goal of counseling infertile couples is not to have a child, but to resolve the crisis of infertility."[64]

PRACTICAL CONSIDERATIONS: ON THE PULPIT, IN THE COUNSELING OFFICE, AND IN THE LIFE OF THE CONGREGATION

In this second part I offer practical advice—in view of the emotional crisis experienced by couples who live with infertility—in three church settings: during congregational services from the pulpit, in pastoral situations in the counseling office, and in the broader life of the congregation as a whole.[65]

---

61. Feske, "Rachel's Lament," 6.

62. Feske, "Rachel's Lament," 6.

63. Feske, "Rachel's Lament," 6.

64. Lawson, "Biblical Model," 12.

65. This section is based on the conclusion of my thesis (Strydom, "Infertility a Female Problem?," 131–37).

The Pulpit as an Opportunity

Churches often have a strong focus on *family ministry*. However, the danger is that parenthood is, to a great extent, elevated in society and in church. As important as families are, the couple unable to conceive should never feel that they are cursed due to their childlessness. Moreover, there may be couples or individuals in the congregation that choose not to have children. Feske raises an important question: "As a place of worship, what is your definition of family? For those who are involuntarily childless, this emphasis can produce a profound sense of isolation, loneliness, and inadequacy."[66]

As a church community we lack *meaningful rituals* that couples who are facing miscarriages and infertility can utilize to symbolize their loss. Rituals for miscarriage are more evident, such as planting of a tree or letting go of balloons on the remembrance day of the loss. However, it appears as if symbolisms or rituals to help a couple demonstrate the loss of what Layne calls a "would-have-been-child," is lacking.[67]

Churches are in the "relationship business"—*relationships* are the DNA of the church. To put it differently and in the words of a familiar African saying, "a person is a person through other persons (*umuntu ngumuntu ngabantu*)." As noted by Sweet, "God even exists in relationship. By yourself you are nothing: in relationship you are everything."[68] Couples struggling with the crisis of infertility need people in whom they can find solace. As noted by Neuger, the infertile couple, just as much as any other persons, seek acceptance, honesty, and understanding.[69]

Ministers or pastors should have a greater sensitivity for special celebrations such as Mother's Day, Father's Day, or even baptism occasions. These are often occasions on which couples who struggle with the crisis of infertility stay away, as these are painful reminders of their loss. One option is to create *liturgical moments* on both Mother's Day and Father's Day for prayer for couples who are struggling to conceive, couples who miscarried, or couples who lost a child during the past year. The church bulletin can also be utilized to communicate such acknowledgment and to make the infertile couple part of the church family.

66. Feske, "Rachel's Lament," 8.

67. Layne, "Breaking the Silence," 309.

68. Sweet, *So Beautiful*, 150.

69. Neuger, *Care of Men*, 223.

In the Counseling Office

Some ministers invest a lot of time and energy into *premarital programmes* in the congregation. Baloyi argues that this is a valuable opportunity to build awareness around realistic expectations of marriage: "(i)t is vital for the couple to know that marriage is not only joyful, but that sorrows are also a part of life and that they need to be ready to deal with those challenging situations."[70] Marriage preparation courses offer the opportunity to lay the foundation of the probability of infertility. It would do well to spend time discussing the topic in an open dialogue when considering the expectations of marriage.

When discussing the possibilities of parenthood, *fatherhood* could also be framed in terms of "social fatherhood"—a way in which the stigma of infertility could possibly subside.[71] If a couple might decide to adopt, or in the case of male infertility the wife may receive a semen sample from a donor, how are especially men guided to address the intersection of masculinity, stigma, and fatherhood?[72] The task of the counselor is to establish the perception of what fatherhood is and guide towards an understanding of social fatherhood. Gravett and Müller build on the foundations of African feminist theology of Mercy Amba Oduyoye who says that we are in desperate need of a theology of procreation that speaks to both those who reproduce and those who do not. Such a theology assists the counselor and minister toward creating respect in the community for the couple struggling with infertility, and toward prevention of further stigmatization of shame or blame.[73]

In the advancement of *medical technology* there is much illiteracy. Ethical questions are often raised not only by the couple but also towards the couple who might begin to consider these medical alternatives or interventions, such as artificial insemination (AI). By encouraging various images of God "and of what it means to be truly human, male and female, in order to decenter the privileging of biological parenting and patriarchal anthropology," we might begin to encourage congregation and community members to think differently about issues such as infertility.[74]

The theological and pastoral task of the minister and pastoral counselor is to guide couples towards *meaning*. We are not able to create meaning on their behalf or to transmit it to them, but they can be guided toward

---

70. Baloyi, "Gendered Character of Barrenness," 4.

71. Hanna and Gough, "Experiencing Male Infertility," 6.

72. Hanna and Gough, "Experiencing Male Infertility," 6.

73. Gravett and Müller, "Poetic Song of Hester," 2.

74. Feske, "Rachel's Lament," 13.

recognizing that there is more than just the crisis at hand. Louw highlights the importance of *promissiotherapy* as a tool for pastoral counselors and ministers. This entails reminding the couple of the promises of God's faithfulness, toward a better understanding of the presence of God and stimulation of hope.[75]

Louw also suggests that couples are encouraged to investigate the use of *lament* as a medium of communication.[76] Lamentation plays a very important role in the Old Testament. It allows people (either as individuals or collectively) to step into conversation with God and to speak to God: "(t)he pain, suffering, unrest, despair and anguish" can be lamented before God.[77] The narrative counseling space is one in which the client is the expert, and where he/she is not prohibited from sharing their experience. This provides a couple or an individual with a safe space where they will not be judged.

Finally, counseling should be approached in such a way that both individuals have the opportunity to *share their stories and experiences*. A space is opened where the client is the expert. The freedom that arises from such an invitation, where there are no scripts, allows men to benefit just as much as women. Men should be allowed to be vulnerable.[78]

A Congregational Approach to Multiple Crises, Such as Infertility

One of the simplest ways in which lay people or congregation members can be of assistance and support to the infertile couple, is by *asking how they are doing* in the infertility crisis. As Feske notes, with any other illness one would be interested in how they are doing. Practical suggestions like cooking a meal for the couple who may have had numerous surgeries, doctor appointments and blood draws, could alleviate some of the physical toll they are experiencing.[79] It is important to bear in mind that for these couples socializing could be problematic, because they do not necessarily fit in with the just-married or married-with-children couples. One of the biggest warnings that Feske highlights is that leaders should encourage congregation members not to give advice to these couples, but to have empathy.[80]

---

75. Louw, *Cura Vitae*, 236.

76. Louw, *Cura Vitae*, 261.

77. Louw, *Cura Vitae*, 261.

78. Neuger, *Care of Men*, 226.

79. Feske, "Rachel's Lament," 7.

80. Feske, "Rachel's Lament," 7.

A big gap in congregations—and specifically also in the Dutch Reformed Church—is the lack of *pregnancy loss support groups*.[81] Although one congregation might not have enough couples struggling with infertility to sustain such a group, neighboring congregations could gather as a group at one facility. The purpose of such a support group for the couple struggling with infertility is "to increase their feelings of control over their lives."[82] Furthermore, these groups can be a safe space to communicate concerns and emotions, and to do so in a confidential, nonjudgmental setting.[83] Support groups can be a prominent space where stigmas are broken and deconstructed. Such a group can become a transformative and healing environment for the couple.

Feske highlights that in popular culture we have not accepted cultural scripts for responding to losses—like infertility and miscarriage. People do not buy you a greeting card if one of these losses has occurred.[84] This is due (at least in part) to the fact that no-one can "see" the loss. It is not that there is not sympathy from family members or friends, but rather that there is an *absence of cultural scripts* for how to behave in such painful circumstances.[85] However, this is an ideal opportunity for the counselor or minister to pay a courtesy visit, or to write a personal letter of sympathy to the couple.

A couple may wish to *challenge the dominant discourses regarding fertility and pregnancy*, amidst their emotional crisis of infertility. It has become customary for couples to make a public and social announcement when they fall pregnant—especially on social media. It may be that a couple chooses to use these platforms to make their struggle with infertility public, and by using similar language and styling as is typically used for pregnancy announcements.[86]

CONCLUSION

In this essay I have tried to not only inform on the topic of infertility, but also to evoke empathy for the couple faced with infertility from a practical

81. Layne, "Breaking the Silence," 297; Lawson, "Biblical Model," 18.

82. Lawson, "Biblical Model," 13.

83. Lawson, "Biblical Model," 14.

84. Feske, "Rachel's Lament," 7.

85. Layne, "Breaking the Silence," 292.

86. An example is that of Whitney and Spencer Blake, a couple from Nampa, Idaho, who journeyed with infertility. They decided to document their journey of numerous unsuccessful IVF treatments with humorous photos and to break the stigma of infertility. They did this by sharing "infertility announcements" on their blog in 2016. Examples include "No Bun in the Oven" and "She's Gonna Pop".

theological perspective. As illustrated in the first part of the essay, the emotional crisis of infertility is incredibly complex, and there is lack of training for ministers, pastors and even pastoral counselors on this crisis that continues to affect more and more congregants. As described in part two by way of practical examples, it is by being informed and by creating awareness from the pulpit, in the counseling office, and in the life of the congregation, that there can be a movement toward assisting couples in this journey in a manner which is helpful, hopeful and filled with grace.

BIBLIOGRAPHY

Anderson, H. "Men and Grief: The Hidden Sea of Tears Without Outlet." In *The Care of Men,* edited by C. C. Neuger and J. N. Poling, 203–26. Nashville: Abingdon, 1997.

Atwood, J. D., and Steven Dobkin. "Storm Clouds are Coming: Ways to Help Couples Reconstruct the Crisis of Infertility." *Contemporary Family Therapy* 14.5 (1992) 385–403.

Baloyi, M. E. "Gendered Character of Barrenness in an African Context: An African Pastoral Study." *In die Skriflig/In Luce Verbi* 51.1 (2017) 1–7.

Berger, R., et al. "Women's Experience of Infertility: A Multi-Systemic Perspective." *Journal of International Women's Studies* 14.1 (2013) 54–68.

Blake, Whitney. "Infertility Announcement #1: No Bun in the Oven." *Spencer and Whitney,* April 25, 2016. http://spencerandwhitneyadoption.blogspot.com/2016/04/.

———. "Infertility Announcement #5: She's Gonna Pop." *Spencer and Whitney,* April 30, 2016.. http://spencerandwhitneyadoption.blogspot.com/2016/04/.

Bosch, David J. *Transforming Mission: Paradigm Shifts in Theology of Mission.* Maryknoll: Orbis, 2011.

Cholette, M. E. "Through the Eyes of a Father: A Perinatal Loss." *International Journal of Childbirth Education* 27.2 (2012) 33–38.

Clarke, L. H., et al. "The Continuity and Discontinuity of the Embodied Self in Infertility." *Canadian Review of Sociology/Revue canadienne de sociologie* 43.1 (2006) 95–113.

Cooper-Hilbert, B. *Infertility and Involuntary Childlessness: Helping Couples Cope.* New York: W. W. Norton and Co., 1998.

Culley, L., et al. "Where are all the Men?: The Marginalization of Men in Social Scientific Research on Infertility." *Reproductive Biomedicine Online* 27.3 (2013) 225–35.

Daniluk, J., and R. Webb. "The End of the Line: Infertile Men's Experiences of Being Unable to Produce a Child." *Men and Masculinities* 2 (1999) 6–25.

Dykstra, P. A., and G. O. Hagestad. "Roads Less Taken: Developing a Nuanced View of Older Adults without Children." *Journal of Family Issues* 28.10 (2007) 1275–1310.

"Fertility and Infertility: Assisting Couples." *World Health Organization.* https://www.who.int/reproductivehealth/topics/infertility/en/.

Feske, Millicent C. "Rachel's Lament: The Impact of Infertility and Pregnancy Loss upon the Religious Faith of Ordinary Christians." *Journal of Pastoral Theology* 22.1 (2012) 3–17.

Gieseler-Devor, N. "Pastoral Care for Infertile Couples." *Journal of Pastoral Care* 48.4 (1994) 355–60.

Gravett, I., and J. C. Müller. "Poetic Song of Hester. Secondary Infertility: Losing Infants, Inheriting a Child." *HTS Teologiese Studies/Theological Studies* 66.2 (2010) 1–5.

Hanna, E., and B. Gough. "Experiencing Male Infertility: A Review of the Qualitative Research Literature." *Sage Open* 5.4 (2015) 1–9.

Keylor, R., and R. Apfel. "Male Infertility: Integrating an Old Psychoanalytic Story with the Research Literature." *Studies in Gender and Sexuality* 11.2 (2010) 60–77.

Kotzé, E., and D. Kotzé. *Telling Narratives*. Pretoria: Ethics Alive, 2001.

Lawson, J. L. "A Biblical Model for Counseling Married Couples Experiencing the Emotional Crisis of Infertility." PhD diss., CBN University, 1988.

Layne, L. L. "Breaking the Silence: An Agenda for a Feminist Discourse of Pregnancy Loss." *Feminist Studies* 23.2 (1997) 289–315.

Louw, Daniël J. *Cura Vitae: Illness and the Healing of Life in Pastoral Care and Counseling: A Guide for Caregivers*. Wellington: Lux Verbi, 2008.

Moss, Candida R., and J. S. Baden. *Reconceiving Infertility: Biblical Perspectives on Procreation and Childlessness*. Princeton: Princeton University Press, 2015.

Neuger, C. C., and J. N. Poling, eds. *The Care of Men*. Nashville: Abingdon, 1997.

Neuger, C. C. *Counseling Women: A Narrative, Pastoral Approach*. Minneapolis: Fortress, 2001.

O'Donnell, E. "Making Room for Men in Infertility Counseling." *SRM* 5.5 (2007) 28–32.

Petok, W. D. "Infertility Counseling (or the Lack thereof) of the Forgotten Male Partner." *Fertility and sterility* 104.2 (2015) 260–266.

"Revised Glossary on Assisted Reproductive Terminology (ART)." *World Health Organization*.   https://www.who.int/reproductivehealth/publications/infertility/art_terminology2/en/.

Skakkebæk, N. E., et al. "Pathogenesis and Management of Male Infertility." *Lancet* 343 (1994) 1473–1479. https://doi.org/10.1016/S0140-6736(94)92586-0.

Strydom, Natalia. "Infertility a Female Problem?: Engaging with Narrative Theory and Biblical Narratives in Pastoral Care for Infertile Couples." MTh thesis, University of Stellenbosch, 2019.

Sweet, L. *So Beautiful: Divine Design for Life and the Church*. Colorado Springs: David C. Cook, 2009.

Vähäkangas, A. *Christian Couples Coping with Childlessness: Narratives from Machame, Kilimanjaro*. American Society of Missiology Monograph Series 4. Eugene, OR: Pickwick, 2009.

Vergin, L. *Infertility: A Guide for Pastoral Care and Counseling*. Ann Arbor: University Microfilms, 1983.

Watkins, K. J., and T. D. Baldo. "The Infertility Experience: Biopsychosocial Effects and Suggestions for Counselors." *Journal of Counseling and Development* 82.4 (2004) 394–402.

Wischmann, T. P. Thorn. "(Male) Infertility: What Does it Mean to Men? New Evidence from Quantitative and Qualitative Studies." *Reproductive Biomedicine Online* 27.3 (2013) 236–43.

14

Transforming Masculinities in the Reformed Church in Zambia?

An Ethnographic Sketch[1]

MIAS VAN JAARSVELD

BACKGROUND INFORMATION

By way of introduction to this essay, the following background information (or disclaimer, if you wish) serves as context for the content provided. As a doctoral candidate, I am currently doing qualitative research for my dissertation on masculinities in the Reformed Church in Zambia (RCZ). In two visits to Zambia, I have conducted 35 interviews, as well as participated in numerous informal conversations. This essay refers to the raw data collected during these visits to Zambia. The information in this essay is based on my personal observations, previous involvement, and the contributions of 10 respondents who agreed to participate voluntarily in face-to-face, semi-structured interviews for this project. In this research project, qualitative research was done, and the narrative and ethnographic research methods were followed within the field of Practical Theology. Ethical clearance was

---

1. This essay is based on the conference paper I presented at the Sexual Reformation Conference held at the University of Stellenbosch, South Africa, May 6–7, 2019.

obtained from the University of the Free State's ethical clearance board, and all research was done according to the terms and conditions as prescribed by the University of the Free State's General/Human Research Ethics Committee (GHREC) (ethical clearance number UFS-HSD2019/0269/1405).

I admit to the challenging context in which this research was conducted, referring to the 72 different tribes, cultures, and languages in Zambia,[2] the unique opinions, expectations, roles, and practices of each congregation, whilst also acknowledging the intersections of culture, language, geography (urban or rural), education, class, sex, and race that come into play when conducting research in the RCZ. In some instances, generalizations are made, and they are undeniably connected to my own subjectivity. My awareness of such subjectivity in this project articulates the infeasibility of objectivity, and the probability of subjective integrity,[3] which also supports the decision on ethnography as research methodology—a method that makes room for the researcher's personal voice, interpretations, and insights.[4] This essay is based on the notes in my field journal and serves as an introduction (or an ethnographic sketch) to my research project on masculinities in the RCZ.

RESEARCH METHODOLOGY

The main focus of this essay is to describe and reflect on my experiences and preliminary findings in the field whilst researching how masculinities are lived and experienced in the Reformed Church in Zambia (RCZ). Choosing a specific research methodology when doing empirical research in another culture and country is a vigilant endeavor. Five respondents at Justo Mwale University[5] disclosed that there had been many international researchers at their institution with a paternalistic attitude and their minds already made up before entering the field, which lead to research that does not necessarily speak to the needs of a group. Having presuppositions when entering the field and the attitude, "You have a problem, and I have come to fix it," is perceived as arrogant, patronizing, and it may even compromise the integrity of the research. Aware and respectful of this statement, I chose to approach

---

2. Pariona, "What Languages," 2017.

3. Van den Berg, "Change of Tongue," 167.

4. Berg, *Qualitative Research Methods*, 134, 142.

5. Justo Mwale University, originally the Reformed Church in Zambia's theological seminary, is an institution of higher learning with university status since 2014, where the ministers of the Reformed Church in Zambia study theology. See the wesbite, https://www.justomwale.net.

this project from a position of "not knowing."[6] I followed the guidelines of practice-orientated research, which is an inductive form of reasoning that states that knowledge should not start with theory, but rather by studying the practice in which theory should suffice.[7] In other words, instead of identifying a specific problem in a specific context before even going into this context, one should first visit, revisit, experience, listen, observe, and let the context speak for itself. It is only thereafter that an issue or phenomenon can be identified or explored.

This is also the premise of ethnographic research. Ethnography is a qualitative approach to empirical research which sees participants as "fellow researchers" or "co-authors" in the research process.[8] The methods of data collection include sincere narrative involvement through appreciative interviewing, actively listening to the complex local stories of a group, becoming an active participant, and immersing oneself in a context.[9] It is advantageous to take on the role of a learner and an observer, paying attention to the finer details—the sights, smells, and tastes of communal life[10]—in order to create a much more authentic, a much richer and a more comprehensive understanding of the cultural narratives in the community of the RCZ. In addition to questionnaires, relevant literature, and studies on institutionalized religion, one should also focus on the cultural and social daily activities, and practices of ordinary people,[11] painting a cultural portrait (or sketch) of what is going on in the RCZ, and thereby contributing to knowledge.

ZAMBIA AND THE CHRISTIAN FAITH TRADITION

Zambia is officially designated as a Christian country. It was declared so by President Fredrick Chiluba on December 29, 1991. This declaration was not discussed, and therefore never contested by his cabinet or by parliament.[12] Even though Zambians claim that they are democratic, the majority of the population simply went along with this autocratic declaration that would influence Zambia's character for many years to come. The irony is that some respondents of this particular study divulged that they do not know if this policy was made out of personal conviction, or if it was done in order to

6. Van den Berg, "Change of Tongue," 174.

7. Hermans, "From Practical Theology," 123.

8. Ward, *Introducing Practical Theology*, 112.

9. Moschella, "Ethnography," 229; Ward, *Introducing Practical Theology*, 112.

10. Ward, *Introducing Practical Theology*, 112.

11. Schoeman and Van den Berg, "Practical Theology," 215.

12. Soko, "Practical Theological Assessment," 38.

leave a legacy, or to obtain popularity during the subsequent election. This decision could be considered President Chiluba's legacy in Zambia.

Today, three decades later, Zambia is still regarded as an official Christian nation—the only one of its sorts in Africa. Being a Christian nation has its benefits: there are numerous Christian holidays, and national days of intercession and prayer; there is a National Department for Religious Affairs (formerly Department of Christian Affairs and Religion);[13] and Zambia is seen as one of the safest and friendliest nations in Africa with few cases of aggressive violence.[14]

In Zambia, expressions of the Christian faith are visible everywhere. On cars and in shops there are depictions of Christian symbols (such as the cross and doves), pictures of a (white) Jesus, and Christian slogans which include "God did this," "Saved by the Grace," "God's time is perfect," "Protected by His blood," "Jesus wins," and "Only God knows."[15] These could be considered liturgical manifestations of the predominantly Christian Zambian people,[16] but some respondents believe that they are smart marketing schemes, since a Christian slogan will make clients subconsciously trust the owner. Other respondents speculated that it has to do with superstition— that using the name of Jesus will ward off all unwanted characters and evil spirits.[17] On a Sunday, you can attend church in any town, where you will find a church on almost every corner. There are also many crusades and travelling pastors, which enjoy a huge following. Even South Africa's evangelist "uncle" Angus Buchan visited Zambia in recent years, with his hat and the message, "It is time!"[18]

To be considered a good Zambian man, you must also be Christian; or as a male respondent said, "You cannot be Zambian and not be a Christian." Many benefit from this statement and use it to their advantage. For example, when the current president, Edgar Lungu, campaigned for his presidency, there were many large billboards in Lusaka depicting Lungu praying for Zambia. This was clearly a marketing strategy employed by the Patriotic Front (PF)—tapping into the fact that being Zambian is synonymous with being Christian, and subsequently a means to gain the favor of the Zambian people. A female respondent (sarcastically) added: "People will think: 'What

13. See the website, https://www.mrng.gov.zm.

14. Owen, "Safest Countries to visit in 2019," line 6.

15. Information based on my field journal.

16. See Wepener, "Liturgical 'Reform' in Sub-Saharan Africa."

17. Cf. Kroesbergen-Kamps, "Dreams and Nightmares of Modernity," 100–112.

18. In Lusaka, I saw large, faded billboards that advertised the "Mighty Men Conference" of August 12, 2018 on a farm near Chisamba (just north of Lusaka).

a good, Zambian man. He believes in God and prays for the people! I will vote for him.'"

Being officially a Christian nation, however, does also have its drawbacks. The majority of respondents agreed that many Zambians read the Bible very literally, which, for example, has led to the criminalization of homosexuality. Respondents agreed that some people use the Bible to uphold and reaffirm traditional practices which are patriarchal and misogynistic in nature. These practices include men's dominance in households, in the workplace, and in church. Some (mostly female) respondents also felt that this type of patriarchy is undeniably linked to high rate of gender-based violence, poverty and HIV/AIDS.

It is significant to note that traditional forms of masculinities are being contested in Zambia today.[19] With the rise of feminist scholarship in Africa, gender inequality and institutionalized patriarchy continues to be criticized anew, and the need to transform masculinities in a patriarchal society is highlighted.[20] According to Louw, men are currently struggling to redefine themselves in a changing society where the traditional roles are contested, and which do not necessarily fit them anymore, and as such could be referred to as "a crisis in masculinity."[21] In rural areas, culture and tribal beliefs are not really contested, but in urban areas, like Lusaka, traditional views of masculinities are being contested, reinterpreted, and even transformed. The church, and then also the RCZ (reformed only in name), undeniably contributes to this phenomenon.[22] This led me to the first question, namely who does research in the RCZ, and why?

WHO DOES RESEARCH IN THE RCZ, AND WHY?

In the Eastern province of Zambia, just outside of the town of Chipata, there is a small village called Magwero. It is in this village, underneath a large wild fig tree (which is still there today), that two Dutch Reformed Church (DRC) missionaries[23] (P.J. Smit and J.M. Hofmeyr) from the former Orange Free State in South Africa, along with Chewa teachers and evangelists from Nyasaland (today known as Malawi), held a worship service on 5 July

19. Zulu, "Zambia."

20. Connell, *Masculinities*, 41, 65.

21. Louw, *Cura Vitae*, 395.

22. Njobvu, "Role of the Reformed Church in Zambia," 31.

23. When referring to the Dutch Reformed Church, I refer to the "Nederduits Gereformeerde Kerk" (NG Kerk), and not the "Nederduitse Hervormde Kerk van Afrika" or the "Gereformeerde Kerk."

1899.[24] Previously, there had been missionaries in Zambia (formerly known as North Rhodesia); the great British explorer and missionary, Doctor David Livingstone, for example, died on 4 May 1873 in the Bangweulu Wetlands, approximately 400 kilometers from Magwero.[25] However, the difference in the case of Smit and Hofmeyr, is that these missionaries were requested there by the chief of the area, Chief Mpenzeni,[26] who was impressed by the work Dutch Reformed missionaries were doing in Nyasaland.

It is told that the Reverends Smit and Hofmeyr were awaited with expectation. The mission grew, and new mission stations were planted in many surrounding towns. In a short period, schools, orphanages, clinics, a theological seminary, and other community projects came into being as a result of the missionaries' (and indigenous evangelists') efforts, all under the same motto as the DRC in the Free State, "Kuunika m'mdima—Light in the darkness." Later, congregations were planted in Lusaka, Zambia's capital city, and also in the Copperbelt province.[27] Since 1966, the RCZ functions as an independent church within the reformed family of churches.[28] The theological seminary in Madzimoyo later became Justo Mwale University in Lusaka, which is today considered a hub for theology in sub-Saharan Africa.[29] It is interesting to note that the RCZ took a strong stance against apartheid legislation in South Africa during the 1980s, declaring that it goes against the heart of the gospel, and that it is an ungodly ideology and policy.[30]

Today, 120 years later, there are more than a million members in the RCZ. It is a growing denomination with 175 congregations, 17 presbyteries, 162 ministers, and 33 full-time evangelists. When looking at the gender demographic of the RCZ, one will see that in urban areas membership consists of 65 percent women and 35 percent men.[31] This majority of women can be ascribed to the reality of largescale labor migration, and the higher life expectancy (on average) of women is in Africa. The majority of respondents, however, felt that men are simply not really interested in attending church. Despite women dominating the membership, many offices in the church are, ironically, still held by men. Of the 162 ministers holding office in the

---

24. Van der Watt and Odendaal, *Family of Reformed Churches*, 16.

25. I visited the Livingstone Memorial Site in the southern parts of the Bangweulu wetlands in Zambia during my pilot study in October and November 2018.

26. Van der Watt and Odendaal, *Family of Reformed Churches*, 63–64.

27. Van der Watt and Odendaal, *Family of Reformed Churches*, 63–64.

28. Soko, "Practical Theological Assessment," 27–28.

29. Van der Watt and Odendaal, *Family of Reformed Churches*, 67.

30. Reformed Church in Zambia Synod Council minutes, 1989.

31. Statistics according to the office of the General Secretary of the RCZ.

RCZ, there are only 18 women who are in full-time ministry. Of the 33 full-time evangelists, only 4 are women. The road to ordaining women as ministers was a lengthy one. In Zambia, the Christian faith is enculturated with some traditional (and patriarchal) practices, which is visible in the way both men and women are treated. In some cases, the Bible is used (or rather misused) to affirm traditional (cultural) views of men and women, including the belief that the order of creation showcases God's intention when it comes to gender: men first, women second.[32]

At the synod of 2000, the RCZ made a progressive decision, allowing women to be ordained in ministry. This decision was made, even though it was turned down at the extraordinary synod in 1999, which formed part of the RCZ's centenary celebration. The first woman to be ordained was Rev. Rose Molowa, who was inducted on 7 January 2001. The decision to allow women to become ordained ministers and to advocate gender equality, was based on the notion that both male and female are "created in the image of God," as well as Paul's words in Galatians 3:28 ("there is neither male nor female").[33] When talking about gender in the RCZ, respondents immediately referred to this synod decision of 2000. It came to my attention that respondents refer to gender as a topic associated with equality, and the inclusion and empowerment of women. However, despite the increasing discussions on gender equality, inclusion and empowerment of women, the topic of what transforming masculinities should look like is rarely a topic that surfaces in RCZ resources.

With this in mind, the focus of this study emerged, namely how masculinities are lived and experienced in the RCZ, according to the respondents of this study.

WHAT ARE MEMBERS OF THE RCZ SAYING ABOUT MASCULINITY(IES)?

During face-to-face, in-depth, semi-structured interviews with male and female ministers of the RCZ, most respondents agreed that being a "real man" in Zambia today could be defined in terms of resourcefulness, authority, dominance, and power. It is expected of a man to get married, have children, and provide for his family. He should take on the role as the head of a household and take responsibility for the family. Men should be physically strong, should be able to give advice, make a success of their lives, and some

32. Phiri, "Church and Culture?," 76.

33. Njobvu, "Role of the Reformed Church in Zambia," 4; Phiri, "Church and Culture?," 76.

respondents divulged that it is expected of a man to be sexually vibrant too. Men who do not meet these expectations are left vulnerable, feeling inadequate, confused, and disappointed. The reality is that not all men meet these expectations. All the respondents in this study admitted that many men in Zambia today are unemployed, and therefore cannot provide for their families. There are also men who are unmarried, disabled, chronically sick, illiterate, or who have difficulties with sexual performance. These men fear that they are considered to be "lesser men."

All the respondents indicated that those men who feel like failures resort to substance abuse. Alcohol abuse is a big problem in Zambia, and respondents who are actively involved in their congregations agree that it could stem from these men's vulnerable position and the need to cope, to feel like a real man, or to numb the reality of their suffering. It does, however, not excuse bad and embarrassing practices that bring shame to the whole family. The tragic irony herein lies in the fact that while many women have taken the place of men as breadwinners and providers of families, many of these (drunk) men still assert their superiority over women.

During an interview, a female respondent disclosed: "The man is a king. They dominate and rule over women. Men in Zambia should be respected, and their authority should not be contested. That is what culture teaches us. A man should have the final say in the house. A woman should never tell a man what to say or what to do."

Five respondents disclosed that in some cultures, it is expected of a man to beat his wife, otherwise a wife may think that he does not love her. Culturally, Zambian women are taught to be submissive. An example of this is the *cinamwali*—an obligatory premarital initiation for young women in rural areas, during which young girls are taught what is expected of them— a sort of finishing school for betrothed Zambian ladies. According to a female respondent, if a man is not satisfied with his new wife, he can either discipline her, take her back to her home to be taught again—which is very humiliating for the family and the shamed wife—or simply get a divorce.

The traditional practice of *lobola* or the bridal price (also called *chimalo*, *impango* or *lubono* in Zambia) is also found in many cultures in Zambia. Even though this cultural practice could be considered a gesture in which a man proves his ability to provide for his bride, the price a man pays could be seen as a transaction between the husband and father-in-law in which a woman's sexual and economic rights are transferred from her family, to her new husband and his family. All the female respondents and two male respondents agreed that this practice is dehumanizing, and it indirectly suggests that women could be, and/or should be treated as commodities, chattels, and sex objects. Female respondents disclosed that this practice makes a man look at his wife as "property," and if he wants to beat her, it is no-one else's business. This way, men uphold the hierarchy and their right to dominate, which some men will even say was bestowed on them by God. Other related cultural practices include child marriages, widow cleansing, and polygamy.[34]

Gender based violence—an umbrella term for physical, sexual, and emotional abuse—is an immense problem in Zambia.[35] All the respondents agreed to this, and the respondents who are actively involved in congregations disclosed that victims of abuse in the RCZ rarely come for help or counseling. Women do not come forward out of fear of their husbands, and men do not come forward out for fear of being shamed in the community. To appear vulnerable, especially in public, is not an option for men. Rather, men's superiority should be maintained, even if it means using violence. To acknowledge that they made a mistake or go for counseling is viewed as being embarrassing and exposing.

This is an indication of a much larger problem about the way men seem to deal with their emotions. A male respondent commented that, "Men are supposed to be brave. They would rather die than show emotions. Even at the funeral of his wife, a man must contain himself. He is not allowed to cry." Another male respondent expressed concern when it comes to men not acknowledging their struggles and vulnerability. "Sometimes men would rather commit suicide to end their suffering, than feel inferior."

These emotions and power struggles are also visible when turning the lens towards the ordination of women ministers. Even though all the respondents felt positive about ordination of women into the offices of deacon and elder, and later as ministers, some female respondents disclosed that being a female leader in the RCZ is an extremely difficult task. Women's authority is constantly challenged, and their abilities questioned. One female respondent voiced her disappointment when men started walking out of church and quitted the church council after being inducted into a congregation. Another female respondent disclosed that some men refuse to take part in the Holy Communion, since they believe the symbols—the bread and wine—have now been "contaminated by the touch of a woman." As one female respondent disclosed, "I constantly have to ask myself: Am I welcome here?" This phenomenon is visible in many RCZ congregations and noticeable on presbytery and synod levels. Women agree that they regularly feel "walked over" and "overlooked."

34. Zulu, "Masks and the Men Behind Them," 81–95.
35. Mwaba, "Gender Based Violence," 106.

It is interesting to note that female respondents gave more thought-through, comprehensive answers than the male respondents when discussing masculinity in light of the Bible and the gospel in particular. This may be because their stories come from a position of being marginalized by the church, by congregations and by male colleagues. One female respondent made a significant contribution, when she said: "I think that if men in Zambia had an encounter with Jesus Christ today, they will not recognize him. He will be seen as weak. He wouldn't be remembered. His death wouldn't be mourned. He broke protocol by dining with sinners, with women and those lesser than him." A male respondent asked an interesting question: "Would Jesus live up to the standards of what it means to be a man in Zambia?" These contributions accordingly became the premise for a theological reflection in this essay.

A THEOLOGICAL RESPONSE TO THESE NARRATIVES

In society and in the media, "real men" are never portrayed as poor, vulnerable, weak, or sick. Even if they are afraid of enemies, are taken advantage of, persecuted, have sins that they cannot do away with, live in extreme poverty, or feel weak, the average Zambian man will not own up to it or admit that they are weak or vulnerable. It is interesting, though, that the message of the gospel actually makes room for vulnerability, because it is weakness that makes room for the grace of God.[36]

During interviews with members, ordained ministers, and theologians in the RCZ, I realized that the average Zambian man cannot really associate with Jesus on the cross. The cross symbolizes weakness, pain, suffering, powerlessness; for Zambians, and the RCZ in particular, the emphasis in sermons would rather fall on Jesus the Victor, the Powerful, the Healer, the one who did miracles and conquered death.[37] I experienced this during my fieldwork trip to Zambia on Easter of 2019. Good Friday was not a somber day of reflection on the cross and the suffering of Jesus Christ. Rather, Jesus's resurrection was already celebrated on Thursday night. It was as though the cross is overlooked. This is ironic, because Zambian men, perhaps even more so than men in some other contexts, know the cost of suffering, and therefore could be expected to associate more with Jesus in terms of his suffering and their suffering.[38]

36. Ellington, "Case of the Missing Cross," 89–91.
37. Ellington, "Case of the Missing Cross," 91.
38. Ellington, "Paul's Way," 62.

It was evident to me that the RCZ and other Christian churches in Zambia preach about social advancement, which includes the themes of health and wealth. Preachers will pray or claim things in the name of Jesus, because this symbolizes power.[39] There is also a large emphasis on "doing" faith, and not much is said about dependency on God from a position of vulnerability—which could be a definition of grace.

The cross, which symbolizes humility and frailty, could bring deep comfort, because it accompanies the message of the New Testament which states that weakness makes one a good candidate for grace. Given their circumstances, it would make sense for Zambians to find comfort in the cross and Jesus's death, but many Zambian men in the RCZ rather focus on the victory of Jesus. It may relate to a "magical way of thinking": that Jesus is a Man of God in a top power position and praying to him can bring about economic and physical benefits.[40]

It is important to consider that the message of the gospel (the Good News) not only stands in conflict with these expectations of men, but also in solidarity with the realities that many Zambian men face today. The Good News teaches us that humility is good, being a servant is just as important as being the head of the house (if not more important), poverty is called "a blessing," and suffering is not something to be ashamed about.[41] Vulnerability is not a unique attribute which only applies to Zambia, but it is a very difficult attribute for Zambian men to admit to.

Maybe men in the RCZ could revisit the phrase that all respondents cited: "being created in the image of God." This God in whose image they were created is also found in the wounded Jesus on the cross, the resurrected Jesus that never gave up his wounds, the Jesus that was ridiculed and judged for embracing the marginalized, and did not care for the prescribed roles and expectations of society.[42] The Jesus that spoke the truth, reacted in love, proclaimed justice and countered intolerance with grace.[43] Perhaps Jesus and his example could once again be the true savior of the men—even the broken and wounded ones—in the RCZ.

---

39. Ellington, "Paul's Way," 47.

40. Ellington, "Case of the Missing Cross," 90–91.

41. Sobrino, *Jesus the Liberator*, 14; Kärkkäinen, *Christology*, 242; Moltmann, *Way of Jesus Christ*, 99–112.

42. Moltmann, *Crucified God*, 197; Ellington, "Is the Prosperity Gospel Biblical?," 37.

43. Kärkkäinen, *Christ and Reconciliation*, 407.

CONCLUSION

In this essay, I presented some of the findings of my research done on masculinities in Zambia. I focused on the answers of respondents who voluntarily participated in this study, as well as observations that are based on my personal experiences during visits to Zambia.

The RCZ is a flourishing and renowned denomination in Zambia. The church has the opportunity and the infrastructure to educate men and women on gender issues, serve communities impacted by gender-based violence, and share the true meaning of the gospel; a gospel that is not only meant for those who fit into the hegemonic structure, but also the broken and vulnerable people, which include the men who cannot admit to this fact.

The RCZ's slogan is "The Light in the Darkness." Maybe the RCZ could shine the light of the gospel that teaches of a frail, vulnerable, and crucified Jesus, who loved unconditionally. Maybe this message could bring light in the lives of those who live in darkness—in a world where weakness, failure, and vulnerability is a reality. Maybe the simple example of the life of Jesus is the good news that men in Zambia need to hear in their struggle to transform toward a new and changing world.

BIBLIOGRAPHY

Berg, Bruce L. *Qualitative Research Methods for Social Sciences.* Needham Heights: Allyn and Bacon, 2015.

Connell, R. W. *Masculinities.* 2nd ed. Cambridge: Polity, 2005.

Ellington, Dustin. "Is the Prosperity Gospel Biblical?: A Critique in Light of Literary Context and Union with Christ." In *In Search of Health and Wealth: The Prosperity Gospel in African, Reformed Perspective,* edited by Hermen Kroesbergen, 36–51. Wellington: Christian Literature Fund, 2015.

Ellington, Dustin W. "Paul's Way of Imparting Jesus Christ Crucified: Self-portrayal, Identity, and Vocation in 1 Corinthians." In *University of the Free State Theological Explorations: Vol. 2, Making Sense of Jesus: Experiences, Interpretations, and Identities,* edited by Francois Tolmie and Rian Venter, 47–65. Bloemfontein: SUN MeDIA, 2017.

————. "The Case of the Missing Cross: Is Conventional Hermeneutics Depriving the Southern African Church?" In *Neo-Pentecostalism in Southern Africa—Some Critical Reflections,* edited by Hermen Kroesbergen, 89–110. Wellington: Christian Literature Fund, 2017.

Hermans, Chris. "From Practical Theology to Practice-Oriented Theology." *International Journal of Practical Theology* 18.1 (2014) 113–126.

Kärkkäinen, Veli-Matti. *Christology: A Global Introduction.* Grand Rapids: Baker Academic, 2003.

————. *Christ and Reconciliation.* Grand Rapids: Eerdmans, 2013.

Kroesbergen-Kamps, Johanneke. "Dreams and Nightmares of Modernity: Accusations and Testimonies of Satanism in Zambia." In *In Search of Health and Wealth: The Prosperity Gospel in African, Reformed Perspective,* edited by Hermen Kroesbergen, 100–112. Wellington: Christian Literature Fund, 2013.

Louw, Daniël J. *Cura Vitae: Illness and the Healing of Life.* Cape Town: Lux Verbi, 2008.

Moltmann, Jürgen. *The Crucified God.* London: SCM, 1974.

———. *The Way of Jesus Christ.* Minneapolis: First Fortress, 1993.

Moschella, Mary Clark. "Ethnography." In *Wiley-Blackwell Companion to Practical Theology,* edited by Bonnie Miller-McLemore, 224–33. West Sussex: John Wiley and Sons, 2012.

Mwaba, S. O. C. "Gender Based Violence: The Zambian Situation." *Studies in Social Sciences and Humanities* 4.2 (2016) 105–18.

Njobvu, Dickson. "The Role of the Reformed Church in Zambia in Promoting Gender Equality: A Case of Lilanda and Garden House Congregations in Lusaka District." MEd diss., University of Zambia, 2017.

Owen, Dannielle E. "Safest Countries to Visit in 2019." *Skyscanner,* December 18, 2018. https://www.skyscanner.com/tips-and-inspiration/safest-countries-visit#.

Pariona, Amber. "What Languages are Spoken in Zambia?" *World Atlas,* October 10, 2017. https://www.worldatlas.com/articles/what-languages-are-spoken-in-zambia.html.

Phiri, Jackson. "Church and Culture?: Exploring the Reception of Women's Ministries in the Reformed Church in Zambia in View of 1 Corinthians 14:26–40." PhD diss., University of Stellenbosch, 2017.

Schoeman, Kobus, and Jan-Albert Van den Berg. "Practical Theology Exploring Interdisciplinary Practices: The Quest for Engaging with Lived Religion in the South African Context." In *Theology and the (Post)Apartheid Conditions. Genealogies and Future Directions,* edited by Rian Venter, 213–31. Bloemfontein: SunMedia, 2016.

Sobrino, Jon. *Jesus the Liberator.* Maryknoll: Orbis, 1993.

Soko, Lucas. "A Practical Theological Assessment of the Schisms in the Reformed Church in Zambia (1996–2001)." PhD diss., Stellenbosch University, 2010.

Van den Berg, Jan-Albert. "A Change of Tongue . . . ?: The Articulation (Picturing) of Pastoral Theological Perspectives." *Practical Theology in South Africa* 1.2 (2006) 164–81.

Van der Watt, Gideon, and Mariëtte Odendaal. *A Family of Reformed Churches in Africa: Remarkable Stories of God's Grace.* Wellington: Christian Literature Fund, 2017.

Ward, Pete. *Introducing Practical Theology: Mission, Ministry, and the Life of the Church.* Grand Rapids: Baker, 2014.

Wepener, Cas. "Liturgical 'Reform' in Sub-Saharan Africa: Some Observations on Worship, Language and Culture." *Studia Liturgica* 44 (2014) 82–95.

Zulu, Brenda. "Zambia: Fighting gender-based violence as fresh cases continue to emerge." *African Renewal,* 2018. https://www.un.org/africarenewal/news/zambia-fighting-gender-based-violence-fresh-cases-continue-emerge.

Zulu, Edwin. "Masks and the Men Behind Them: Unmasking Culturally-Sanctioned Gender Inequality." In *Living with Dignity: African Perspectives on Gender Equality,* edited by Elna Mouton et al., 81–95. Stellenbosch: SUN MeDIA, 2015.

15

Invisible No Longer

*In Search of the Lived Experiences of Transgender
People in African Independent Churches*

Sizwesamajobe (Sizwe) Sithole

INTRODUCTION

Coming out as a transgender man in my church was not an easy thing to do,
simply because my church was and has been very silent on issues of sexuality and sexual diversity. As my identity was constantly discussed, certain
concepts were communicated to me in an attempt to try to explain why I
was feeling and identifying masculine in a female body. My identity and
sexuality were always seen as a string of occurrences tied up and influenced
by the ancestral spirit of my brother who comes after me, and I was told that
he lives through me. Such comments and concepts spiked my curiosity and
led me to investigate and explore how other transgender individuals negotiate their gender identities in the African Independent Churches (AICs). I
further searched for literature on the AICs and sexuality, but to my surprise
I could not find anything referring to sexuality or gender identities—only
articles and journals on the position of women in the church. I was dis-
turbed by this silence as I believe that the AICs form a large proportion of
the Christian faith community in South Africa. Therefore, I embarked on a

study to explore the lived experiences of transgender individuals in the Zion churches in KwaZulu-Natal.

Firstly, this essay aims to reflect on the religio-cultural concepts used to negotiate and engage transgender individuals located within the landscape of the African Independent Churches.[1] Secondly, and more importantly, I reflect on the experiences of transgender people in the development of their gender identity, and how faith features in this process of transitioning and embodiment. The questions informing this part of the study include: how is transgender identity embodied in the Zion churches? And how do transgender individuals respond to an embodiment of their identity in these churches?

DEFINING THE TERM TRANSGENDER

Scholars have defined the term transgender as an umbrella term used to refer to diverse transgender queer individuals. Scholars have defined transgender as a term that denotes a range of gender experiences, subjectivities, and presentations that fall across, between or beyond stable categories of "man" and "woman."[2] Stryker has defined the term transgender as an extensive and inclusive term for diverse gender-variant practices and identities such as transsexuality, transvestism, intersex, genderqueer, gender fucking, female and male drag, gender blending, cross-dressing and others.[3]

The term transgender refers to a diverse group of transgender people, such as transgender non-binary or gender non-conforming people, that is transgender people whose identity falls outside the gender binary. Then there is also the transgender binary, referring to transgender individuals whose identity falls within the binary gender construction. Transgender queer are transgender individuals who identify with and in between the binary. Transgender individuals identifying within the binary are transgender individuals who experience the incongruency between their gender identity and the sex assigned at birth, namely a transgender woman (Male to Female

1. I am aware of the research argument on the terminology of AICs. In this essay, I prefer to use the term African Independent Church/es, as I understand the Ethiopian Zion churches to be the Zion churches that broke away from the missionary churches yet kept some elements of worship and liturgy that are found in the mission churches. Although these Ethiopian Zion churches were founded by black African people, they kept the elements of the mission churches and infused elements from African traditional religion to Africanize Christianity. See Hayes, "African Independent Churches," 139–46.

2. See, for example, Hines and Sanger, "Introduction," 1–24; Yarhouse, *Understanding Gender Dysphoria.*

3. Stryker, "Contexts, Concepts, and Terms," 1–44.

or MTF) and transgender man (female to male or FTM). Transgender individuals loyal to the binary have been identified as transgender people who show a high level of experiencing gender dysphoria. Gender dysphoria refers to a deep and abiding discomfort over the incongruence between one's biological sex and one's psychological and emotional experience of gender.[4] However, it is important to note that one cannot conclude that other transgender diverse people do not experience gender dysphoria.

Transgender identity is mostly a personal identity, as transgender individuals may self-identify and express their gender in different ways depending on the individual concerned.[5] In this chapter, I use the term transgender in its narrow meaning to refer to transgender individuals who experience the incongruency between their gender identity and sex assigned at birth. These transgender individuals feel obliged to be loyal to the gender binary of masculinity or femininity. This choice of terminology is because of the fieldwork data collected amongst the four transgender individuals in KwaZulu-Natal who identified as either transgender men or transgender women.

THEORY AND RESEARCH METHOD

This chapter draws from the insights of feminist, queer, and transgender theorists as proposed by Nagoshi and Brzuzy (2010), to engage the lived experiences of transgender individuals. Feminist theory addresses the cultural-historical context and biological premises of gender, as well as the issues of sexism and the intersectionality of multiple forms of oppression. Hawkesworth notes that feminist scholars have defined gender in numerous contexts, from an attribute, to a type of social organization and as an ideology, to sex roles, power differentials, and analytical categories.[6] Nagoshi and Brzuzy emphasizes that "(q)ueer theory developed from feminist and the constructivist theories that posited that normative and deviant sexual behaviors and cognitions are social constructs."[7] Much of the philosophical and political understanding of non-heteronormative gender identity and sexuality are derived from queer theory. Though queer theory developed from feminist theory, Nagoshi and Brzuzy highlight that

> . . . (t)he social constructivist approach was a rebellion against the "essentialist" ideas that developed in Western societies

---

4. Yarhouse, *Understanding Gender Dysphoria.*

5. Gender Dynamix, *Transgender Lives in Southern Africa.*

6. Hawkesworth, "Gender as an Analytic Category," 145–75.

7. Nagoshi and Brzuzy, "Transgender Theory," 434.

beginning in the late 19th century. Such essentialist ideas came to link gender roles, gender identity, and sexual orientation tightly within a binary, biologically based, heteronormative gender schema. . . (q)ueer theory is in many ways a challenge to feminist theory.[8]

McLelland mentions that queer theory "concerns itself with the effects which arise from modern societies' preoccupation with consigning individuals into two opposite and mutually opposed camps based on the gender of their preferred sexual partner."[9] Though we appreciate the insights of feminist and queer theory, in dealing with the nuances and the ambiguities of transgender identities an appropriate theory would be that which transcends both the feminist and queer theory. Nagoshi and Brzuzy illustrate that

> (t)ransgender theory encompasses and transcends feminist and queer theory by explicitly incorporating ideas of the fluidly embodied, socially constructed, and self-constructed aspects of social identity, along with the dynamic interaction and integration of these aspects of identity within the narratives of lived experiences.[10]

The combination of these theories embodies the fluidity of human identity from a personal or an individual's lived experience, which provides a helpful framework for the discussion in this essay. It contests the hierarchical, binary construction of gender as the normal and the only way of perceiving gender, which informs our sexuality. Moreover, this essay will draw from my own experience as a transgender man and from my Master's research study produced under the Gender and Religion program at the University of KwaZulu-Natal.

For this study, I gathered empirical data through individual in-depth interviews. The participants included four transgender individuals and two key informants from the Zion church. Interviews were conducted between June 2018 and September 2018. The age of participants ranged from twenty to sixty years old. A requirement was that participants had to have been members of the Zion church[11] for two years or more, and that participants resided in KwaZulu-Natal as the study concerned itself with Zion churches

---

8. Nagoshi and Brzuzy, "Transgender Theory," 434.

9. McLelland, "Inside Out," 259.

10. Nagoshi and Brzuzy, "Transgender Theory," 432.

11. This essay is only concerned with data gathered amongst members of the Ethiopian Zion churches in KwaZulu-Natal. On issues of terminology and typology of AICs, see Anderson, "Challenges and Prospects," 283–94; Zwane, "African 'Independent' Churches."

in KwaZulu-Natal. Snowball sampling was employed to identify participants who will best co-produce relevant data. Noy Chaim defines snowball
sampling as,

> A sampling when the researcher accesses informants through
> the contact information that is provided by other informants.
> This process is, by necessity, repetitive: informants refer the
> researcher to other informants, who are contacted by the re-
> searcher and then refer her or him to yet other informants, and
> so on.[12]

I will structure my reflections around three key central themes that
form an important part in the development of the transgender identity,
namely, naming, body, and cultural identity. From the key central themes,
several subthemes emerged. They are grouped as follows: under the key
theme "naming" I will discuss first, sexual identity and sexual diversity as a
difficult subject; second, the experience of being called *Inkonkoni* without
being asked; and third, elderly people who still use the dead name. Under
the key theme "body," the following subthemes emerged: first, my body as
shame; second, my body as cause of depression; and third, expressing love of
my body. In the last key theme, "cultural identity," the following subthemes
are explored: first, *Inkosana*—when gender identity, tradition, and culture
meet; and second, Sangomahood[13] as a safe space.

SUMMARY OF FINDINGS

Naming

*Gender trouble? Sexual identity and sexual diversity, not an easy
subject*

Sexuality and gender identity have proven to be a difficult topic for the
church, and it continues to tear the church apart. The Zion churches are not
exempt from such an observation, though they may come across as a silent
faith community when it comes to issues of sexuality and sexual diversity.
I say that they are a silent faith community, because a recent research study
has highlighted that there has been minimal research done on Zion churches and sexuality.[14] This particular study was inspired precisely by such si-

12. Noy, "Sampling Knowledge," 330.
13. A Sangoma is a highly respected healer in Nguni society.
14. Sithole, "Exploration of Religio-Cultural Concepts."

lence from the Zion churches when it comes to issues of sexuality. African Independent Church scholars have highlighted that these churches advocate for conservative gender roles.[15] This observation suggests that these churches operate within the heteronormative construction as their gender framework is that of a gender binary, which is a social construct informing patriarchy. The heteronormative hierarchy of these churches was displayed clearly when I was scouting for the participants. Both the church leaders were male individuals and they both shared that their church committees only comprised of male individuals, and mostly also old men. Siphokazi* and Nhlakanipho*[16] also highlighted these heteronormative structures in the Zion church as they described the seating arrangements and the uniform worn in these churches. This is how they cited their experiences:

Nhlakanipho*: *I was made to wear the female's uniform.*[17]

Siphokazi* had this to say about the hierarchical structure found in her Zion church:

Siphokazi*: *As you may well be aware, that at the Zion church you never wear make-up, no nails and whatsoever, so I guess they know me. It's just that sometimes I get a sense that they fail to separate gay from Trans and vice versa. But because they know that I was born male they make me sit with males, which is very uncomfortable for me.*[18]

The two key church informants highlighted the instabilities the Zion churches are facing as they lack the correct and the right theories and vocabulary to negotiate and engage transgender individuals. This is how the key informants reflected on their churches engaging with transgender members:

Bishop Nxele*: *We do have oNgqingili and at the moment the church is still discussing the sexuality and gender identity issue as a critical issue that still needs to be discussed further in our upcoming meeting. This came up as we were amending the church constitution. This issue is still in question in the church, because we raised this issue as a question to say what does the church say about LGBTIQA+ people, because we see them in the church. Let me make an example: as you may know our church has a uniform*

15. Ohlmann et al., "African Initiated Churches' Potential."

16. The asterisk (*) indicates that these are not the real names of participants.

17. Nhlakanipho,* interviewed on July 19, 2018.

18. Siphokazi,* interviewed on July 15, 2018.

> *for boys and a uniform for girls, so what we usually do, we wait*
> *to be guided by the person concerned because we may not always*
> *know how they identify.*[19]

Deacon Mkhize* had this to say about his church in engaging with transgender individuals:

> Deacon Mkhize*: *We have not had a topic or discussion in the*
> *church about transgender, and I must say it is not easy to talk*
> *about such topics when no one has mentioned it before or come*
> *forward to mention it. For me, I believe it is a matter of transgen-*
> *der people coming forward. However, it seems as if this topic does*
> *not bother people much, because it has never been discussed or*
> *brought forward to be negotiated.*[20]

Such observation and highlights point out how these Zion churches still find issues of sexuality and gender identity difficult to tackle, and how heteronormative structures operating in the church hinder progress in negotiating and engaging transgender individuals. These churches still maintain the patriarchal orientation which has always existed amongst these churches.

They call me Inkonkoni but they never asked me

As a Zulu speaking person, I remember how frustrated and angry I would be when a person called me *Inkonkoni* or *Isitabane*. These two words are known within the Zulu community as derogatory words, used to undermine and insult LGBTIQA+ persons or any other person who does not conform to the societal normative gender roles. Research indicates that transgender individuals within the landscape of African independent Churches still face the challenge of being referred to as *Izinkonkoni or Izitabane*. These Zulu words have mostly been used to refer to gay and lesbian individuals and any persons not fitting within the heteronormative gender binary. This highlights that gay and lesbian identities have become containers of any sexual identity outside of heteronormative gender identity. This also highlights how the homogenization of gay and lesbian studies has overlooked the experiences of transgender individuals, hence transgender individuals face such erroneous judgment of their gender identity as that of sexual orientation. Amanda Swarr articulates this very well, ". . . those identified and referred to as *stabane* rarely have intersexed bodies; instead, in contemporary Soweto and elsewhere, there is a widespread assumption and co-created

19. Bishop Nxele,* interviewed on June 27, 2018.
20. Deacon Mkhize,* interviewed on June 26, 2018.

understanding that those who self-identify as lesbian or gay or engage in particularly gendered same-sex encounters may be intersexed."[21]

Elderly people still use my dead name

The notion of changing and appropriating one's name, forms an important part of the development of the transgender identity. In many cultures names are gendered—we have boy names and girl names, and subsequently transgender individuals have often been given names that do not match their gender identity. This disconnection becomes difficult for transgender individuals. Transgender individuals who are loyal to the gender binary as they transition, choose a different name that aligns with their gender identity. The birth name then becomes referred to as a dead name. However, in the research findings transgender individuals highlighted that elderly people in the church find it hard to adapt to this change. As Van der Schans notes, names invoke some form of identity in understanding who the individual is, that is they invoke ethnic, social, and religious backgrounds. More importantly, names become a source of empowerment to allow us to be who we want to be.[22] This study confirmed Van der Schans' reflections, as some of the participants mentioned that they understand that the elderly people are not using their dead names to insult them. Rather, for some it is simply the name they have always known or used to refer to an individual, often from an early age. It is also serves as a connection of an individual to the family name. As Philani* and Siphokazi* articulated in their experiences,

> Philani*: Yes, most people in the church use my nickname I first used when I came to church because as I might have mentioned I am not a very talkative person so I created a nickname trying to explain what I am or who I am. Few of them call me by my surname and I would say most people who use my birth name are the pastors and the elders. I understand that when elderly people call you by your surname it is some level of respect for your family name. Sometimes even your name given at birth to them is not an insult but some level of respect for you and your family line.[23]

> Siphokazi*: I am not sure, but as you may know, people from the local community sometimes have this belief that when they call you by your surname, they are respecting you. I would like to

21. Swarr, "Stabane," 525.
22. Van der Schans, "Role of Name Choice," 1–21.
23. Philani,* interviewed on August 23, 2018.

think of it that way because I have never had a chance to speak with them about it.[24]

For this study, it was interesting to learn that these transgender individuals have formulated a form of resilience and resistance as elderly people continue to use their dead names, the names which they no longer identify with. They also vouched to continue educating people who still misgender them by continuously using wrong pronouns and dead names.

Body

I am a bread spoiled from the bakery, my body was a shame

Transgender individuals who experience the incongruence between their gender identity and sex assigned at birth, have shown to experience the same kind of incongruence between their anatomic body and lived gender body. Therefore, for those transgender individuals loyal to the gender binary, body alignment is important as these individuals experience incongruence between their lived gender body and anatomic body. Two participants in this study highlighted the importance of body alignment. This is what these two participants had to share about their body experience as transgender individuals who have started the transition process:

> Philani*: *Before I started hormones, I was not happy to see hips in my body, breasts, and periods. After taking hormones I am beginning to see changes in my body and I am happy with these changes. My wish one day is to remove breasts and be free of this binder I am using to flatten my chest. I am now free from the periods and my body is changing shape to be more male, so indeed I am happy.*[25]

Mirender highlighted how she used stuffing to create the alignment of her anatomic body and her lived gender identity:

> Mirender: *At first, it was not easy, my body was a shame to me. I was not comfortable because I was not as feminine as I wanted or hoped my body to be as a woman. I was tired of having to stuff my chest with all sorts of things making fake breasts, because that is what I wanted to have. When you are transitioning you have to be sure of your story—that is why we attend so many therapy sessions. So after three months, I started to see changes and I was*

24. Siphokazi,* interviewed on July 15, 2018.
25. Philani,* interviewed on August 23, 2018.

happy because even the beard was fading away. After all, before hormones, I had to shave every three days. So I was excited with the changes that I was seeing in my body, because they fitted exactly as I was picturing them in my mind.[26]

My body as a cause of depression

Not all transgender individuals who participated in the study have started the transition process. One participant highlighted how such a delay in starting the transition process creates anxiety and depression, as the anticipated and needed changes for transitioning to become the visible lived gender identity has not happened. This is how he shared his experience:

> Nhlakanipho*: *Yes, I would say even now I still have the problem with my body concerning my identity. Even the way I used to dress, I would not wear tight clothes, because I would be offended when people compliment my body in a feminine manner and that makes me a very emotional person. I started counseling sessions because I became depressed whenever such comments are made, I did not want my schoolwork to suffer as well. The more people commented on my body in a female manner, the more I became depressed.*[27]

Nhlakanipho*'s experience highlights the sensitive and vulnerable position transgender individuals find themselves in when they are not able to start the process of transitioning, which would produce the desired results in terms of the body. This confirms research that has highlighted that the high prevalence of suicide amongst transgender individuals is at times caused by anxiety and depression due to lack of access to transition, family rejection, victimization, discrimination, stigmatization, physical, and verbal abuse.[28]

I don't need to wear makeup to be feminine - I love my body

Not all transgender individuals loyal to the gender binary, feel the need to align their anatomic bodies to their lived gender identity. Within the transgender binary identity, individuals are beginning to reject the normative gender performance of how a transgender individual ought to look like.

26. Mirender gave consent to use her real name as she felt that this study is a contribution to the visibility and the realities faced by transgender individuals. Mirender, interviewed on September 2, 2018.

27. Nhlakanipho,* interviewed on July 19, 2018.

28. Virupaksha et al., "Suicide and Suicidal Behaviors," 505–09.

Such an example is Siphokazi* who identifies as a transgender woman who appeared in her male clothing and expressed that she did not need to wear make-up to be accepted as a transgender woman. She expressed that she is female enough without makeup and female clothing, as her identity lies with the self. This experience highlights a diverse and very complex conceptualization of transgender bodies in the formulation of gender identity. Siphokazi* had this to say about her gender identity:

> Siphokazi*: *I love my body. I was doing grade 9 when my body started to change, and I am happy with how I look. I refuse to think that I need feminine make-up to make me feel and look feminine. I am comfortable in my looks and happy as I am, though I would like to transition at a later stage in my life when I have consulted with my ancestors and they agree for me to transition.*[29]

Such reflections speak to the unspeakable and undeniable fluidity of transgender identities. This reflection is the push back against the general and the considered normal construction of binary transgender identities, and this experience highlights the complex and diverse conceptualization of gender identity amongst transgender individuals. It is reflections like these that push against traditional, hetero-patriarchal binary constructions that trouble societies—in some cases resulting in the extreme of sexual abuse or gender discrimination against transgender individuals. This push against the "norm" leads to transgender individuals being seen as "outcasts" or the "other" in our society, forcing them to live on the margins of society. Hence as transgender people, we constantly have to fight for acceptance and visibility in faith, traditional, and cultural spaces, as captured in Mirender's experience in the following section.

Cultural Identity

You are an Inkosana: Gender identity, tradition, and culture meet

Despite a progressive and enlightened constitution in South Africa, transgender people in South Africa continue to face stigma, prejudice, ignorance, and discrimination from the faith community, in addition to a huge societal pressure to conform to socially constructed sexual stereotypes.[30]

The study highlighted that there are enormous challenges and contradictions between gender identity, culture, and tradition. As transgender

---

29. Siphokazi,* interviewed on July 15, 2018.
30. Bateman, "Transgender Patients Sidelined," 91–93.

individuals who do not identify within the normative gender identity, our identity often challenges the societal expectation of how gender roles should be maintained. Therefore we push back against communities' gender prejudices of conforming to normative gender roles. Mirender is a good example of such a push back. As a firstborn child (born in a male body) in a polygamous family, she was expected to lead by example as *Inkosana*.[31] However, all of this changed when "he" identified as a female or as a woman. This is what Mirender had to say:

> Mirender: *My father was very strict when it came to culture and tradition and was a much-respected member of the community, more like a king. He had status, so for him it was like he cannot have "his" son, his eldest son, turn into something else. You understand the status of having a son in the local community as a family; it kind of earned you respect, so I guess that is why he decided to kick me out.*[32]

Other participants revealed that culture was never used to discriminate or violate their lived gender identity. Therefore, this study suggests that culture and tradition are fluid and not static, as we may have been led to believe in our communities. However, this cannot be said to be the general experience for all transgender individuals. As indicated in Mirender's story, some transgender people face being disowned by their families because they are seen as people defying the cultural and traditional norms and practices. However, it was very interesting to hear one of the participants who identify as a transgender woman sharing her story as a Sangoma, bringing a dynamic experience of how they navigate the Sangomahood space which is considered to be sacred in the Zulu culture. Sangomahood is a highly held position within the Zulu culture as Sangomas are appreciated as custodians of tradition and culture.

Sangomahood as a safe space

One of the participants identified herself as a Sangoma and mentioned how her position as a Sangoma creates a safe space for her to be accepted in public. She is elevated into an extraordinary being as a Sangoma. Within the Zulu culture and tradition Sangomas are believed and known to be under the protection of the ancestors, hence they are regarded as extraordinary

31. *Inkosana* is a Zulu term that is given to a male firstborn child. *Inkosana* is second in command to the father in the household.

32. Mirender, interviewed on September 2, 2018.

beings in society. This is how Siphokazi* reflected on her position as a Sangoma in her local church:

> Siphokazi*: *Yes, I think the fact that I am a Sangoma is one of the things that provides me a space to be still a member of that church. I once had a vision that I shared with them and it became true, so I would like to believe that from there they started to tolerate me, but other than that I do not think they are as welcoming as they think they are.*[33]

This highlights the position of safety, as most transgender individuals are faced with issues of sexual violence, corrective rape, and transphobia. Siphokazi*'s safety is on the basis that she is a Sangoma/Diviner. The question remains, would she still be safe in her church if she was not gifted with the Divinity/Sangoma powers? The participant mentioned that she believes that she is being tolerated in the church for who she identifies as because of her spiritual powers, and she is being used in church as a medium between the ancestors and the church. What are the possibilities of seeing Siphokazi* being fully accepted and included in her church for who she identifies as concerning her gender identity, as opposed to who she is concerning her spiritual powers?

CONCLUSION

In conclusion, this study highlights that for many Christians and Christian institutions transgender issues still pose a dilemma. Christian institutions find it difficult to talk about issues of sexuality in general and it becomes even worse for issues related to transgender people. As is seen in this study, the Zion churches find it difficult to embody the gender identity of transgender people. The vernacular language used to refer to transgender people reflect that transgender people are somehow understood and embodied as people involved in or identifying with homosexual relationships. This only adds to the limitation of transgender identities and leaves little room for appreciating diversity within transgender identities. As such, this study is a contribution to the visibility of transgender people navigating the spaces of faith and culture and adds to the growing body of literature and work done by organizations fighting for the visibility of transgender people in KwaZulu-Natal and South Africa. It aims specifically to benefit the African Independent Churches in their engagement and theoretical reflection on human sexualities. It is a challenge to the silence of African independent scholars on issues of sexuality

---

33. Siphokazi,* interviewed on July 15, 2018.

and sexual diversity. Lastly, the study seeks to give voice to transgender individuals within faith communities and further contribute to African literature on issues of human sexuality. As Mkasi pointed out, "lack of literature and African scholars who are interested in African indigenous same-sexualities is problematic for students who want to study this subject, because using Western literature to analyze African same-sexualities weakens the analysis."[34] Silence from both the church and from African independent scholars is not a life-affirming answer that empowers transgender individuals to be open about their experiences, nor their realities.

The main contribution this essay hopes to achieve, is to call for the church and community to open itself up to questions that are uncomfortable, to listen to the experiences of vulnerable bodies, and to begin recognizing that transgender individuals count as the body of Christ that has to be embodied and appreciated in its diverse, complicated and transcending identity. Recommendations from this essay would include carrying out further research on the praxis of African Independent Churches, to assist these churches to formulate theories and adequate vocabulary to allow spaces of engagement with transgender members in the church. I hope to cover this in my doctoral studies. Moreover, these churches need to open themselves up to sex, gender, sexuality, and gender identity training and workshops to learn more about transgender people. These trainings can assist in lessening the confusion between gender identity and sexual orientation which seems to be driving further the discrimination of LGBTIQA+ people within African faith communities. Finally, and most important, is for African Independent Churches to invite and encourage transgender people in and to allow them to have a platform to share their experiences and share the development of their identity. This may shed a bit of light on the type of support that transgender individuals need or require from their churches.

BIBLIOGRAPHY

Anderson, A. "Challenges and Prospects for Research into African Initiated Churches in Southern Africa." *Missionalia* 23.3 (1995) 283–94.

Bateman, Chris. "Transgender Patients Sidelined by Attitudes and Labelling." *SAMJ* 101.2 (2011) 91–93.

Gender Dynamix. *Transgender Lives in Southern Africa: The State and Nature of Transgender People's Lives in the Southern African Sub-region.* Cape Town: South Africa, 2016.

34. Mkasi, "African Same-Sexualities," a1576.

Hawkesworth, Mary. "Gender as an Analytic Category." In *Feminist Inquiry: From Political Conviction to Methodological Innovation*, edited by Mary Hawkesworth, 145–75. New Brunswick: Rutgers University Press, 2006.

Hayes, S. "The African Independent Churches: Judgement through Terminology?" *Missionalia* 20.2 (1992) 139–46.

Hines, Sally, and Tam Sanger. "Introduction." In *Transgender Identities: Towards a Social Analysis of Gender Diversity*, edited by Sally Hines and Tam Sanger, 1–24. New York: Routledge, 2010.

McLelland, Mark. "Inside Out: Queer Theory and Popular Culture." In *Aesthetics and Experience in Music Performance*, edited by E. Mackinlay et al., 255–81. Newcastle: Cambridge Scholars, 2005.

Mkasi, Lindiwe. "African Same-Sexualities and Indigenous Knowledge: Creating a Space for Dialogue within Patriarchy." *Verbum et Ecclesia* 37.2 (2016) a1576. http://dx.doi.org.ez.sun.ac.za/10.4102/ve.v37i2.1576.

Nagoshi, Julie, and Stephan/ie Brzuzy. "Transgender Theory: Embodying Research and Practice." *Affilia: Journal of Women and Social Work* 25.4 (2010) 431–43.

Noy, Chaim. "Sampling Knowledge: The Hermeneutics of Snowball Sampling in Qualitative Research." *International Journal of Social Research Methodology* 11.4 (2008) 327–44.

Ohlmann, Phillip, et al. "African Initiated Churches' Potential as Development Actors." *HTS Teologiese Studies/Theological Studies* 72.4 (2016) a3825. http://dx.doi.org/10.4102/hts.v72i4.3825.

Sithole, Sindisiwe. "An Exploration of Religio-Cultural Concepts of Transgender Identities in the Ethiopian Zion Churches in KwaZulu-Natal, Midlands." Unpublished Master's thesis, University of KwaZulu-Natal, 2018.

Stryker, Susan. "Contexts, Concepts, and Terms." In *Transgender History: The Roots of Today's Revolution*, 1–44. Berkeley: Seal Studies, 2008.

Swarr, Amanda. "'Stabane,' Intersexuality, and Same-Sex Relationships in South Africa." *Feminist Studies* 35.3 (2009) 524–48.

Van der Schans, Arielle. "The Role of Name Choice in the Construction of Transgender Identities." *Western Paper in Linguistics/Cahiers Linguistiques de Western* 1.2 (2015) 1–21.

Virupaksha, Hasiruvalli, et al. "Suicide and Suicidal Behaviours among Transgender Persons." *Indiana Journal of Psychological medicine* 38.6 (2016) 505–09.

Yarhouse, Mark. *Understanding Gender Dysphoria: Navigating Transgender Issues in a Changing Culture*. Westmont: InterVarsity, 2015.

Zwane, Sithembiso. *African "Independent" Churches and Postcolonial "Development."* Uppsalla: Ujamaa Centre for Community Development and Research, 2017.